The Economics of
Power System Reliability
and Planning

A World Bank Research Publication

Mohan Munasinghe

The Economics of
Power System Reliability
and Planning

Theory and Case Study

with contributions by
Walter G. Scott *and* Mark Gellerson

Published for the World Bank
The Johns Hopkins University Press
Baltimore and London

McK
HD
9685
.A2M85

The views and interpretations in this book are the author's and
should not be attributed to the World Bank, to its affiliated
organizations, or to any individual acting in their behalf.

Library of Congress Cataloging in Publication Data

Munasinghe, Mohan.
    The economics of power system reliability and planning.

    Bibliography: p. 306.
    1. Electric power systems—Reliability—Economic
aspects.   2. Underdeveloped areas—Electric utilities—
Case studies.   I. Scott, Walter G.   II. Gellerson,
Mark.   III. Title.
HD9685.A2M85   338.4'3   79–2182
ISBN 0–8018–2276–9
ISBN 0–8018–2277–7 PBK.

Foreword

▀▄

In evaluating the merits of the investment programs it finances, the World Bank has generally sought to adopt a national viewpoint, by considering not only the supply costs incurred by the borrowing institution, but also the effect of these investments on other individuals and enterprises in the economy. In view of the increasing dependence of modern economies on electric power, the capital-intensive nature of the power sector, and the shortage of economic resources in the developing countries, the Bank's wider concerns have focused on, among other things, the trade-off between the rising unit costs of electricity supply and the costs imposed on consumers by the reduced reliability or quality of supply.

I believe that this is the first book that seeks to provide a well-balanced and integrated economic-engineering treatment of the topic of power system reliability. It demonstrates that in order to maximize the net social benefit of consuming electric power, it is necessary to minimize total social costs, which consist of both the supply costs to the power authority and the costs to the consumer that are likely to result from supply shortages or power outages. This approach, which establishes socially optimum reliability levels, subsumes the traditional system planning criterion based upon minimization of system costs alone. Thus the methodology presented here is both timely and relevant, not only in the Third World, but also in the developed countries.

This book is an integral part of the World Bank's continuing research program in energy, and as such it is linked to and contributes to other elements in the overall research effort. Thus, the book analyzes the subject of optimum system reliability within a broader context by discussing a range of related topics that are of more general application, including demand forecasting, system expansion planning, shadow pricing, and optimum tariff policy.

YVES ROVANI
Director
Energy Department
The World Bank

Contents

~~~~~~

Part Two. Case Study   117

Appendixes   197

Figures

~~~~~~

xi

Tables

●▼●▼●▼●▼●▼●▼●▼●▼●▼●▼●▼●▼●▼●▼●▼●▼●▼●▼●▼●

Preface

‸‸‸

The original impetus for this research arose from the need to examine
all opportunities for using the scarce resources of the developing countries as efficiently as possible in the electric power sector. The World
Bank has pursued the goal of economically efficient use of limited resources in the power sector in two principal ways.

On the demand side, basic research and case studies in marginal cost
pricing have been carried out. The Bank is now encouraging and assist-
ing the electricity authorities in Third World countries to develop and
to implement power tariff structures based on long-run marginal costs.

On the supply side, the Bank has researched and promoted the use
of system planning and cost minimization techniques. This work has
focused on the application of economic principles for choosing among
established technologies, while leaving the research and development
of new hardware to manufacturers and other institutions, which are better equipped to address such problems. In this spirit, the Bank's research
study, "Standards of Reliability of Urban Electricity Supply" (RES
670-67), from which this book stems, was originally designed to examine the possibilities for realizing system cost savings by varying power
supply reliability standards.

My previous work in least-cost system expansion planning had left
me dissatisfied with the common practice in the developing countries
of using reliability standards that often were arbitrarily borrowed from
the industrialized nations. Then, about two years ago, while we were
working on the applications of optimal electricity pricing rules, Jeremy
Warford drew my attention to a hitherto neglected aspect of power
economics involving system reliability. He suggested that it might be
interesting to examine the possibilities of broadening the cost savings

approach to include the notion of outage costs or costs incurred because of poor reliability and resulting power failures.

I felt that it was logical, therefore, to combine the study of reliability standards, system planning, and outage costs by expanding the basic framework of research project RES 670-67. Richard Sheehan, who was overseeing the research effort, quickly supported the idea. The economic principle developed in the study was the planning of power systems to minimize the total costs to society, defined as system costs plus outage costs. This criterion for power system planning leads to the development of economically optimal reliability levels. Therefore, this broader criterion subsumes the more traditional principle of minimizing just the power system costs to meet some (arbitrary) target reliability level.

The results of the research project also illustrate the close links between different aspects of electricity economics, such as marginal cost prices, optimal reliability levels, and system planning. In particular, cost savings are important, because several factors have recently contributed to massive increases in both the developing and developed countries' power system expansion requirements. The 1973 OPEC oil price increases have resulted in a shift to more capital-intensive plants involving hydroelectric, coal, and nuclear generators. At the same time the possibilities for realizing significant cost savings through economies of scale and technological advances have diminished, while the progressive electrification of rural and other areas of low consumer densities at relatively high unit costs is accelerating. Potential net savings to society resulting from the use of the new method could arise from voluntary decreases in reliability and resultant system cost decreases, from planned improvements in reliability and consequent outage cost reductions, or from a combination of both effects in different geographic areas.

Although the case study presented here involved distribution system planning in a city of a developing country, the theory and principles are general enough to be applied, with some modifications, to total system planning, including generation and transmission system optimization. The method is also applicable in the developed countries. It is fitting that this research study, which was designed to improve developing country reliability standards, because these standards were borrowed ad hoc from the industrialized countries, should produce results that were also relevant to the developed world. The issue of optimum reliability levels has recently attracted increasing attention in North America and Europe, especially following several recent major power failures, such as the New York City blackout of July 1977 and the widespread blackouts in Western Europe during the winter of 1978–79.

I am grateful to my colleagues Walter Scott and Mark Gellerson for their contributions, especially their work on the case study. I enjoyed collaborating with them both in Brazil and the United States. I am also indebted to the management and staff of the Compania Paranaense de Energía Elétrica (COPEL), including Arturo Andreoli, Edson Neves Guimaraes, Joaõ Calvo, Roberto Schulman, Amadeu Busnardo, Antonio Marcos Ferreira, Alceu Pacheco, Claudio Mesniki, Ademar Luiz Pastro, and especially Victor Waszczynskyj, for their hospitality and assistance with the case study.

Thanks are due to many Bank staff members, including Yves Rovani, Richard S. Sheehan, Herman van der Tak, Fred Howell, Edward Moore, John Davis, Charles MacNealy, Carlos Mena, Cheruvari Chandran, Orville Grimes, the Research Committee, Vinod Dubey, Ardie Stout-jesdijk, David Green, Benjamin King, Frank Lamson-Scribner, Everardo Wessels, and Vatsal Thakor, for general advice and support; and to Jeremy Warford, Yuji Kubo, DeAnne Julius, Robert Saunders, Ted Minnig, Jim Fish, Colin Warren, Dennis Anderson, Alistair Stone, David Hughart, Robin Bates, Karl Jechoutek, Joseph Gilling, Ibrahim Elwan, Anandarup Ray, Lyn Squire, and Johannes Linn for illuminating discussions of a more technical nature. Among those outside the Bank, comments from Robert L. Sullivan, Alton D. Patton, Ezra Mishan, and Ralph Turvey were most helpful.

Acknowledgments are also due to Añura De Silva, Michael Telson, Gerry Farnell, and John Chang for general assistance; to Monica Scott, David Teitelbaum, Emerito Asuncion, and Maria de Guillen for helping with the computations; to the municipal authorities of Cascavel, Brazil, for helpful information; and to Julieta Valencia and the staff of the MTST unit, as well as Beverley Rollins, Cindy Urban, Cecily Orr, and Pattie Koh for preparing the manuscript. My thanks also to Romesh Dias-Bandaranaike for careful proofreading and final corrections.

Last but not least, I owe much to my wife Sria and children Anusha and Ranjiva for their patience, understanding, and support, and to my parents and siblings for their constant encouragement. Needless to say the responsibility for all remaining errors in the text is mine.

An early draft of the text was edited by Roberta Maggenti; the final draft was edited by Judy Barry. The charts were prepared by Raphael Blow and the text was indexed by Professional Indexing of Atlanta, Georgia.

Definitions

ARI	Accounting rate of interest
AWG	American Wire Gauge
CCL	Critical consumption level
CES	Constant elasticity of substitution
CF	Conversion factor
Cr$	Cruzerio = US$0.081 (end 1976)
DU	Dwelling unit
EHV	Extra high voltage
ESWR	Efficiency shadow wage rate
EUSE	Expected unserviced energy
FAD	Frequency and duration of outage
FC	Factor cost
FTER	Free trade exchange rate
HV	High voltage
IFC	Idle factor cost
LDC	Load duration curve
LF	Load factor
LOEE	Loss of energy expectation
LOLP	Loss of load probability
LRMC	Long-run marginal cost
MCM	Thousands of circular mills
MOC	Marginal outage cost
MRS	Marginal rate of substitution
MSB	Marginal social benefit
MSC	Marginal social cost
MSC	Marginal supply cost
NFC	Nonfactor cost
OC	Outage cost
OCC	Opportunity cost of capital
OCF	Outage cost function
OCK	Outage cost per kilowatt-hour lost

OE	Outage energy
OER	Official exchange rate
OLSQ	Ordinary least squares (regression)
OR	Outage rate
PDV	Present discounted value
R	Reliability level
R*	Reliability expectation of consumers
RC	Recovered cost
SC	System supply cost
SCF	Standard conversion factor
SER	Shadow exchange rate
SPC	Spoiled product cost
SRMC	Short-run marginal cost
SWR	Shadow wage rate
TC	Total cost
VAR	Reactive volt-amps
XLOL	Expected loss of load

Part One

~~~~~~

Theory

During the twentieth century, the electric power industry has emerged as one of the most vital and capital-intensive sectors of the economy in almost every country. In 1978 the United States used about 560 gigawatts of installed capacity to generate 2,200 terawatt-hours of electrical energy, or approximately 10,500 kilowatt-hours annually per capita, making it the largest and the second most energy-intensive economy in the world.[1] The United States devoted more than US$30 billion to investments in the electric power sector in that year.[2] With electric energy requirements growing at an average rate of more than 4 percent during the 1980's, these investments will exceed US$70 billion by 1990.[3] In the developing countries the 1978 installed capacity and production of electricity were about 210 gigawatts and 820 terawatt-hours, respectively.[4] Rates of growth of the demand for electricity are expected to average nearly 10 percent and will have to be met by investments of approximately US$25 billion a year during the next decade, accounting

1. Gigawatt $= 10^6$ kilowatts; terawatt-hour $= 10^9$ kilowatt-hours.
2. "Twenty-ninth Annual Electrical Industry Forecast," *Electrical World* (September 15, 1978), pp. 61–76.
3. All investment costs are given in constant 1978 dollars.
4. Edward A. Moore, "Electricity Supply Forecast for the Developing Countries," Energy, Water, and Telecommunication Department, the World Bank (a restricted circulation document) (Washington, D.C., December 1978; processed).

1

for more than 20 percent of all public sector investments in these countries.

The worldwide trend of increases in the real costs of supplying electric power is likely to continue, because of the rapid growth of demand and such factors as the shift, following the oil crisis, toward more costly coal and nuclear generating plants and the dwindling availability of cheaply exploitable hydroelectric sources. Also, there are few opportunities to realize further significant economies of scale, especially as systems continue to expand into areas of lower population density at higher unit costs.

The massive investment needs for power imply that even small improvements in efficiency will lead to significant savings. These are especially important for those developing countries that face shortages of both local and foreign-exchange resources. Traditionally, the major emphasis has been placed on improving technical and financial efficiency through least-cost, long-range planning for system expansion, as well as by optimizing short- and medium-term system operation and providing better management of utilities. These considerations on "the supply side" of the supply-demand equation have been tackled with a remarkable degree of success, usually by engineers using technically and financially oriented solutions. More recently, power economists have focused attention on the objectives of economic efficiency in the national context. These developments will have a growing and significant effect on "the demand side," chiefly by the application of the principles of marginal cost pricing. On the supply side as well, the acceptance of economic arguments is reflected in the use of economic opportunity costs. These costs are represented by shadow prices that are the true costs of economic resources, instead of purely financial or accounting costs.

Chapter 1

~~~~~~

Objectives and Methodology

The current emphasis on economic efficiency in the electric power sector, especially in the areas of marginal cost pricing and improved tariff policy, is welcome and long overdue. But the topic of electric power system reliability, or dependable quality of electricity service, has previously received detailed treatment only from the supply side, using engineering models and analysis. The socioeconomic effect of the reliability of electricity supply on consumers has been examined in a more general and descriptive way. Thus, the traditional design and planning of power systems has been based on the principle of minimizing the supply costs required to meet a certain load at a given level of reliability. Increasingly, economists are realizing that even the most sophisticated planning models for least-cost expansion of power systems are usually developed with respect to arbitrary standards of supply reliability. These standards are derived from past practice and vague notions about the quality of service that would be acceptable to the electricity-consuming public.

Until recently, investigators have ignored the effects on the demand side that relate to the economic worth of reliability. The problems involved in measuring the economic benefits of improved quality of service were the primary reasons for this neglect. As reliability is presented in this book, the imbalance is addressed by considering the level of reliability as a variable for which optimum values would be developed during the system planning process, rather than as an arbitrarily imposed stand-

Figure 1.1. *Flowchart of the Principal Steps in the Methodology*

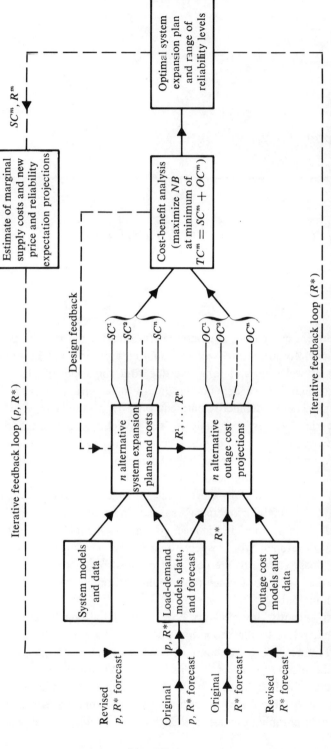

Note: p = price; R^* = consumer's reliability expectation; R = reliability level; SC = supply costs; OC = outage costs; TC = total costs; and NB = net benefits. Maximizing NB yields the optimal system plan m and the corresponding reliability R^m at the minimum value of $TC^m = SC^m + OC^m$.

ard. To achieve this goal, a social cost-benefit analysis is needed to evaluate the inherent tradeoff between the increase in the power system supply costs required to achieve a higher level of reliability and the corresponding decline in outage costs: that is, the economic costs incurred by electricity consumers because of power shortages. In other words, at a given electricity price the optimum reliability level, which maximizes the benefits that consumers receive by using electricity after subtracting the supply costs, should be established at the point at which the marginal increase in the supply costs is exactly offset by the marginal decrease in outage costs. In most countries such a plan would result in significant net economic savings.

This study highlights the importance of developing and applying a new criterion for power system planning that is based on optimal reliability levels. Using a dual economic-engineering method, it is shown both theoretically and operationally that it is possible to establish an optimum plan for long-run power system expansion and a corresponding range of reliability levels that will produce the greatest net social benefits. Such a balanced treatment of the effects of reliability on both the supply and demand side requires accurate estimates of system costs and outage costs. Estimates of system costs may be determined from straightforward engineering-economic considerations normally associated with power system design and planning. Estimating outage costs is a more difficult task, however. Therefore, new models and detailed methods are presented for analyzing the various ways in which electricity is used by different categories of consumers.

Summary of Methodology and Conclusions

Figure 1.1 is a schematic representation of the basic steps involved in the methodology presented in this book. There are two major parts to the text: the theory and a case study. The order of the chapters follows the logic of the flow chart shown in the figure.

First, a framework and a set of models are developed to analyze the economic costs incurred by different categories of consumers—residential, industrial, and others—as a result of electric power shortages of varying intensity. Concurrently, a disaggregate long-range, load-demand forecast of perhaps twenty years is estimated, based on an assumed evolution of electricity prices within the area to be served by the electric power utility. Next, using system models and data, several alternative (least-cost) power system plans are prepared that will meet this future load at different levels of reliability. The expected annual frequency and the duration of power failures associated with each alternative system design or plan are estimated for the entire period that is forecast. In addition, the time these shortages occur and the average numbers and kinds of consumers affected are also projected.

To determine the total future outage costs for each system plan, the outage frequency and duration results are used in the consumer outage-cost models. On the supply side, the investment and operating costs of each alternative design can also be estimated. A cost-benefit model is then used to compare the outage costs with the corresponding power system costs attributable to each alternative plan. At this stage, some preliminary feedback of forecast frequency and duration data, as well as disaggregate outage costs and system costs from the cost-benefit module, may be used to improve system design even further. Finally, the optimum long-run system expansion plan and a range of associated reliability levels are established, which maximize the net social benefits or, equivalently, minimize the total costs to society—both system costs and outage costs. At this optimal point, the marginal supply costs of improving system reliability are equal to the corresponding benefits from the expected marginal outage costs avoided.

Two further possibilities exist for incorporating feedback effects, as shown by the optional iterative loops in figure 1.1. The principal return path is through the effect of electricity prices on the load forecast. This would occur if the new optimized system plan requires changes in the original assumptions regarding the future prices that were used to make the initial projection of demand. A similar but less important feedback effect may also be incorporated into the analysis. This would involve the effect of changes in consumers' reliability expectation on both demand and outage costs. Therefore, if necessary, it is possible to repeat these computations by iterating through the model several times to arrive at a mutually self-consistent set of price, demand, and optimal reliability levels. Generally, such feedback effects would be important mainly in the theoretical sense, and, therefore, in practice a single iteration may often be considered sufficient.

This optimizing methodology adds an extra dimension to the more traditional procedure followed by system designers. In this approach, the reliability level is treated as a variable. The sum of the outage and the power system supply costs is minimized, while the system meets the load requirements without violating various technical and other constraints. This broader framework effectively subsumes the conventional technique of system planning, in which only the supply costs are minimized, subject to meeting some predetermined target level of reliability, the load requirements, and all other constraints. The model presented here is flexible enough to permit a further level of sophistication in the analysis by allowing the demand forecast to be varied by the effects of price feedback. The theoretically important point concerning the simultaneous optimization of both price and reliability levels is also accounted for in this practical way.

The costs consumers incur as a result of electric power shortages may be either direct or indirect outage costs. The direct costs occur when an outage actually takes place. Indirect costs arise if consumers adapt their activities by paying more to become less susceptible to outages, or if they resort to standby energy sources. Therefore, the relative importance of the direct and indirect components in total outage costs depends on consumers' expectations about the reliability of future supply and the extent of behavior changes to avoid outages.

In estimating outage costs, disruptions in the productive activity of electricity users is a better indicator than consumers' surplus. If consumers' surplus is used, outage costs probably will be underestimated because the customers' "willingness-to-pay" for planned electricity consumption is generally much less than the economic costs incurred because of an unexpected outage. System supply costs must be based on the physical and operating characteristics of the power system. These costs should be estimated in the national economic context, by using shadow prices when market prices are distorted. This method is preferable to the common practice of using only financial or accounting concepts and costs, which are more relevant from the viewpoint of a private electric power utility company.

To test the methodology, a case was designed that optimized the reliability of the distribution system in Cascavel, Brazil—a small city in a developing country. The study demonstrated that it was possible to optimize the long-range design of a distribution system to minimize the total costs to society and thereby realize substantial net social savings. The results also indicated that a better optimum may be achieved by varying the reliability of the distribution system according to the intensity of outage costs imposed on consumers in different geographic areas. In general, the practical implementation of the theory was quite straightforward, using data as inputs to three basic computerized models developed specifically to determine (a) the demand forecast, (b) the alter-

native designs of the distribution systems, and (c) the corresponding
system costs and outage costs. Since the economic aspects of the methodology used were quite general, it would be possible to treat generation
and transmission system reliability in the same way: that is, to optimize
the design of the entire electric power system.

From the theoretical model of household behavior presented here,
two conclusions may be reached. First, to the residential electricity consumers, the principal outage cost incurred is the loss of evening leisure
caused by lack of electricity. It is assumed that daytime domestic activities interrupted by outages could be rescheduled without much inconvenience. Second, the marginal monetary value of this leisure is equal
to the net effective wage or income earning rate of the household, on
the basis of the consumers' labor-leisure choice. Both hypotheses were
verified in the case study. The survey showed that residential consumers
were willing to pay in the short-run to avoid unexpected outages.

Industrial outage costs by major kinds of industrial users also were
analyzed in detail. They included spoilage, idle factors of production,
and recovery of lost production during regular working hours, as well
as overtime. The analysis was helpful in identifying the industries that
are most sensitive to outages. Such information would be useful in the
context of load shedding, for example, to rank industries by outage cost
per kilowatt-hour lost. Techniques for measuring the outage costs of
other kinds of consumers are also discussed, but these were found to
be rather insignificant in the case study.

Because every country and power system has unique characteristics,
the results of the case study cannot be used to draw wide-ranging conclusions regarding generally desirable levels for power system reliability
in other countries. The overall methodology, however, remains valid
and could be applied elsewhere. The net savings to society that could
have been realized by adopting the reliability-optimizing approach
amounted to approximately 0.04 percent of the total value added, or
about 5 percent of power system investment in Cascavel. If a conservative estimate of one-half of these figures were accepted as a benchmark,
the total potential net savings on the sum of system and outage costs
in the capital-scarce developing countries alone would amount to approximately US$4 to 5 billion (in constant 1978 dollars) during the
next ten years. Before these estimates can be confirmed, however, the
new methodology must be applied further to problems of power system
optimization, especially at the generation and transmission level. The
potential case studies should involve several consumer categories in
different physical and socioeconomic environments.

Chapter 2

~~~~~~

Introduction to Reliability

Electric power system reliability and security is a broad topic with a voluminous bibliography.[1] This chapter summarizes those aspects of reliability that are relevant to the economics of power systems, but no attempt is made to review the literature completely.[2] The various measures of reliability currently used are defined and described, and the weaknesses of the existing concepts of reliability are discussed, as well as the need for developing reliability standards that are based on explicit economic criteria.

Reliability Concepts

A relatively simple concept of reliability applicable to nonrepairable systems was originally developed in the aerospace industry. Reliability

1. See, for example, S. Vemuri, "An Annotated Bibliography of Power System Reliability Literature," *Proceedings of the IEEE Power Engineering Society Summer Meeting, Los Angeles, July 1978*, paper no. A78548-0; and Roy Billinton, "Bibliography on the Application of Probability Methods in Power System Reliability Evaluation," *IEEE Transaction on Power Apparatus and System*, vol. PAS-91 (March–April 1972), pp. 649–60.
2. See, for example, A. D. Patton and A. K. Ayoub, "Reliability Evaluation," *Systems Engineering for Power: Status and Prospects, USERDA Conference, Henniker, New Hampshire, August 1975*, NTIS no. CONF-750867, pp. 275–89; N. D. Reppen, R. J. Ringlee, B. F. Wollenberg, A. J. Wood, and K. A. Clements, "Probabilistic Methodologies—A Critical Review," *Systems Engineering for Power: Status and Prospects*, pp. 290–310.

was broadly defined as the probability that a component or system would perform its intended functions satisfactorily during a given period of time under actual operating conditions.[3] The more modern and appropriate concept is to think of the repairable electric power system component as existing in one of many possible states. The simplest example would involve two states typically labeled "up," or functioning, and "down," or unavailable (see appendix A for details). When the component fails, it undergoes a transition from the up to the down state, and, conversely, when repairs are completed, it returns from the down to the up state. The concept of reliability during some period may then be introduced as the fraction of total time that the component spends in the up state. Greater sophistication of analysis is possible by defining additional intermediate states in which the component is only partially functioning.

The concept of reliability for an electric power system is similar, but more difficult to determine, because the system consists of many components, and their interaction adds greatly to the complexity of the analysis. Thus, the reliability or ability of the system to perform its task satisfactorily will depend on the functioning of many components. Also, because of redundancy, the system may perform adequately even though some of its components are nonfunctioning or not functioning perfectly. The interaction of individual components in the system is easiest to analyze when their failures are mutually independent; if the failure of one component is related to or influences the failure of others, the determination of overall system reliability again becomes more complicated.

Clearly, the definition of system reliability requires that acceptable levels of performance for the system be carefully defined in relation to its purpose. An electric power system must supply electricity to consumers at the power level they want and at the time and place of their choosing, while maintaining an acceptable quality of service: that is, voltage and frequency levels must lie within specified limits. Therefore, before discussing reliability concepts, the different components of a typical power system are described briefly. The basic constituent elements of a power system may be analyzed in terms of their functions: generation, transmission, and distribution. The concept of a generating

3. See Igor Bazovsky, *Reliability Engineering and Practice*, Prentice-Hall Space Technology Series (Englewood Cliffs, N.J.: Prentice-Hall, 1961).

source or power plant is relatively unambiguous. Both transmission and distribution facilities carry the electric power from the source to the consumer. These ideas are further clarified in figure 2.1, a schematic diagram of a simple power system.

The output from two power generating plants G_1 and G_2 (hydro-electric or thermal) is increased to the high voltage (HV) level at source by the respective transformers TF_1 and TF_2 and is fed into the busbars in transmission substation TS_1 via the HV transmission links T_1 and T_2. At TS_1 the voltage is further increased to the extra high voltage (EHV) level, before the power is transmitted through the EHV line T_3 to substation TS_2. A voltage reduction occurs at TS_2, after which the electric power is fed, through HV transmission lines T_4 and T_5, into the distribution substations DS_1 and DS_2 located close to the load centers. Another voltage reduction occurs at DS_1 and DS_2, and then power flows out of the distribution substation busbars, through primary feeders such as F_1, to various distribution transformers (for example, DT_1), where the voltage is decreased further. Finally, the power is delivered to a representative consumer, through the secondary distribution line S_1, and service inlet and meter M_1.

In transporting power the general principle is that voltage level depends on distance and power flow. Transmission lines are used to carry large amounts of power over long distances, while distribution lines involve smaller power flows over shorter distances. The technical distinction between transmission and distribution facilities is usually made on the basis of their operating voltages. Although voltage standards vary greatly from country to country, broadly accepted definitions for voltage levels are as follows: EHV transmission, more than 220 kilovolts; HV transmission, 45 to 220 kilovolts; primary distribution, 6 to 25 kilovolts; and secondary distribution, 110 to 380 volts. In practice, considerable overlap is likely, and facilities operating at voltages in the range of 25 to 45 kilovolts (often called subtransmission), may be included within the distribution or transmission category, depending on their function.

An operating power system is much more complex than the one described above and in general has many generating sources linked to many load centers via an interconnected transmission network. Transmission interconnections may be used to tie the power systems of several different utilities together to form an even larger power pool. The distribution grid at a single load center would serve thousands of consumers. Furthermore, many other components, including protective and

Figure 2.1. *Schematic of a Simple Electric Power System*

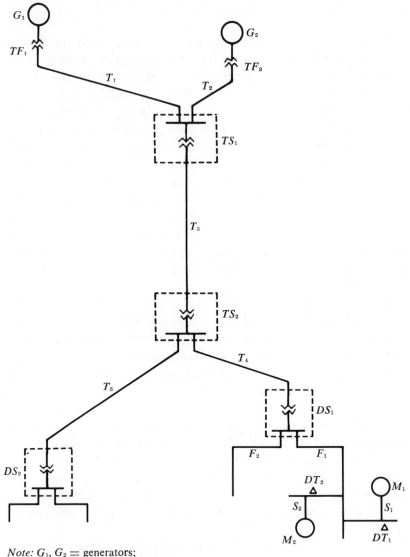

Note: G_1, G_2 = generators;
      TF_1, TF_2 = voltage transformers;
      T_1, T_2, T_4, T_5 = HV transmission lines;
      TS_1, TS_2 = transmission substations;
      T_3 = EHV transmission;
      DS_1, DS_2 = distribution substations;
      F_1, F_2 = primary feeders (or circuits);
      DT_1, DT_2 = distribution transformers;
      S_1, S_2 = secondary lines;
      M_1, M_2 = customer service inlets and meters;

relaying devices as well as load control and dispatching equipment, would play important roles in a large interconnected system.

Therefore, an ideal electric power system that unfailingly supplies power to consumers whenever required is by definition a perfectly reliable one, and, conversely, a system that is never able to deliver electricity to users could be termed totally unreliable. All real world power systems lie between these two extremes. As a system's reliability level is improved, a trade-off occurs between increased costs of supply and reduced inconvenience and costs to consumers from fewer power shortages. Therefore, criteria and methods to assess and rank systems by reliability level must be developed. Before discussing measures or indexes of reliability, an examination of the causes and manifestations of supply shortages would be helpful.

As in the case of any other good or service, electric power shortages occur when demand exceeds supply. Power systems are usually planned so that the supply is sufficient to meet forecast demand. In general, however, there will be unexpected variations in both projected supply and demand which would result in shortages; that is, less than perfect reliability of supply. The stochastic or random nature of demand is manifested by unforeseen increases in the magnitude of the load. One example is the demand placed on a system when unusually warm weather causes consumers to use their airconditioners unexpectedly. Similarly, the supply of power may also be subject to random variations. The unexpected failure or outage of the various components of a power system or the lack of water for hydroelectric generation caused by an unusual drought are two examples of potential supply problems.[4]

In recognition of these random changes in supply and demand, system planners accept that any system will suffer a certain number of future shortages. The expected long-run level of these built-in shortages, which may be estimated with the help of past data, constitutes the static element of system reliability. There is also a dynamic component of reliability, because to the extent that the planners have failed to correctly anticipate and analyze these supply and demand uncertainties, the actual incidence of shortages will not correspond to the planned static level. Furthermore even when the demand forecast is accurate and the system is well planned, the level of long-run reliability may fall

---

4. For a detailed definition of a component outage, see *IEEE Standard* no. 346-1973 (New York: IEEE, 1973).

below the expected level because of inadequate short-run operating criteria and procedures, as described later in this chapter.

From the consumers' viewpoint, power shortages manifest themselves in several ways, including complete interruptions of supply (blackouts), frequency and voltage reductions (brownouts), and unstable service caused by erratic frequency fluctuations and power surges. Although all these phenomena are likely to inconvenience and to impose costs on consumers, the consequences of supply interruptions are the most severe. For example, supply interruptions at night will disrupt most activity, but a voltage reduction may cause lesser effects, ranging from the inconvenience of dimmed lights to excessive current drain, overheating, inefficient operation, and reduced lifetime of electric motors. The decreased life-span of fluorescent lights is another long-term result of brownouts. Frequency variations would affect a power system's automatic control equipment, as well as other synchronous devices such as electric clocks. Power surges could also damage some equipment, but these consequences are difficult to identify. The definition of outage costs and the theoretical framework developed in chapters 4 to 7 for estimating these costs encompass the expenses consumers incur because of all types of shortages. In practice, however, the principal emphasis will be on the effect of supply interruptions. Moreover, the effects of random or unexpected interruptions will be stressed, since they are likely to impose much greater hardships on users than known or planned power cuts. (See chapter 4, Estimation of Outage Costs.)

Sufficient redundancy and excess capacity throughout the system to meet unexpected contingencies are the major safeguards against shortages. Once a failure has occurred, the cause of the problem should be analyzed as quickly as possible, and a set of predetermined emergency procedures implemented to restore the system rapidly to normal operation.

At the generation level, excess capacity is expressed in the form of reserves. In the short-run context, spinning reserves are maintained by practically all systems to follow minute-by-minute load variations and to meet sudden contingencies, such as the forced outage or unexpected failure of a generating unit. These reserves consist of generators that are already connected to the busbars and are ready to take the load immediately, for example, machines that are operating at less than full output. Rapidly interruptible loads and generators, such as hydroelectric units operating in the pumping mode, are also considered equivalent to spinning reserves and are often loosely included in this category. Machines that require longer times to connect to the system to carry load constitute the system's nonspinning reserves, typically ranging from fast-starting hydroelectric units and gas turbines to slow-starting thermal units.

In the longer run, the system's operating reserves, which include both spinning and nonspinning components, are available to meet supply shortages. Operating reserves are especially useful when the need for more generation is predicted sufficiently in advance of the shortage for example, when it is anticipated that load would build up more rapidly than originally projected because of a load forecasting error. The terms hot and cold reserves are also used in system operation. Hot reserve usually refers to a thermal plant available for service within a few minutes, such as a generator with a hot boiler, that only requires startup of the turbine. Cold reserve consists of a plant that has to be brought into operation from "cold" conditions, with startup times ranging from several minutes for hydroelectric generators to many hours for thermal units.

In an emergency, as the demand approaches the total supply (including all reserves, generators operating at overload levels, and the maximum possible amount of power purchased from neighboring systems), measures must be taken to reduce the load. These would include voluntary decreases in demand, voltage and frequency reductions, and either operator-controlled or automatic load shedding.[5] The connecting and disconnecting of generators and loads to the system also cause technical problems involving sequencing, matching, and synchronization, that may affect the level of reliability, but these are usually handled routinely. If the excess demand is not curtailed in this way, the system could become unstable, with frequency fluctuations and power surges, the tripping of and damage to generators and lines, and so on, that finally culminate in widespread and unpredictable blackouts. Therefore the orderly reduction of load will help to limit shortage costs, especially by decreasing the number of consumers who would suffer the most drastic form of shortage—a supply interruption.

Decreasing the system voltage and frequency levels constitutes one of the most effective methods of reducing modest amounts of load and thereby significantly lowering the incidence of supply interruptions. Voltage reductions are generally preferred, because decreasing the sys-

5. See, for example, U. Di Caprio and R. Marconato, "Automatic Load Shedding in Multiarea Elastic Power Systems," *Electric Power and Energy Systems*, vol. 1 (April 1979), pp. 21–29.

tem frequency is often unacceptable where the system is interconnected with other systems, and it also results in stability and synchronization problems with the generators within the system. For example, the Central Electricity Generating Board (CEGB) in England, which operates one of the world's largest fully integrated systems, can rapidly shed up to 7.5 percent of the load by appropriate voltage and frequency reductions of 6 percent and 0.5 hertz, respectively, before disconnecting consumers. These measures would result in about a tenfold decrease in the risk of interruptions.[6] In a typical large interconnected system, a 0.2 percent drop in the operating frequency is likely to be associated with about 0.5 percent reduction in the demand, whereas 0.5 percent drop in the voltage level of the system would also have a comparable effect on the load.

Bulk transmission reserve capability is ensured by following basic design principles such as: (a) having adequate thermal margins (to prevent overheating); (b) ensuring steady state, dynamic, and transient stability against disturbances such as the buildup of large voltage oscillations following a lightning stroke; (c) avoiding bottlenecks in power flows; and (d) providing alternative pathways to feed load centers by using ring systems. In an interconnected system, it is important to avoid prolonged and extensive blackouts caused by the progressive overloading and cascading failure of many lines, following the initial outage of a single link resulting, for example, from a three-phase fault to ground.[7] The design of distribution networks also provides some redundancy. These design techniques allow extra safety margins for substation capacity and for power flow along feeders, and use switches to isolate faulted sections of line and to connect customers temporarily to circuits unaffected by the outage.

Measures of Reliability

Two different but related concepts will be discussed in this section: the assessment of power system security and the use of system reliability measures. The first has an essentially short-term objective of

6. See: R. W. Werts, "International Criteria and Practices for System Reliability," *Symposium on Reliability Criteria for System Dynamic Performance,* IEEE Publication no. 77Ch1221-1-1PWR (New York, 1977), pp. 24–28.

7. See, for example, G. L. Wilson and P. Zarakas, "Anatomy of a Power Failure," *IEEE Spectrum* (February 1978), pp. 39–46.

guiding system operations on an hourly or daily basis; the second in-volves reliability evaluation for the long-range planning and design of power systems over many years. Since this book is particularly concerned with the long-run potential tradeoff between system costs and outage costs, the second concept is more relevant. To provide a more complete perspective, however, the first viewpoint is briefly summarized before the second aspect is discussed in greater detail.[8] Because of the basi-cally mathematical nature of the models underlying these concepts, some jargon is unavoidable, but an attempt is made to keep the presentation as nonmathematical as possible. A more rigorous treatment of some of the more important mathematical concepts is given in appendix A.

Power system security assessment and enhancement in the short run involve the use of preventive measures and on-line decisions to main-tain or to improve the security level of a power system in operation. In the modern (probabilistic) view of a secure operation, the system is essentially characterized by several states.[9] A contingency may cause the transition of the system from the normal or secure state, in which loads are met subject to the operating constraints, to the alert or insecure state. Unless preventive action is taken to restore the secure state, a further transition to the emergency state could occur. This is equivalent to the conditions of shortage described earlier. Corrective or emergency controls are required to return the system directly, or through the "re-storative" state, to the alert state, from which a further transition to the secure state may be made. Security assessment helps to characterize the various states in relation to security indexes or functions, and to deter-mine the appropriate response of the system controller.[10]

Control may be exercised by taking simple (deterministic) but in-herently inflexible actions, for example, implementing a predetermined operator response to a specified contingency. More sophisticated re-

8. For details, see, A. R. Debs and A. S. Benson, "Security Assessment of Power Systems," *Systems Engineering for Power: Status and Prospects*, pp. 144–76; and L. P. Hajdu and R. Podmore, "Security Enhancement for Power Systems," *Systems Engineering for Power: Status and Prospects*, pp. 177–95.

9. See Thomas E. DyLiacco, "The Emerging Concept of Security Control," *Proceedings of the 1970 Symposium on Power Systems* (Lafayette, Ind.: Purdue University, May 1970).

10. See Tor-odd Berntsen and Arne T. Holen, "Security Control in Network System Operation," *Reliability of Power Supply Systems*, IEE Conference Publi-cation no. 148 (London: Institute of Electrical Engineers, February 1977), pp. 154–57; and Karel Janac, "Control of Large Power Systems Based on Situation Recognition and High Speed Simulation," *IEEE Transactions on Power Apparatus and Systems*, vol. PAS–98 (May/June 1979), pp. 710–15.

sponses would involve rapid on-line analysis of a (probabilistic) computer model of the system, such as the one described earlier. The model would use an existing data base and on-line telemetered input values of key system variables to identify and to characterize the contingency. The essential link between this concept of system security and the long-run viewpoint used in system planning is the use of probabilistic security/reliability indexes to describe the state of the system. The models used in each case are generally different, however, with system security assessment relying on time-dependent probabilities to characterize system states, whereas long-run system reliability (discussed below) is based on corresponding steady-state probabilities.

In the context of long-range system expansion planning, reliability concepts are required to establish target reliability levels and to analyze and compare the future reliability levels of different system design options with these target values. The initial use of reliability criteria in system planning relied on simple rule-of-thumb, deterministic approaches. For example, the concept of ensuring an adequate reserve margin (such as 20 percent above the expected peak demand) or use of a single or double-worst-fault design criterion (that is, the capability of the system to meet the load after the loss of the largest or the two largest generating units respectively) was common for many years in generation planning. Such rules are still used by some smaller systems. Combined deterministic criteria may also be used, for example, one requiring sufficient capacity to withstand the loss of the largest unit, and to still retain an adequate reserve margin.

Given the basically probabilistic character of system reliability and component outages, the next stage of sophistication in reliability analysis led to the development of combinatorial (probabilistic) methods. These combinatorial models made it possible to compute the long-run expectation of the future state of a large and complex system. One example would be the system's inability to meet the predicted load. In these models relevant load data and information regarding the probable availability of the individual system components are appropriately combined according to the axioms of probability.[11] Familiar reliability indexes such

---

11. The basic laws of probability involved are the well-known ones that define additivity, multiplicability, and complementarity. In this context, the assumption regarding the independence of random events is particularly critical and should be carefully verified, since it implies that different system components fail and are repaired independently of one another. (See appendix A for a more detailed discussion.)

as the loss-of-load-probability (LOLP) and loss-of-energy-expectation (LOEE) were estimated using this approach.[12]

The latest generation of probabilistic tools for power system reliability analysis involves overlaying the combinatorial method by the more recent concept of the system viewed as a stochastic process evolving over time. In this instance, the system commonly is modeled as a discrete-state, continuous-transition Markov process, which is discussed below.[13] At any given moment the system may change from one state to another, because of events such as component outages or actions designed to restore normal operation. The system may be analyzed when all the possible states are identified, and the rates of transition between them are known. The transition rates are determined by the corresponding contingencies or restorative control actions. The transition rate matrix, which specifies the transition rates between all possible pairs of states, provides a useful mathematical summary of the Markov process. The latter also may be visually depicted by a state-space diagram, with several closed boxes representing the system states and with a series of lines joining the boxes representing the possible transitions. This type of model facilitates the estimation of the expected frequencies and durations of outages, the modeling of the effect of exogenous shocks, such as the imposition of a sudden load on the system, and the treatment of nonindependent events, for example, the failure and repair of different system components. Given its importance, a mathematical treatment of the Markov model is provided in appendix A.

The several indexes of reliability currently used are summarized in this section, including their advantages, disadvantages, and the methods of computing them. The following discussion begins with the probabilistic measures of system reliability, since the simple rule-of-thumb criteria, such as the reserve margin, have already been described.

The LOLP criterion is commonly used, especially in generation planning. System failure is most often defined in terms of inability to meet the daily peak load. (See chapter 8, Power System Supply Costs, for a

12. The LOLP measure was introduced first in 1947; see G. Calabrese, "Generation Reserve Capacity Determined by the Probability Method," *AIEE Transactions*, vol. 66 (1947), pp. 1439–50. For a more recent review of probabilistic reliability indexes, see Roy Billinton, Robert J. Ringlee, and Allen J. Wood, *Power System Reliability Calculations* (Cambridge, Mass.: MIT Press, 1973).

13. See Chanan Singh and Roy Billinton, "Frequency and Duration Concepts in System Reliability Evaluation," *IEEE Transactions on Reliability*, vol. R-24 (April 1975), pp. 31–36.

discussion of the load characteristics.) Therefore, in the context of a generation study, the LOLP is usually computed not as a strict probability, but rather as an expectation; this may be interpreted as the average number of days over a long period, during which the daily peak demand is expected to exceed the available generating capacity. With this definition the LOLP is also less frequently, but more correctly, referred to as the loss-of-load expectation or LOLE. For example, the target LOLP frequently used in the United States is one day in ten years; in European countries, the corresponding standard varies from one day in fifteen years to one day in two and a half years. In transmission and distribution planning, time is measured continuously, rather than in terms of the daily load cycle, and therefore the LOLP is given in terms of the long-run average fraction of total time the system is expected to be in a state of failure.[14] The latter might be defined as an interruption of supply, or sometimes as a voltage reduction or component overload.

The LOLP is often supplemented by the expected-loss-of-load (XLOL) index, which indicates the expected magnitude of the unsupplied load, given that a failure has occurred; therefore, XLOL is a conditional expectation. Another index that measures the magnitude of system failure is the loss-of-energy expectation or LOEE (also called the expected unserviced energy or EUSE). The LOEE is the expected amount of energy not supplied because of outages in the long run, and it may be expressed in units of energy or as a fraction of the total energy demanded during a certain period. The expected frequency or mean recurrence time between outages and their expected duration is another pair of reliability indexes (frequency and duration or FAD). These indexes are used widely in transmission and distribution system planning, but rather infrequently in generation studies.

Several general points about measures of reliability should be noted. First, each of the indexes has its strengths and weaknesses, and cannot individually provide a complete description of outages. For example, although it is a measure of the probability of system failure, the LOLP does not indicate the expected magnitude of the load lost during such a contingency. In contrast, the XLOL provides the expected magnitude, but neither the probability nor the average duration of an outage. Like

14. See T. P. Hayes, Jr., R. P. Webb, and J. T. Day, "A Quantitative Method for Transmission System Reliability Calculations," *Proceedings of the IEEE Power Engineering Society Summer Meeting, Los Angeles, July 1978*, paper no. A78566-2.

the LOLP, the FAD measure also does not indicate the mean size of the failure, but because the FAD indexes are specified at the load-point or particular point of consumption, the number of affected customers and the magnitude of the interrupted load may be deduced.

Second, because the underlying models, the methods of computation, and their interpretation may vary considerably, the indexes are generally neither comparable, nor consistent in the sense that they could yield different rankings of systems by reliability level. Often, even the same index may be calculated in more than one way. For example, the LOLP can be derived by using a conventional model in which each generator is represented in two or more discrete states, or alternatively, by modeling the whole generating system as a normal distribution.[15] Similarly, the FAD measure of outages would be interpreted differently, if it is defined at the load-point than if it is specified as a systemwide generation-transmission index.[16] Finally, if the LOLP and LOEE criteria are compared, the former index will rank a system that has a long-lasting failure on one day above a system with two short failures on separate days, whereas the latter measure is likely to reverse the order of ranking.

The third and perhaps the most important point is that because of the way that reliability indexes are usually computed as predictors of long-run average system performance, they often do not reflect actual experience well. The basic reason for this divergence between prediction and observation is that the effects of operating procedures and constraints are rarely considered when long-run reliability indexes are computed. These operating criteria are important in short-run security assessment models, as discussed earlier, and, therefore, also modify the long-run system reliability. In particular, including operating considerations in generation and transmission system reliability studies leads to formidable computational difficulties, especially those caused by genera-

15. See, for example, R. N. Allan and F. N. Takieddine, "Generation Modelling in Power System Reliability Evaluation," *Reliability of Power Supply Systems*, IEEE Conference Publication no. 148 (London: Institute of Electrical Engineers, February 1977), pp. 47–50.

16. See, for example, R. N. Allan and F. N. Takieddine, "Network Limitations on Generating Systems Reliability Evaluation Techniques," *Proceedings of the IEEE Power Engineering Society Winter Meeting, New York, January–February 1978*, paper no. A78070-5; and G. E. Marko, "A Method of Combining High Speed Contingency Load Flow Analysis with Stochastic Probability Methods to Calculate a Quantitative Measure of Overall Power System Reliability," *Proceedings of the IEEE Power Engineering Society Summer Meeting, Los Angeles, July 1978*, paper no. A78053-1.

tor dependencies. Therefore, their effects traditionally have been ignored, except in Monte Carlo simulation and in advanced analytical models. These methods are described later in this chapter. Furthermore, reliability indexes that encompass large blocks of load and a chain of voltage levels cannot capture the variations in reliability experienced by individual consumers. For these reasons, the estimated indexes may be much more significant in the relative rather than the absolute sense. In this respect, forecast values of distribution system reliability indexes are likely to be somewhat more accurate than comparable generation and transmission system indexes.

Two broad categories of mathematical techniques are used to calculate the values of power system reliability indexes. The analytical methods rely on the direct, or analytical, manipulation of the basic probability axioms.[17] In contrast, the Monte Carlo methods use the computer first to simulate various random events in a way that is similar to throwing dice. The simulated events include the mean time to failure and repair time of components. Then, the system reliability levels are estimated (see appendix A).[18]

Analytical models tend to be compact and elegant, but become increasingly difficult to solve as the complexity of the system increases. Monte Carlo methods, however, always yield results with a minimum of assumptions and without explicit specification of stochastic system behavior. Yet they generally use large amounts of computer time and often require resimulation of the entire system, even when small parameter changes are made. Using the analytical methods, a partial or perturbation technique could suffice. Two types of Monte Carlo techniques, called sequential simulation and independent increment simulation, are in use; the second method is faster, but, unlike the first, it provides no information on the frequency and duration of outages. Generally, this method would be appropriate when the failure and repair of individual system components are mutually independent of each other. A recent assessment, in which a relatively simple system is modeled, shows that both the conventional analytical and the Monte Carlo simulation meth-

17. See Roy Billinton, *Power System Reliability Evaluation* (New York: Gordon and Breach, 1970).

18. See P. L. Noferi, L. Paris, and L. Salvaderi, "Monte Carlo Methods for Power System Reliability Evaluation in Transmission and Generation Planning," *Proceedings of the Annual Reliability and Maintainability Symposium, Washington, D.C., January 1975*, pp. 460–69.

ods are likely to yield closely similar results of reliability indexes, provided that the assumptions underlying the models are specified clearly and consistently.[19]

Analytical studies of generation systems usually require explicit specification of discrete generating capacity as well as load models; both generators and loads are assumed to be aggregated or lumped, and to be connected to a common terminal. The LOLP is the most commonly computed index, although the FAD measure is becoming increasingly popular. Techniques are also available to evaluate energy-limited, rather than capacity-limited, generating systems.[20] Monte Carlo sequential simulation methods are useful when no analytical method exists. An example would be systems with severe operating constraints, such as heavy reliance on energy-limited hydro or peaking units.[21]

Both analytical[22] and Monte Carlo[23] methods have been used in transmission and distribution system reliability analysis. The FAD measure is computed most often in these studies. The analytical approach includes techniques that directly solve an explicit Markov model, as well as those that implicitly use Markov concepts to compute reliability indexes on a step-by-step basis. This is done after determining the minimal cut sets of the system: that is, the least number of components whose failure will cause a supply interruption. Transmission and distribution studies have also been made using the Monte Carlo sequential and the independent increments simulation techniques. The latter method only provides the probability of system failure, as mentioned earlier.

For this discussion, the most relevant studies are those that treat the

19. See Khai D. Le, "Conventional Probability Methods and Monte Carlo Simulation Techniques: A Comparison of Results," *Proceedings of the IEEE Power Engineering Society Winter Meeting, New York, January–February 1978*, paper no. A78238-8.

20. See Roy Billinton and P. G. Harrington, "Reliability Evaluation in Energy Limited Generating Capacity Studies," *Proceedings of the IEEE Power Engineering Society Winter Meeting, New York, January–February 1978*, paper no. F78004-4.

21. See L. Paris and L. Salvaderi, "Optimization of the Basic Characteristics of Pumped Storage Plants," *Proceedings of the IEEE Power Engineering Society Winter Meeting, New York, January–February 1974*, paper no. C74158-2.

22. See Roy Billington and M. S. Grover, "Reliability Evaluation in Distribution and Transmission Systems," *Proceedings of the IEEE*, vol. 122 (May 1975), pp. 517–23.

23. See P. L. Noferi, L. Paris, and L. Salvaderi, "Monte Carlo Methods for Power System Reliability Evaluation in Transmission and Generation Planning."

system as a whole. The problem of unifying the evaluation of generation, transmission, and distribution system reliability is complicated by the large and intractable number of network capacity states. Analytical techniques are available, however, for combined generation and transmission reliability analysis. Some of these studies basically deal with the LOLP;[24] others yield the FAD indexes either at the load point[25] or for the entire generation-transmission system.[26] A basic choice arises with analytical methods. Should generation and transmission failures be modeled independently to derive separate reliability indexes that may be combined later? Or are transmission flow patterns and the status or behavior of generators so closely linked that an integrated and inherently more complicated treatment of the generation/transmission composite is required?[27] The Monte Carlo independent increments simulation method has also been applied to system-wide reliability studies.[28]

The Need for Economic Criteria

The earlier discussion of reliability focused almost exclusively on the analysis of the system in relation to the supply side. Target levels of reliability, however, are required for planning, against which the reliability indexes of future system performance could be compared. The determination of such standard levels requires analysis of demand side considerations as well, and this constitutes a difficult problem that has not yet been addressed successfully. More specifically, rational economic criteria have not been used to establish target reliability levels.

Most current reliability standards are based on past practice, and general notions regarding the quality of service that would be acceptable to electricity users. Sometimes, when the reliability level could be raised

24. See, for example, C. K. Pang, R. L. Watt, and J. A. Bruggeman, "Multi-Area Generation Reliability Studies," *Proceedings of the IEEE Power Engineering Society Summer Meeting, Los Angeles, July 1978,* paper no. A78546-4.
25. See G. E. Marko, "A Method of Combining High Speed Contingency Load Flow Analysis with Stochastic Probability Methods to Calculate a Quantitative Measure of Overall Power System Reliability."
26. See R. N. Allan and F. N. Takieddine, "Generation Modelling in Power System Reliability Evaluation."
27. See Roy Billinton, "Composite System Reliability Evaluation," *IEEE Transactions on Power Apparatus and Systems* (April 1969), pp. 276–80.
28. See P. L. Noferi, L. Paris, and L. Salvaderi, "Monte Carlo Methods for Power System Reliability Evaluation in Transmission and Generation Planning."

at relatively little expense, it has been increased to the point where further improvements would sharply increase system costs, that is, until the sharp "knee," found in most curves of supply costs versus reliability level, was reached (see figure 13.1, chapter 13). Because of the formidable problems associated with estimating the economic worth or benefits of improved reliability, however, only very recently have some preliminary attempts been made to measure the benefits of the quality of service in relation to the corresponding costs.[29] (For a review of these earlier studies, see chapter 4, Estimation of Outage Costs.)

Given the highly capital-intensive nature of the electric power sector and the increasing demand, massive investments in power systems will continue to be needed. (See chapter 1, Overview.) Whereas the costs of electricity supply will remain high, modern nations are so heavily dependent on electric power that disruptions caused by power failures would also be considerable. Therefore, given the large investment involved and the significance of the quality of electricity supply, the reliability standard must be based on economic considerations, rather than on arbitrary choice. The situation is particularly serious in the developing countries that are capital and foreign exchange scarce and that often adopt inappropriate reliability standards borrowed from industrialized nations.

Clearly, a balanced analysis of both the supply and the demand of electricity is required. Therefore, the basic economic criterion presented in this book would establish socially optimal reliability levels at the point where the marginal benefits of further improvements in reliability (measured in terms of avoided shortage costs) are equal to the marginal costs of supply.[30] A cost-benefit model is developed in the next chapter to achieve this objective.

In theory, the optimal power system expansion plan, which is the least-cost long-range design corresponding to the optimal reliability level,

29. See, for example, Michael L. Telson, "The Economics of Alternative Levels of Reliability for Electric Power Generation Systems," *The Bell Journal of Economics*, vol. 6 (Autumn 1975), pp. 675–94; and Z. Reguly, "Costs Evaluation of Power Supply Reliability," *Reliability of Power Supply Systems*, IEE Conference Publication no. 148 (London: Institute of Electrical Engineers, February 1977), pp. 13–16; and Mohan Munasinghe and Mark Gellerson, "Economic Criteria for Optimizing Power System Reliability Levels," *The Bell Journal of Economics*, vol. 10 (Spring 1979), pp. 353–65.

30. For a true social optimum, both the electricity price and the reliability level should be optimized together, as discussed in the next chapter.

could be determined independently of the specific measure of reliability used. As the case study indicates, however, in practice it is important to develop reliability indexes that satisfy two basic criteria. These indexes must not only characterize future system performance in a way that is helpful for traditional system planning, but also should be meaningful at the consumer level, and easily usable to determine the costs of shortages incurred by users, as discussed in chapters 4 to 7. From this viewpoint, load-point indexes of the FAD type, by time of day, referred to individual consumers on a disaggregate basis, would be the most convenient measures to use. In particular, in estimating these indexes, the effect of operating criteria on system reliability should be considered wherever possible, as previously discussed.

Generally, the more disaggregate and complete the information regarding the reliability indexes, the greater would be the accuracy of the corresponding estimates of outage costs. For example, since outage costs are generally a nonlinear function of outage duration, ideally, the probability distribution of outage duration should be computed. In general, this would be possible with Monte Carlo simulation methods.[31] But, given the many other sources of error in the estimation of outage costs (see chapters 4 to 7), it would be difficult to justify devoting considerable effort to estimating probability density functions for outage duration. Therefore, in practice, a knowledge of the average duration at specific times may be sufficient, for example, during the periods of peak, shoulder, and off-peak demand. Knowing the mean outage duration during given periods of the day would improve the accuracy of the outage cost estimates in two ways. First, if the day were subdivided into smaller intervals of time, the actual values of outage duration estimated for these periods would be more tightly clustered around the corresponding expected values, because the duration could vary by time of day, depending on such factors as the load and the availability of repair crews. Second, even the costs associated with an outage of fixed duration would tend to vary by time of day.

By estimating reliability indexes (and consequently outage costs) at specific times that coincided with the rating periods used in tariff setting,

---

31. An analytical model for incorporating the effect of uncertainty in LOLP-LOLE calculations by estimating the variance of this index is discussed in Roy Billinton and G. Hamond, "Considerations in Including Uncertainty in LOLE Calculations for Practical Systems," *Proceedings of the IEEE Power Engineering Society Winter Meeting, New York, 1979*, paper no. A79075-3.

it would also be possible to establish links with optimum electricity pricing policy. This is because the theory of peak load pricing suggests that the marginal capacity costs of supply be allocated among the different rating periods—such as peak, shoulder, and off-peak—in proportion to the corresponding marginal outage costs in each period. (See chapter 3, Method of Optimizing Reliability, for a discussion of the relations between optimum reliability and price levels.)

Method of Optimizing Reliability

The discussion in the previous chapters indicates that the procedure for optimizing reliability levels should be both theoretically rigorous and operationally useful: that is, it should bring together supply and demand side effects within a consistent economic-engineering framework that would be relatively simple to apply and would use readily available information. Accordingly, the economic theory for the optimization model that follows is drawn mainly from cost-benefit analysis, whereas the engineering aspects are strongly influenced by the practical approach used in power system planning. A range of optimum reliability levels, which maximizes the net social benefit of electricity consumption, may be determined by identifying the system expansion program that minimizes the sum of system and outage costs to society during the planning period. Equivalently, the reliability level should be increased up to the point at which the marginal supply costs of increasing reliability are equal to the expected benefits from the marginal shortage costs avoided because of the improvements in reliability.

Features of the Model

Several important features of the reliability optimizing planning model presented here should be emphasized. First, this method adds a new dimension to traditional system expansion planning. Usually, the power authorities examine several alternative long-range power system plans designed to meet a basically fixed-load forecast at some predetermined, desired level of reliability. The plans are also subject to other political, environmental, and legal constraints, and often variation in the growth of demand may be considered for sensitivity testing. (For details, see chapter 2, Introduction to Reliability.) Then, the plan with the lowest value of the present discounted value (PDV) of total costs is chosen. The PDV concept is defined in the next section. This cost minimization method is equivalent to the maximization of net benefits criterion used in cost-benefit analysis if the benefit streams of the alternatives being compared are identical.

In the more general approach described in the next section, the reliability level is also a variable to be optimized. The system planner must design a number of alternative systems to meet the future demand, which is initially assumed to be fixed, at each of several target reliability levels, still subject to the other constraints mentioned above. Then these alternatives are compared, and the one that minimizes the total costs, defined as the sum of the outage costs and the system costs, is chosen. Therefore, the more conventional system planning criterion of minimizing only the system costs is subsumed within the broader procedure of minimizing total costs that is presented here.[1]

Second, the new reliability model introduces another level of sophistication to system expansion planning by considering variations in the demand forecast. This method focuses primarily on the reliability level, which is optimized subject to a fixed initial forecast of load growth. It follows logically that a fixed evolution of electricity prices is assumed. Although it would be ideal from an economic point of view to optimize price and reliability simultaneously, electricity tariffs in the real world usually are fixed, and not necessarily at optimum levels. In this model, it is more practical to assume a given evolution of prices when the first round of optimum reliability levels is determined. Any changes in the pricing assumptions resulting from the first iteration can be fed back into the model to improve the optimal choice.

Third, this approach underlines the importance of accurately measuring outage costs based on detailed economic activity models for different kinds of electricity consumers. Outage costs should be estimated in

1. See Mohan Munasinghe, "A New Approach to Power System Planning," *IEEE Transactions on Power Apparatus and Systems*, vol. PAS-99 (January/ February 1980).

disaggregate form, in particular, using load point frequency and duration reliability indexes rather than aggregate measures such as the loss-of-load-probability (LOLP), and recognizing variations in outage costs by time of day, by outage duration, and by specific type of customer, rather than using average concepts such as costs per kilowatt-hour or kilowatt not served. The framework for evaluating outage costs as well as system costs is basically economic and is more appropriate in the context of the national economy, or society as a whole, rather than from the financial or accounting viewpoint of a private power utility company. Thus the goods and services used as inputs to the electric power system—such as labor, land, physical assets, and materials—are considered scarce economic resources, which could be used in alternative production, and they are valued accordingly. In particular, if markets are highly distorted, shadow prices may be used (see chapter 9, Shadow Pricing). Such an approach is especially relevant in the case of a publicly owned power utility, a situation that occurs very often in the developing countries. As examined below, however, the proposed approach does not require explicitly the existence of a single nationwide power system.

Fourth, the model facilitates optimization of power systems at various levels of aggregation. It may be applied to any complete power system or subsystem, even in cases when there are many such entities serving a single country. Thus, the planning of several power systems could be optimized: (a) globally, assuming full interconnection among them; (b) partially, with only limited interties and possibilities for buying and selling capacity (that is, reliability); and (c) singly, allowing no provisions for interties. Clearly, the global optimum would be the best and most economically rational one, providing the maximum net benefit of electricity consumption to society. Political, administrative, and other constraints, however, may force decisionmakers to adopt the options with limited or no interties, leading to local optima for each of the systems, which are collectively not as good as the global optimum for the country.

Similarly, although it would be best to optimize the planning of a power system in its entirety (that is, generation, transmission, and distribution), it is still possible to apply the proposed method to a subsystem, such as a distribution network. Thus, the case study presented in Part II is an example of such a distribution subsystem optimization, in which the generation and transmission reliability of bulk supply to an urban distribution grid is assumed to be fixed. Once again, system-wide planning is superior to partial (or subsystem-by-subsystem) planning.

If the latter option is pursued, however, the transfer price for bulk services between different parts of the system (for example, bulk power sales from a generation to distribution utility) should reflect the true incremental economic costs of the service. As discussed next, this point has much wider relevance to the establishment of prices that accurately signal the cost of service to customers (whether they are individuals or utilities), so that they may adjust their purchases of electricity to economically efficient levels.

Before developing the cost minimizing model, the simultaneous optimization of price and reliability or capacity levels should be discussed further, given its theoretical importance.[2] The closely related issues of optimal capacity levels and electric power system reliability have received attention recently as part of the more general economic literature concerning public utility pricing under conditions of uncertainty: that is, with stochastic demand and supply.[3] In this case, the utility is typically modeled as a net welfare maximizer, where net social welfare equals the expected willingness-to-pay for electricity, minus either the expected supply costs (Brown and Johnson) or the sum of expected supply costs plus the costs of rationing electricity according to consumers' willingness-to-pay (Crew and Kleindorfer, 1976, 1978). Such studies indicate that, ideally, both price and reliability should be simultaneously optimized to achieve maximum net social welfare.

This complex analysis can be expressed simply.[4] Economic efficiency would be maximized if the price were set equal to marginal cost and the capacity level were fixed at the point where the marginal cost of adding to capacity (net of the energy saved) was equal to the marginal con-

2. Optimizing reliability and capacity are equivalent in this context.
3. See, for example, Gardner Brown Jr., and M. Bruce Johnson, "Public Utility Pricing and Output Under Risk," *American Economic Review* (March 1969), pp. 119–28; Michael A. Crew and Paul R. Kleindorfer, "Peak Load Pricing with a Diverse Technology," *The Bell Journal of Economics* (Spring 1976), pp. 207–31; Roger Sherman, and Michael Visscher, "Second Best Pricing with Stochastic Demand," *American Economic Review* (March 1978), pp. 41–53; Michael A. Crew and Paul R. Kleindorfer, "Reliability and Public Utility Pricing," *American Economic Review* (March 1978), pp. 31–40; Ralph Turvey and Dennis Anderson, *Electricity Economics* (Baltimore: Johns Hopkins University Press for the World Bank, 1977), chap. 14.
4. See Mohan Munasinghe, "Electric Power Pricing Policy," *LDC Energy Management Training Seminar, State University of New York–Brookhaven National Laboratory, Stony Brook, New York, November 1978*; and Mohan Munasinghe and Mark Gellerson, "Economic Criteria for Optimizing Power System Reliability Levels," *The Bell Journal of Economics* (Spring 1979), pp. 353–65.

sumer benefits from averted corresponding electric power shortages. Setting the capacity level would also automatically determine the reliability level.

The optimal pricing and capacity rules interact in several ways. First, if system capacity is optimally planned (and operated), then the short- and long-run marginal costs (SRMC and LRMC) are equal, where SRMC and LRMC are defined as the costs of meeting one unit of incremental electricity consumption with capacity fixed and with capacity varying optimally, respectively. If the system plan is suboptimal, SRMC and LRMC diverge, and the pricing policy must reflect some appropriate compromise between these values. Second, the marginal costs of supply include both capacity and energy components. For pricing purposes, the optimal marginal capacity costs may be allocated among different rating periods in proportion to the corresponding expected marginal shortage costs during these periods.[5] In the simple case of a peak and off-peak pricing model (where it is assumed that no shortages occur during the off-peak period), all marginal capacity costs would be imposed on peak consumers. Both peak and off-peak users would have to pay marginal energy costs.

Given a rationing or load-shedding scheme, previous studies maximized net welfare by satisfying simultaneous first-order conditions: that is, by equating to zero the partial derivatives of net welfare with respect to prices and capacity. This indicates that partial models attempting to optimize reliability subject to given prices would not guarantee the maximization of net benefits. That is, satisfying the first-order condition with respect to capacity alone does not ensure that the objective function is maximized, because a different combination of prices, capacity, and, therefore, reliability may lead to greater net social benefits.

Since electricity tariffs are in practice often not readily subject to change, it is appropriate to try to optimize reliability, subject to fixed tariffs, at least to a first approximation. To the extent that this is accomplished, the net benefits derived from the provision of electricity should

5. See, for example, Yves Balasko, "On Designing Public Utility Tariffs with Applications to Electricity," *Electricité de France Report, Paris* (1974); and Joseph Vardi, Jacob Zahavi, and Benjamin Avi-Itzhak, "Variable Load Pricing in the Face of Loss of Load Probability," *The Bell Journal of Economics,* vol. 8 (Spring 1977), pp. 270–88; where it is proposed that marginal capacity costs be allocated in inverse proportion to a reliability index such as the loss-of-load probability (LOLP). This would be inappropriate, however, because these aggregate indexes are poor proxies for prorating outage costs.

at least increase. Therefore, it is possible to develop a method of optimizing reliability by comparing the costs and benefits associated with
alternative levels of reliability. The costs incurred by consumers because
of electricity supply interruptions or outages decrease as reliability increases, and the costs of providing electric power increase. Therefore,
given a demand forecast based on the assumed tariffs, reliability should
be optimized where the marginal system costs of further increasing
reliability are equal to the marginal social costs of outages that are
averted because of greater reliability. Moreover, as shown in the model
developed in the next section, this method of optimizing reliability, given
the tariff level, can be used iteratively to optimize reliability and price
simultaneously. Supply and demand uncertainties are implicitly recog-
nized in the model by considering outage costs. To simplify the presentation, however, supply and demand are not modeled as stochastic
processes, and the conditions for simultaneous optimization of price and
reliability have not been derived. Incorporation of these features in the
model would not alter the basic results developed here.

Reliability Optimizing Planning Model

The first step is to formulate the hierarchical model of an electric
power system required to serve a large region consisting of N smaller
geographic areas for a long time interval, which also may be divided into
τ distinct periods. Consider M alternative long-run investment plans or
expansion paths arising from different power system designs prepared by
the system planners. Let the set $\mathbf{R}^i$ that characterizes the global reliability level for the region and is associated with the ith power system
expansion plan, be defined as:

$$\mathbf{R}^i = R^i_{jt} \qquad j = 1 \text{ to } N, \text{ and } t = 1 \text{ to } \tau, \text{ for } i = 1 \text{ to } M;$$

where the superscript i and the subscripts j and t relating to the variable
R denote values of R corresponding to system expansion plan i, in
geographic area j, and during time period t, respectively.

Generally in any given area j, there are limits to the variation of the
reliability level in adjacent time periods, and the values taken by R^i_{jt}
over time will be related because of the indivisibility or lumpiness of
power system investments.

Next, the set representing global demand for electricty services is defined by:

$$\mathbf{D} = D_{jt} \qquad\qquad j = 1 \text{ to } N \text{ and } t = 1 \text{ to } \tau.$$

Each component of demand is a function of other variables and the equation may be written:

(3.1) $$D_{jt} = D_{jt}(P_{jt}, Y_{jt}, R^*_{jt}, \mathbf{Z}_{jt})$$

where P is the electricity price, Y is the income variable that represents the level of economic activity, R^* is the expected value of reliability, and $\mathbf{Z}$ is a vector of other independent variables affecting demand. Initially, it is assumed that the demand forecast is determined by the exogenously given evolution over time of the values of arguments on the right-hand side of equation (3.1).

As described in chapter 4 (Estimation of Outage Costs), the costs suffered by electricity consumers because of electric power shortages may be represented as a geographically localized function of the target reliability level, forecast demand, and reliability expectation:

(3.2) $$OC^i_{jt} = OC^i_{jt}(R^i_{jt}, D_{jt}, R^*_{jt}).$$

Power system supply costs, incurred as a consequence of providing electricity services, may be written:

(3.3) $$SC^i_t = SC^i_t(\mathbf{R}^i, \mathbf{D}).$$

Both outage and supply costs are defined as economic costs; the methods of estimating them are described in chapters 4 to 9.

If the system planners must consider several alternative designs associated with any single reliability configuration $\mathbf{R}^i$, they would select the plan with the lowest present discounted value (PDV) of total costs (PDV is defined in the next paragraph). The supply costs described in equation (3.3) correspond to such least cost system designs, where appropriate. SC^i should include the capital and operating expenses as well as the kilowatt and the kilowatt-hour losses in the system, appropriately valued (at the marginal cost of supply), but net of the marginal supply costs of kilowatt-hours not delivered because of outages. Disaggregation of system costs by geographic area would not be meaningful, because the effect of certain investments, primarily at the generation and transmission levels, are unlikely to be localized. A similar argument may be advanced regarding disaggregation by time period, but this breakdown is required to facilitate discounting over time, as described later. The arguments on the right side of equation (3.3) further emphasize that because power system investments are lumpy, in general, the supply cost in any given period could be associated with several components of reliability and demand, spanning many geographic areas and time periods.

A simple expression for the present discounted value of the net benefit of electricity consumption resulting from system expansion plan i is:

$$(3.4) \qquad NB^i = \sum_{t=0}^{T} \left\{ \sum_{j=1}^{N} (TB_{jt} - OC_{jt}^i) - SC_t^i \right\} / (1 + r)^t$$

where $TB_{jt} = TB_{jt}(D_{jt})$ is the total benefit of electricity consumption in the absence of outages, and r is the appropriate discount rate or accounting rate of interest, as described in chapter 9, Shadow Pricing. Because of the long lifetime of some investments, the discounting time horizon T is usually chosen to be greater than the planning time horizon, τ to eliminate end-effects.[6]

Consider what happens when system expansion plan $i + 1$ is derived from plan i by changing plan i slightly. At one extreme, a change in the generation expansion plan may alter the reliability level globally in all the geographic areas served by the power system; at the other extreme, a modification in local distribution system design would affect only the reliability level in a single area. Using equations (3.1), (3.2), (3.3), and (3.4), the resultant change in net benefit is given by:

$$(3.5) \quad \Delta NB^i = NB^{i+1} - NB^i$$

$$= \sum_{t=0}^{T} \left\{ \sum_{j=1}^{N} \left[\frac{\partial}{\partial D_{jt}} (TB_{jt} - OC_{jt}^i) \cdot \Delta D_{jt} - \frac{\partial OC_{jt}^i}{\partial R_{jt}^i} \cdot \Delta R_{jt}^i \right] \right.$$

$$\left. - \frac{\partial SC_t^i}{\partial \mathbf{R}^i} \cdot \Delta \mathbf{R}^i - \frac{\partial SC_t^i}{\partial \mathbf{D}} \cdot \Delta \mathbf{D} \right\} / (1 + r)^t,$$

6. For the period τ to T, TB_{jt} and OC_{jt}^i may be held constant, and only operating and maintenance costs are included in the SC_t^i stream. Since the lifetime of some system components could exceed T, it may be necessary to deduct the residual depreciated value of such items from the cost stream in the final year T. The large discount factor will minimize the effect of this correction.

where $\Delta R^i_{jt} = R^{i+1}_{jt} - R^i_{jt}$, $\Delta D_{jt} = (\partial D^i_{jt}/\partial R^i_{jt})\cdot\Delta R^i_{jt}$, and so on. The respective terms $[(\partial SC^i_t/\partial \mathbf{R}^i)\cdot\Delta \mathbf{R}^i]$ and $[(\partial SC_t/\partial \mathbf{D})\cdot\Delta \mathbf{D}]$ are not vector expressions in the strict mathematical sense, but rather, symbolically represent partial changes in supply costs associated with (a) changes in the set of reliability levels alone, that is, holding demand constant; and (b) variations in the set of demand levels induced by the changes in the corresponding set of reliability levels. The secondary effect on demand and outage cost occurs because of a change in the reliability expectation, which is induced by the change in the reliability level. Derivatives of the form $\partial D_{jt}/\partial R^i_{jt}$ and $\partial OC^i_{jt}/\partial R^i_{ij}$ could be defined so as to include this effect.

Equation (3.5) may be greatly streamlined by assuming that $\partial D_{jt}/\partial R^i_{jt} = 0$, at least in the first approximation so that $\Delta D_{jt} = 0$, and $\Delta \mathbf{D} = 0$. On the basis of equation (3.1), this assumption has two implications. First, the direct effect of reliability level changes on demand via the reliability expection R^* is negligible. Such a supposition is particularly true when the range of variation in R being considered is relatively small. Furthermore, to be practical, the problems of estimating such direct feedback effects of reliability on predicted demand are likely to outweigh by far any resulting advantages from the small refinement in the numerical results. Second, the indirect effect of reliability-level changes on demand resulting from any associated price change is also ignored. Both these assumptions may be modified later, however, by iterating, or running, through the model on subsequent rounds, as discussed later in this chapter.

On the basis of the foregoing discussion, a simplified version of equation (3.5) can be written:

(3.6) $\Delta NB^i = -\Delta OC^i - \Delta SC^i$

where $\Delta OC^i = \sum_{t=0}^{T} \sum_{j=1}^{N} [(\partial OC^i_{jt}/\partial R^i_{jt})\cdot\Delta R^i_{jt}]/(1 + r)^t$,   and

$\Delta SC^i = \sum_{t=0}^{T} [(\partial SC^i_t/\partial \mathbf{R}^i)\cdot\Delta \mathbf{R}^i]/(1 + r)^t$.

To interpret equation (3.6), it is assumed that the change from system expansion plan i to plan $i + 1$ involves an overall unambiguous improvement in reliability, specifically that each component of $\Delta \mathbf{R}^i$ is nonnegative. In general, this implies correspondingly that $\Delta OC^i \leq 0$ and $\Delta SC^i \geq 0$. In this case, equation (3.6) yields:

(3.7) $|\Delta NB^i| = |\Delta OC^i| - |\Delta SC^i|.$

Therefore, to maximize the net economic benefits of supplying electricity to society, the reliability level should be increased as long as the corresponding decrease in incremental outage costs exceeds the increase in incremental supply costs and vice versa. An equivalent way of interpreting equation (3.7) is to state that the net benefit NB is maximized when the present discounted value of the sum of outage costs and supply costs is minimized, since the total benefit TB is assumed to be independent of reliability R.[7]

Outage Simulations and Optimum Reliability Levels

In this section, the characteristics of the model and the methodology are further explored. (See also figure 1.1, chapter 1, Objectives and Methodology.) To analyze and present the results so that the practical implications of this approach are emphasized, it is necessary to simplify the theoretical model. First, the measure of reliability R, which was introduced earlier in a rather abstract way, will be defined more precisely. Second, ways of meaningfully aggregating variables such as R, OC, and SC will be developed after they have been estimated at the disaggregate level. One specific load point reliability measure could be written:

$$R_{jt}^i = (f_{jt}^i, d_{jt}^i)$$

where f and d are the mean frequency and duration of outages, respectively, during the period, t. As discussed in the previous chapter, accurate estimation of outage costs generally would require further detailed information relating to f and d, such as the time of day outages occur and

---

7. This formulation may be modified in various ways. For example, the total available investment funds (I) for the power system may be fixed over the planning period. In this case NB would typically have to be maximized subject to a budget constraint of the form:

$$I - \sum_{t=0}^{T} SC_t^i / (1 + r)^t = 0,$$

using the method of Lagrangian multipliers.

the numbers and types of consumers affected. For the exposition of the model, however, it is more convenient to use the simpler measure:

$$(3.8) \qquad\qquad R^i_{jt} = 1 - (OE^i_{jt}/TE^i_{jt})$$

where OE is the electric energy not supplied because of outages, and TE is the total energy that would have been supplied if there had been no outages. The above measure is analogous to the loss-of-energy-expectation (LOEE) criterion used in generation system planning (see chapter 2, Introduction to Reliability) and is related to the bulk power energy curtailment index defined by IEEE.[8]

For a given plan i, and area j, the local reliability R^i_{jt} may be plotted against time t. Figure 3.1 depicts three such evolutionary paths of local reliability for a given demand forecast, starting from the existing level a_o and extending over the planning horizon, 0 to τ. Each path corresponds to a system expansion plan i that seeks to achieve the desired local reliability level a_i. In general, the paths will vary about the target values because of capital indivisibilities (or lumpiness). A similar figure may be plotted for each of the N geographic areas served by the power system. Furthermore, by appropriately specifying the scalar index:

$$\Re^i_t = 1 - \sum_{j=1}^{N} OE^i_{jt} / \sum_{j=1}^{N} TE^i_{jt},$$

it is possible to depict graphically the evolution of global reliability for the entire system over time ($\Re^i_t$).

The impact of the global reliability level on the present value of outage and supply costs may be summarized by the following global scalar measures:

$$\Re^i = 1 - [\sum_{t=0}^{T} \sum_{j=1}^{N} OE^i_{jt} / (1+r)^t] / [\sum_{t=0}^{T} \sum_{j=1}^{N} TE^i_{jt} / (1+r)^t],$$

8. Reliability indexes for evaluating system adequacy are discussed in IEEE PES Working Group, "Reliability Indices for Use in Bulk Supply Adequacy Evaluation," *IEEE Transactions on Power Apparatus and Systems*, vol. PAS-97 (July–August 1978), pp. 1097–1103; and Roy Billinton, T. K. P. Medicherla, and M. S. Sachdev, "Adequacy Indexes for Composite Generation and Transmission System Reliability Evaluation," *Proceedings of the IEEE Power Engineering Society Winter Meeting, New York 1979*, paper no. A79024-1.

$$OC^i = \sum_{t=0}^{T} \sum_{j=1}^{N} OC_{jt}^i / (1 + r)^t,$$

$$SC^i = \sum_{t=0}^{T} SC_t^i / (1 + r)^t, \quad \text{and}$$

total costs: $TC^i = OC^i + SC^i$.

The model developed in the previous section indicates that the optimum expansion path, i, is the one in which TC^i is minimized. It should be re-emphasized that before the simplifying aggregations described above, values of R, OC, and SC are assumed to have been estimated at a very disaggregate level, for example, by starting with values of the underlying frequencies and durations of outages.

A typical set of results might appear as shown by the solid curve in figure 3.2. Starting with the low reliability run $\mathfrak{R}^1$, increasing the overall reliability level results in decreasing socal costs, TC, to a minimum at $\mathfrak{R}^m$. Further improvements in reliability are not justified beyond this

Figure 3.1. *Reliability Level Trajectories over Time Associated with Three Alternative Expansion Plans—i = 1, 2, and 3— for the Given Local Service Area,* j.

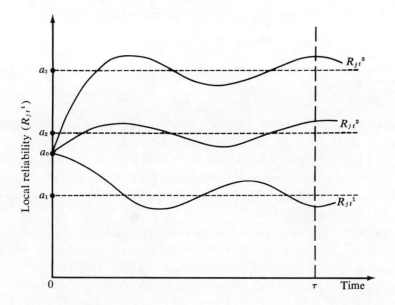

Figure 3.2. *Total Costs Curve*

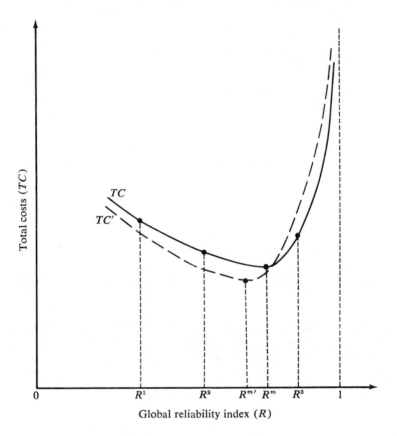

Global reliability index (R)

Note: TC = first-round estimate; *TC'* = revised estimate after feedback and reiteration.

point, because the marginal costs of supply exceed the marginal benefits due to averted outage costs. The same result is shown in somewhat different form in Figure 3.3. The optimal reliability level $\mathcal{R}^m$ corresponds to the point at which marginal supply costs (*MSC*) are equal to negative marginal costs outage ($-MOC$), reflecting the optimality condition $\Delta NB = 0$ in equation (3.6).

In this formulation, the reliability measure is defined only generally. Therefore, in the context of the theoretical model, the selection of the optimum system plan and the associated reliability level may be made on the basis of economic cost-benefit analysis and is quite independent

Figure 3.3. *Marginal Supply Costs (MSC)*
and Negative Marginal Outage Costs (—MOC)
as Functions of Reliability

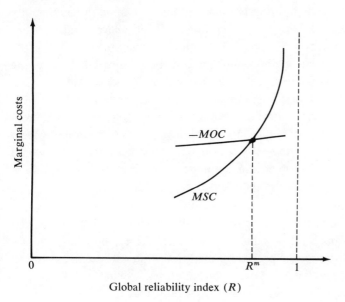

Global reliability index (R)

of the actual index of reliability. In practice, however, the nature of
the specific reliability measure to be used is important, because it would
be required for the empirical estimation of all outage costs. Because
of the large number of variations possible, especially at the distribution
level, each global alternative expansion path i is likely to have a unique
set of indexes $\mathbf{R}^i$ associated with it. Yet, more than one such path may
correspond to a single value of the global index $\mathfrak{R}^i$, a highly aggregate
scalar quantity. Furthermore, if R^i_{jt} is defined as in equation (3.8), in
theory, two separate expansion paths with different values of outage
frequency and duration might even yield the same sets of indexes $\mathbf{R}^i$,
although this would be highly improbable in practice.

Given this discussion, two slightly different conceptual interpretations
of the method of optimization become possible. In the first, each long-
range system design and corresponding index set $\mathbf{R}^i$ may be considered
as a strictly distinct one. Therefore, the system planner designs several
alternative expansion paths that span a sufficiently wide spectrum of
reliability levels, and then directly determines the optimum one that
has the minimum value of the sum of outage and supply costs. In the

other interpretation, the optimization procedure may be broken down into two stages. Initially, several specific levels of the global, scalar index $\Re^i$ that fell within a suitable range would be selected, and the alternative systems would be designed to be clustered tightly around these reliability values. For example, if there are m target reliability levels and a cluster of n distinct system plans associated with each level, then a total of mn alternative expansion paths would have to be considered. In any one cluster the global supply costs (SC^i) could vary widely, but the total outage costs (OC^i) would be similar. The first step in this method essentially consists of choosing the cheapest alternative system design from each cluster. This technique closely parallels the conventional system planning process. In the next step, these m least-cost alternatives would be compared to determine the optimum long-range system expansion plan, which minimized the total social costs (TC^i).

The first interpretation is theoretically more correct because no assumption is required regarding the equality of values of OC^i for different expansion plans in the same cluster. The second, however, follows more naturally from the procedure used in traditional system expansion planning. In practice, the two interpretations would tend to merge, since the system designing process is discrete: that is, it does not move smoothly or continuously from one path to the next, and time constraints prevent simulation of too many alternative system designs. Thus, engineering judgment often must be relied on to reduce the number of least-cost expansion paths to be considered. By choosing sensible nonintersecting and smoothly varying trajectories for R^i_t, situations in which paths with lower $\Re^i$ values corresponded to higher expenditures (SC^i) can be avoided. Because such variations are possible, it would be better to speak of a target band of optimum reliability levels around $\Re^m$, rather than a unique optimum value. A similar conclusion would apply in cases where the graph of total costs versus reliability had a fairly broad and flat minimum.

In particular, varying the reliability at the generation, transmission, and distribution levels must be done in a balanced way, as implied by equation (3.6). Suppose that starting from the value $\Re^m$ within the optimum reliability range, a small improvement ΔR^m in the reliability level and a corresponding decrease in outage costs $-\Delta OC^m$ may be realized by an increase in only the incremental costs of generation ΔSC^m_G, keeping transmission and distribution costs constant. Similarly, let ΔSC^m_T and ΔSC^m_D be the increments in transmission costs only and distribution costs only, respectively, each of which will separately bring about the same reliability increase ΔR^m and outage cost decrease $-\Delta OC^m$. Then the optimality condition for balanced improvements in generation, transmission, and distribution would require that:

$$\Delta SC_G^m = \Delta SC_T^m = \Delta SC_D^m = -\Delta OC^m .$$

Equivalently and with a change of notation, it is possible to write this condition in the forms:

$$(3.9) \qquad \frac{\partial SC_G^m}{\partial R} = \frac{\partial SC_T^m}{\partial R} = \frac{\partial SC_D^m}{\partial R} = \frac{-\partial OC^m;}{\partial R} \quad \text{at} \quad \Re = \Re^m.$$

The partial derivative $\partial SC_G^m/\partial R$ symbolically represents the ratio $\Delta SC_G^m/\Delta R^m$ where only the costs of generation are permitted to change, and $\partial SC_T^m/\partial R$ and $\partial SC_D^m/\partial R$ may be similarly interpreted. If, for example, $\partial SC_D^m/\partial R = -\partial OC^m/\partial R \neq \partial SC_T^m/\partial R \neq \partial SC_G^m/\partial R$, then this represents a partial optimization of the distribution subsystem alone. The case study of urban distribution network optimization presented in Part Two of this book corresponds to the above situation. A more global optimum for the whole system as represented by equation (3.9) would be better than the aggregate of three separate optima—one for each of the generation, transmission, and distribution subsystems. This is because the global optimum will result in a lower minimum value of total costs TC, or equivalently, a higher value of net social benefits NB. In cases involving the interaction of several different power systems, similar optimality conditions and arguments may be developed concerning the superiority of the global optimum for fully interconnected systems relative to the group of separate optima on a system-by-system basis.

Finally, consider a situation in which the stream of system supply costs SC_i^m associated with the optimum expansion plan $i = m$, on the first round, requires significant changes in the assumptions about the evolution of prices that were used to determine the initial demand forecast. For example, the application of a marginal cost pricing rule or a simple financial requirement, such as an adequate rate of return on fixed assets, may require previously unforeseen changes in future electricity tariffs to compensate for the new supply costs. Such a shift in prices would directly affect load growth. Furthermore, the new target reliability levels implied by the first round optimum path $i = m$, may affect reliability expectation, thus having a secondary effect on demand and outage costs (see equations (3.1) and (3.2)).

In the situation described above, the effect of the new sets of price and expected reliability levels on the demand forecast and outage cost estimates may be determined by iterating through the model again. In general, this reiteration would shift the whole total cost (TC) curve as shown by the broken line in figure 3.2, leading to a new optimum plan m'. In this way, the direct and indirect feedback effects of reliability on demand may be considered iteratively, until the optimum set of self-consistent (simultaneous) price, demand, and reliability levels are determined (see feedback loop in figure 1.1, chapter 1). Clearly, the implementation of such an iterative procedure would require considerable additional information, such as the probable evolution of pricing policy, the elasticities of demand with respect to price for various types of electricity consumers, the effects of changing outage expectation on outage costs, and so on. Therefore, although the simultaneous optimization of price and reliability is theoretically elegant, in practice only a single iteration through the model probably would be attempted, assuming exogenously fixed prices and demand.

If the first-round iteration results indicate that prices and reliability levels do have to be changed, often it would be more practical to implement these changes and to then observe their effect on demand and outage costs over some period of time. The optimizing procedure then could be repeated in the light of revised forecasts. The emphasis would be on recalculating results at different times to approach the optimum gradually over the years, rather than on attempting to compute the optimum by repeated iteration right at the beginning. This procedure is also more sensible in light of uncertainties in demand forecasts, system costs, and outage costs, which may require application of statistical decision theory, scenario analysis, or fuzzy set theory, as discussed in chapter 8, Power System Planning and Supply Costs.

Chapter 4

▄▀

Estimation of Outage Costs

Throughout this book, the term "outage costs" is used to encompass all the economic costs suffered by society when the supply of electricity is not perfectly reliable or when it is not expected to be perfectly reliable. In this chapter the types of outage costs and the general problems associated with estimating them are discussed in relation to previous attempts to measure costs. It is concluded that outage costs should be estimated on the assumption that all electricity is used for productive purposes: that is, electricity is combined with other inputs and intermediate products to produce various outputs. These outputs either would be marketed by industrial, commercial, and agricultural producers; consumed directly, by households, for example; or distributed without specifically related charges by the public sector. Since electricity is used in all these production processes, the economic costs associated with imperfect actual, or expected reliability levels can be measured relative to their effects on production. Detailed methodologies and models of outage cost estimation for different categories of electricity consumers are presented in subsequent chapters.

Nature of Outage Costs

As discussed in chapter 2, Introduction to Reliability, electric power supply shortages are manifested in various ways, ranging from power surges, frequency variations, and voltage level drops (brownouts) to load shedding and complete interruptions of supply (blackouts). These effects impose certain economic costs on consumers, of which the most important and perhaps the most simple to measure are the costs of interruptions.

Outage costs are direct when they occur during or following an outage, but are considered indirect when they are incurred because an outage is expected. For example, during an outage, consumers will suffer direct outage costs, since normal productive activity is disrupted. Indirect outage costs are incurred because consumers may adapt their behavior patterns in ways that are less efficient or more costly, but less susceptible to outage disruptions. They may also purchase alternative (standby) sources of energy. Although indirect outage costs do not result from a specific outage, they should be considered when attempting to estimate the economic costs associated with alternative reliability levels, because they depend on the general level of reliability and represent real resource costs. Generally direct outage costs are related more to the short-term effect of unexpected outages; indirect outage costs arise from longer-term considerations of outage expectation, including the effects of planned power cuts. In practice, it would often be difficult not only to estimate total outage costs associated with a particular level of reliability, but also to distinguish clearly between the direct and indirect components.

The direct and indirect outage costs associated with a given level of reliability depend, other things being equal, on both the expected and the actual levels of reliability. The nature of this dependence can best be illustrated by considering the following two situations.

(a) If a low level of reliability is expected (R^{L*}), then, to reduce direct outage costs, consumers are likely either to adjust their household and productive activities or to purchase alternative sources of energy. As noted earlier, these behavior modifications result in indirect outage costs. Total outage costs also depend on the actual level of reliability. If the latter is low, direct outage costs are still significant despite the indirect or preventive outage costs consumers incur. In this case, total outage costs will likely be high. With high actual reliability, direct outage costs will be smaller, and, therefore, total outage costs will be less than in the case of low actual reliability.

(b) If high reliability is expected (R^{H*}), individuals probably do little to adjust their behavior and, therefore, few indirect outage costs are incurred. In this instance, total outage costs will be relatively high if the actual reliability level is low, and these costs will be smaller if actual reliability is high.

The effects that the relation between expected and actual reliability has on outage costs is demonstrated graphically in figure 4.1. Consider a field of curves, each of which is a graph of total outage costs against the actual level of reliability, but parametrized by a given level of expected reliability. In general, at a given level of actual reliability, outage costs are higher when the difference between actual and expected reliability is greater. Also, outage costs will typically decrease with increasing reliability for any given level of expected reliability. These relations are depicted in the figure. Overall, total outage costs are likely to be highest with high expected reliability and low actual reliability (R^H*, R^L). Lower total outage costs are likely to occur in the case of low expected and actual reliability levels (R^{L*}, R^L), whereas total outage costs will be even lower when there is low expected and high actual reliability

Figure 4.1. *Relation between Total Outage Costs and the Levels of Actual and Expected Reliability*

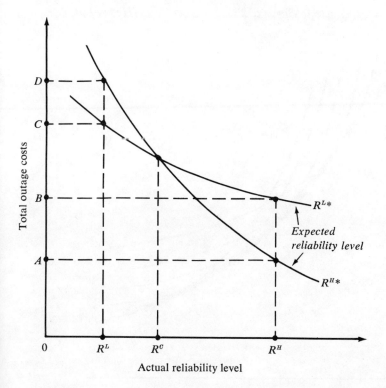

Note: R^H = actual high reliability level; R^L = actual low reliability level; and R^v = critical reliability level. R^{H*} = expected high reliability level, and R^{L*} = expected low reliability level.

(R^{L*}, R^{H}). Finally, total outage costs will be lowest of all when there is both high expected and actual levels of reliability (R^{H*}, R^{H}).

In reality, reliability expectations might lie anywhere between R^{L*} and R^{H*}, assuming that these are the limits. Thus, there will be many curves relating the reliability level to outage costs, one curve representing each level of reliability expectation. At each level of actual reliability, the curve that indicates the lowest possible outage costs is the one for which the actual and expected reliability levels are equal. Therefore it is possible to draw an envelope curve indicating those outage costs which would result if individuals could anticipate correctly the actual level of reliability and would take rational steps to minimize the resulting outage costs. Such an envelope curve is represented by the bold line in figure 4.2.

In practice, it will be difficult to determine how changes in actual reliability affect consumers' expectations of reliability. It may be necessary to estimate outage costs based on the assumption that expectations

Figure 4.2. *Envelope Curve of Total Outage Costs (Heavy Line)*

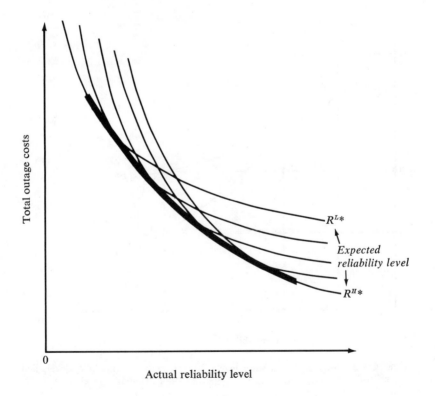

remain essentially unchanged over some range of actual reliability levels. With this simplified approach, adaptations to avert outage costs, such as purchasing a standby generating plant, would presumably occur only after the level of reliability falls below some critical value, which would vary for different consumers. For example, as shown in figure 4.1, if reliability level is reduced from R^H to R^L, outage costs will appear to increase by AD, given the assumption that reliability expectations remain unchanged at the high level $R^{H}*$. The increase in outage costs, however, may be only AC if consumers' expectations and their consequent behavior adjusted to the lower level of reliability $R^{L}*$. This would occur after the critical reliability level R^c has been passed. Actually, expectations would take time to adjust, and therefore the resulting increase in actual outage costs would lie somewhere between AC and AD.

In conclusion, by ignoring possible feedback effects between changes in reliability and reliability expectations, some relatively small errors in outage cost estimation are likely to be introduced. Since little is known in advance about the extent of such feedback effects, however, sophisticated attempts to correct for them could easily result in even greater errors.

Methods of Estimating Outage Costs

In the recent economics literature, there are two schools of thought concerning how outage costs should be estimated. One approach is to estimate them on the basis of observed or estimated willingness-to-pay for planned electricity consumption.[1] The other approach, the one used in this book, estimates outage costs by the effects of outages on the production of various goods and services.[2]

1. See Gardner Brown Jr. and M. Bruce Johnson, "Public Utility Pricing and Output Under Risk," *American Economic Review* (March 1969), pp. 119–28; Michael A. Crew and Paul R. Kleindorfer, "Peak Load Pricing with a Diverse Technology," *The Bell Journal of Economics* (Spring 1976), pp. 207–31; Roger Sherman and Michael Visscher, "Second Best Pricing with Stochastic Demand," *American Economic Review* (March 1978), pp 41–53; and Michael A. Crew and Paul R. Kleindorfer, "Reliability and Public Utility Pricing," *American Economic Review* (March 1978), pp. 31–40. Crew and Kleindorfer also recognize that there are other costs associated with outages: that is, the rationing costs of determining how to shed loads at the lowest cost, but these costs are not well defined.
2. See Michael L. Telson, "The Economics of Alternative Levels of Reliability for Electric Generating Systems," *The Bell Journal of Economics*, vol. 6 (Fall

As mentioned in chapter 3, Method of Optimizing Reliability, attempts to estimate outage costs according to willingness-to-pay are actually part of a more general literature on optimal pricing for public utilities under conditions of uncertainty: that is, stochastic demand and supply. In this approach the variable to be maximized is net welfare, which is generally set equal to the expected area under the demand curve corresponding to planned electricity consumption, minus the sum of the expected costs of supplying electricity, plus any expected costs of rationing available electricity among consumers if an outage occurs. Thus, outage costs are measured by the expected reduction in net welfare or the amount those deprived of electricity would be willing to pay for it, minus the costs saved by not supplying it.

Studies that estimate outage costs on the basis of willingness-to-pay assume that electricity provides direct satisfaction to its consumers. Outage costs are therefore estimated in terms of lost consumers' surplus. Other studies that estimate outage costs by the effect of outages on various types of production do not make this assumption. Instead, they treat electricity as an intermediate input used to produce various goods and services that provide consumers with satisfaction, rather than as a final good that provides satisfaction to consumers. Outage costs are therefore measured primarily by the costs to society of outputs not produced because of outages.

The studies that estimate outage costs on the basis of willingness-to-pay have several important shortcomings. (a) It seems clear that observed willingness-to-pay for planned electricity consumption is not an accurate indicator of what an individual would be willing to pay to avoid an unplanned outage.[3] This type of outage is apt to disrupt activities involving electricity consumption, and, therefore, actual outage costs

---

1975), pp. 679–94; Ralph Turvey and Dennis Anderson, *Electricity Economics* (Baltimore: Johns Hopkins University Press for the World Bank, 1977), chap. 14; Mohan Munasinghe, "Costs Incurred by Residential Electricity Consumers Due to Power Failures," *Journal of Consumer Research* (March 1980); and Mohan Munasinghe and Mark Gellerson, "Economic Criteria for Optimizing Power System Reliability Levels," *The Bell Journal of Economics*, vol. 10 (Spring 1979), pp. 353–65.

3. For example, Michael Webb, in "The Determination of Reserve Generating Capacity Criteria in Electricity Supply Systems," *Applied Economics* (March 1977), pp. 19–31, suggests using electricity tariffs as a lower bound on the estimate of outage costs. This is inappropriate because even at the margin, the cost of an unexpected interruption in the supply of electricity will exceed what consumers are willing to pay for the planned consumption of electricity.

may be greatly in excess of observed (long-run) willingness-to-pay. (b) These studies measure losses of consumers' surplus on the basis of their assumption that load shedding takes place according to willingness-to-pay: that is, those with the lowest willingness-to-pay are the first to have their electricity cut off. Thus, with reference to figure 4.3, the marginal consumers' surplus lost is the triangle-shaped area, ABC, defined by the downward sloping demand curve, DD, the horizontal line at the price, $\bar{p}$, and the vertical line representing the quantity, Q_A, of electricity supplied in spite of the outage. In many instances, however, it is not reasonable to assume that load shedding takes place according to willingness-to-pay. For example, if the outage is caused by a distribution system failure rather than a generation system failure, the ability to carry out load shedding according to some predetermined order may be severely limited. If this is the case, the resulting loss in consumers' surplus is the trapezoid-shaped area, $EFGH$, defined by the demand curve, the price line, and the inframarginal units of electricity not supplied, ΔQ_2. The implication of these arguments is that actual outage costs will exceed outage costs estimated on the basis of the marginal consum-

Figure 4.3. *Marginal and Inframarginal Consumer's Surplus Lost*

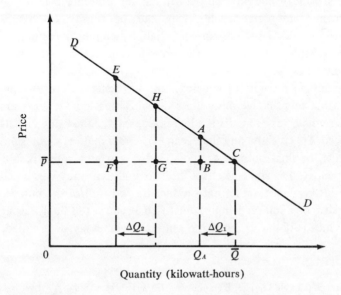

Note: ABC = consumer's surplus lost because of marginal energy lost, ΔQ_1; $EFGH$ = consumer's surplus lost because of inframarginal energy lost, ΔQ_2.

ers' surplus lost. Finally, with this approach, the empirical estimation of outage costs requires exact knowledge of various consumers' demand functions for electricity. Given the problems associated with empirically estimating these demand functions, it is likely that any estimates of outage costs obtained in this way will be subject to considerable error.[4]

Therefore, outage costs would be more appropriately measured in relation to the effects of outages on a variety of productive activities. A general methodology for estimating outage costs consistent with this conclusion is developed in this chapter, and attempts to estimate direct outage costs in relation to the effects of outages on production are reviewed.

Production is a process in which capital and labor are combined with other inputs, such as raw materials and intermediate products, to produce a stream of outputs over time. Under conditions approximating those of perfect competition, the net social benefit of a marginal unit of output in a given time period equals the value of the output minus the value of inputs. For inframarginal units of output, producers' and consumers' surpluses must be included when measuring the net benefits of production. When market distortions are present in the economy, appropriate shadow prices must be used to value inputs and outputs (see chapter 9, Shadow Pricing, for details). The net social benefit resulting from a time stream of marginal outputs equals the present value of the resulting stream of net social benefits. Thus, the opportunity cost of supplying electricity with less-than-perfect reliability can be measured in terms of the resulting reduction in the present value of this stream of net social benefits.

When an outage disrupts production, the net benefits derived from all activities that rely on electricity are reduced. Direct outage costs are incurred, since the costs of inputs are increased, and/or the value of outputs is reduced. Specifically, an outage can cause raw materials, intermediate products, or final outputs to spoil, and it can also result in idle productive factors. The spoilage effect leads to an opportunity cost equal to the value of the final product not produced as a result of the outage, minus the value of additional inputs not used because the final output was not produced. If the value of the output is not easily determined,

4. See Lester D. Taylor, "The Demand for Electricity: A Survey," *The Bell Journal of Economics*, vol. 6 (Spring 1975), pp. 74–110; and chapter 8, Power System Supply Costs.

however, as in the case of household and public sector outputs that are not sold directly on the market, then it is necessary to use the cost of producing the spoiled product or output as a minimum estimate of the resulting cost of the outage.

When productive factors become idle because of an outage, an opportunity cost results. The magnitude of the opportunity cost depends on the nature of the production process and on the producer's decision whether or not to work overtime to make up the lost output. The idle factor cost when lost output is not recovered equals the foregone value-added: that is, the value of the lost output minus the value of materials and intermediate products involved in its production. Again, when the value of outputs cannot be easily determined, then this cost may be estimated by the cost of idle productive resources during the outage period, assuming that factor payments equal marginal revenue products. This measure of outage costs also ignores the losses of consumers' surplus, which is apt to be small because of the marginal reduction in output resulting from most outages. Any offsetting benefits realized during outage periods when production has stopped, such as workers' enjoyment of the forced idleness, is also neglected.

Lost output might be made up in the short run by overtime production. An opportunity cost would result in this case, since output is produced later in the time stream and factor costs, especially labor, increase. In practice, it is better to ignore the longer-term possibility that the productive life of capital might be extended by the length of the outage, since the capital is not used during this period. It would not be realistic to assume that lost output could be recovered during this "extra" production period at the end of the machines' lifetime, unless physical depreciation was strictly a function of usage. Instead, if depreciation were a function of time, technical change, or changing factor prices, then the life of the equipment would not be significantly extended. Even if the lost output were produced later, the present worth of the resulting net benefits would generally be small because of the effect of discounting.

This approach for estimating outage costs can be simplified so that it can be applied when there are few details available about the response of various economic units to outages. In most cases an industrial user of electricity would not have an economic incentive to make up lost output with overtime. Similarly, electricity used in the home and for street lighting produces outputs that are integrally related to the time of production. Since these outputs are essentially consumed at the time of production, there is little likelihood of overtime production.

Review of Previous Studies

Several previous studies have attempted to estimate outage costs.[5] Given the preceding discussion of the general nature of outage costs, these studies are now briefly reviewed with respect to: (a) the actual measure of outage costs that they develop; (b) the way in which this measure is utilized to obtain outage cost estimates for various types of electricity consumers; and (c) the extent to which these studies investi-

---

5. The studies reviewed in this section are: Dahlin Lalander, "Memorandum Concerning Estimation of the Costs of the National Economy in the Event of a Loss of Supply" (Vattenfall, 1948); Swedish Joint Committee for the Electricity Council, "Cost of Interruptions in Electricity Supply" (Stockholm: September 1969); R. Bruce Shipley, Alton D. Patton, and John S. Denison, "Power Reliability Cost vs. Worth," *IEEE Transactions on Power Apparatus and Systems*, vol. PAS-91 (September/October 1972), pp. 2204–12; World Bank, EMENA Projects Division, "Appraisal of the Istanbul Power Distribution Project, Istanbul Electricity, Tramway, and Tunnel Company (IETT), Turkey" (a restricted-circulation document) (Washington, D.C., April 1973, processed); Pablo Jaromillo and Esteban Skoknic, "Costo Social de las Restricciones Energía Eléctrica," Oficina de Planificación, Chile (August 1973); Taiwan Power Company, "Evaluation of Generating Capacity Reserve for Taiwan Power Company"; Jamaica Public Service Company Planning Department, "Reliability Dollar Value Analysis," and "The Selection of a Generation (Static) Reliability Criteria for the Jamaican Public Service Company, Ltd" (November 1975); Alvin Kaufman, "Reliability Criterion—A Cost-Benefit Analysis," Office of Research, New York State Public Service Commission (August 1975); Michael L. Telson, "The Economics of Alternative Levels of Reliability for Electric Generating Systems"; DeAnne S. Julius, "The Economic Cost of Power Outages: Methodology and Application to Jamaica," report no. *RES7* the World Bank, Energy, Water, and Telecommunications Department (a restricted-circulation document) (Washington, D.C., August 1976, processed); Michael Webb, "Determination of Reserve Generating Capacity Criteria in Electricity Supply Systems"; and D. Priestman, "The Cost of a Long Term Electrical Energy Shortage Due to Underplanning" (paper presented at the Eleventh Annual Pacific Northwest Regional Economic Conference, May 1977, Eugene, Oregon; processed. Other relevant studies include: H. Weber, "Evaluation of the Damage to the Economy Caused by Losses of Electricity Supply," *Energetik*, vol. 2 (1966), pp. 22–26; J. Fabres and A. Bonnardot, "The Cost of Energy Not Applied in Electrical Networks," *Electrical Review* (November 1971), pp. 737–39; G. F. L. Dixon, "British and French Views on Security of Supply," *Electricity Review* (November 1971), pp. 735–37; S. Schulte, "Problems in the Evaluation of Costs Incurred Due to Electricity Supply Failures," *Elektrizitatswirtschaft*, vol. 70, no. 23 (Nov. 1971), pp. 656–61; and L. Lundberg, *Quality of Service from the Consumer's Point of View* (report of the Group of Experts, no. 60/D1, International Union of Producers and Distributors of Electrical Energy) (Paris: UNIPEDE, 1972). Further references are given in appendix E.

gate the relation between the duration of an outage and its resulting cost. For more specific details readers are referred to the original studies.

Measurement of outage costs

None of the studies reviewed in this section explicitly discusses the fact that there are two general types of outage-related costs: the direct costs of spoiled products and idle factors, as well as the indirect costs of obtaining standby sources of energy and of adopting less efficient production techniques. Since these studies did not attempt to measure indirect outage costs as defined earlier in this chapter, only their attempts to measure direct outage costs are discussed here.

Previous attempts to measure the direct component of total outage costs were unsatisfactory because they did not recognize production as a process through which inputs are combined with raw materials and intermediate products to produce a stream of outputs over time. Therefore, these studies do not estimate the effects of outage costs on the stream of final outputs. The exception is the Jamaica study by Julius, which implicitly recognizes how these costs affect industrial consumers by allowing for the possibility of overtime production. This study also attempts to measure the effects of outages on industry on the basis of opportunity costs.

Several studies use the simplistic assumption that outage costs are directly related to the average level of output per unit of time or electricity. A major weakness of this approach is that such average measures cannot be used in general to estimate the marginal effect of an outage, as discussed at greater length in the section on the relation between outage cost and duration. In the Istanbul study, for instance, the average value added per hour of work day in 1971 was multiplied by the number of hours of outages during work days in that year, to estimate the costs of outages in 1971. Similarly, in the study by Shipley and others, an estimate of outage costs per kilowatt-hour of electricity not consumed because of outages, was obtained by dividing the gross national product (GNP) in a given year by the kilowatt-hours consumed in that year.

The studies in Taiwan and Chile as well as those by Kaufman, Telson, and Priestman also use estimates of either output or value added per megawatt-hour or kilowatt-hour to measure the costs of outages to industrial consumers. The Taiwan study first determined production values per megawatt-hour for various industries, and then assumed that load shedding would occur according to the value of production per megawatt-hour. Costs of outages of various durations were calculated based on the assumption that load shedding occurred strictly in accordance with priority: that is, the supply of electricity to the industry with the lowest output per megawatt-hour would be curtailed first. For example, given a shortage of generating capacity, the electric energy made available to the industry with the lowest output per megawatt-hour would be cut off first, and so on. The product of megawatt-hours curtailed times the value of lost production per megawatt-hour over all the industries affected provided an estimate of the cost of a particular outage.

In many cases it may be inappropriate to use ratios of output or value added per kilowatt-hour to compare the losses among industries. Given an electricity-intensive industry and a nonelectricity-intensive industry, the former would have a lower production value per kilowatt-hour than the latter. It cannot necessarily be concluded from this alone, however, that electric energy is more important to the low-electricity-intensive industry than to the high-intensive one. Industry production functions and the availability of electricity substitutes would actually determine the importance of electricity. Thus, load shedding strictly according to the ratio of value added per unit of electricity might not minimize the value of reduced production.[6] Furthermore, load shedding according to some fixed order may be difficult to accomplish when outages are related to transmission or distribution: that is, when the nature of the system failure determines which consumers are not supplied with electricity.

The Chilean study estimates costs per kilowatt-hour of outage for twenty industrial users of electricity by employing an input-output approach. More specifically, a vector of input-output coefficients, b_{ij}, which indicates the reduction of electricity consumption in sector j, given a US$1.00 reduction in final demand for the output of sector i, is determined. If the output of sector j is not an input to sector i, then $b_{ij} = 0$. Thus, $(b_{ij} \times C_j)$, where $C_j =$ electricity consumption in sector j, measures the total reduction in electricity consumption in sector j resulting from a US$1.00 reduction of output in sector i, whereas the reciprocal of this measure is an estimate of the value of lost production in sector i, resulting from a 1 kilowatt-hour reduction in the electrical energy supplied to sector j. Similarly, the Priestman study uses a regional-

6. This point is emphasized in: Michael L. Telson, "The Economics of Alternative Levels of Reliability for Electric Generating Systems," p. 688.

ized input-output model to estimate shortage costs for each kilowatt-hour of electricity not supplied.

Kaufman estimates outage cost for New York State in value added for each dollar of electric utility revenues in 1972. He first estimated the state utilities' lost revenues and then multiplied this figure by the ratio of value added to electric utility revenues. Such outage costs are calculated on a yearly basis for 1974 to 1985. This assumes that the value of production for each dollar of revenues would be increased 2 percent annually to account for the expected growth of electricity inputs.

Finally, Telson suggests two upper-bound estimates of the costs per megawatt-hour of outages. The first of these is the large upper-bound estimate, which is defined as the ratio of the gross product of an area to the electric energy consumed by commercial and industrial users in the area. The small upper-bound estimate is the ratio of wages and salaries in a given area to the electric energy consumed by commercial and industrial users.

The Swedish and Jamaican Public Service Company studies use a more sophisticated approach to determine outage costs. Both employed interviews and questionnaires to determine the effect of electric power outages on industrial output. In the Swedish study, estimates of outage costs for industrial consumers of electricity were obtained from questionnaires completed by approximately seventy firms, which account for 28 percent of total industrial consumption. Total costs for the industrial sector were calculated as weighted averages of the costs in the twelve industries considered; the weights were the levels of electric energy consumption of each industry in 1965. These costs were estimated for outages of various durations and were measured in value-added terms, to avoid double-counting when aggregating across sectors.

The study by the Jamaican Public Service Company initially calculated the amount of gross domestic product (GDP) in value-added terms accounted for by each sector, and then the sensitivity of each sector to electricity outages: that is, the percent by which production would be reduced as a result of an outage was determined by averaging the estimates of three experts. The product of GDP for each sector times the sector's sensitivity to outages provided an estimate of the cost of an outage to each sector, based on the so-called "dollar value effect." The empirical results obtained should be viewed with caution, since the sensitivity estimates used assumed an outage of undetermined length, rather than of 1 megawatt-hour, as suggested in the report. By summing the above costs across all sectors and dividing by the total megawatt-hours of electricity consumption in Jamaica, a weighted measure of the value of production per megawatt-hour was obtained. This served as an estimate of the cost to society of each megawatt-hour of electricity not supplied, and is called the "reliability dollar value." The estimate of the value of production per megawatt-hour is biased downward, since residential electric consumption was included in the denominator, whereas the value of household production was excluded from the numerator.

Finally, this study measured the opportunity costs of outages caused by ruined and idle productive resources of industrial consumers. In some cases this cost might be roughly equivalent to the financial cost of outages, particularly when prices reflect opportunity costs, and there is neither slack productive capacity nor overtime production. If some production is recovered, however, either by using existing productive capacity more intensively after the outage or by overtime production, then the opportunity cost and financial cost measures may differ, and the former would provide a better estimate of the economic resource cost.

In summary, this review makes clear that most studies estimate outage costs as the value of production foregone during an outage. This lost production is assumed, in most cases, to be proportional to either the total length of outages or to the total amount of electricity not supplied. Such an approach leads to overestimates of outage costs if there is (a) some possibility of substituting other energy sources for electricity in production processes; (b) some production processes that either do not use electricity at all, or use it for noncritical aspects of production; (c) excess production capacity; or (d) sufficient inventories to cover lost production together with some excess capacity that allows lost production to be recovered eventually. Conversely, this approach could lead to an underestimate of outage costs if production cannot restart immediately after the supply of electricity is restored, or if materials are spoiled because of outages. The use of direct questionnaires or expert estimates would reduce the possibility of such over- or under-estimates.

Treatment of electricity consumers by category

Applying the general techniques of estimating outage costs described in the previous section to the specific types of electricity consumer affected by outages is particularly relevant. Many studies only consider the cost of outages that affect industrial users of electricity, including those focusing on Istanbul, Taiwan, and Jamaica (Julius), and those by Kaufman and Telson. The work on Sweden and Chile, and the Ja-

maica Public Service Company and Priestman studies, attempt to estimate the costs that outages impose on residential as well as on industrial
consumers. The Swedish study estimates outage costs for "typical" residential consumers. These costs include expenses associated with alternative energy sources needed, reduced efficiency of domestic work,
interference with food preparation, and restrictions on leisure activities.
The procedures used to obtain these specific cost estimates, however,
are not described in detail.

The Chilean study uses a fundamentally different approach to estimate
the costs that outages impose on residential consumers of electricity.
In this study, such costs are estimated in terms of two components: (a)
the per-kilowatt-hour tariff based on the assumption that consumers
value the electricity they use, or want to use, but cannot obtain because
of outages, at least as much as they pay for it; and (b) the implicit cost
of temporarily useless appliances. This latter cost is determined by dis-
tributing the annuitized purchase price and operating cost of the appliances over their useful lifetimes, and then dividing this annual cost by the
appliances' annual usage of kilowatt-hours. The result is an estimate of
the implied appliance cost per kilowatt-hour of outage. The method used
in the Jamaica Public Service Company's study to estimate outage costs
for residential consumers is similar to the technique used in the Chilean
study. Although the implicit capital cost of temporarily useless appliances is calculated in the same way in both studies, the kilowatt-hour
tariff was not included in the estimated outage cost because these electricity charges are not incurred during the outage. Outage costs will be
less than those estimated by this approach to the extent that (a) some
of the appliances considered will not be in use at the time of the outage,
(b) the outage will not affect the quality of service provided by some
appliances, such as refrigerators when the outage is relatively short, or
(c) the use of some of the appliances can be rescheduled without inconvenience. Other more fundamental problems with this approach are
discussed later. Finally, the study by Priestman uses the lost consumers'
surplus approach to measure residential outage costs, which would underestimate these costs significantly, as discussed previously in this
chapter.

Only the Swedish study attempts to estimate outage costs for those
other than industrial and residential consumers. Specifically, an attempt
is made to estimate these costs for agricultural consumers. These estimated costs are determined on the basis of a hypothetical "average"
farm. In this case, outage costs result from less productive labor for hand
milking, other milk production, and animal husbandry; loss of some

egg and poultry production; interference with food preparation and domestic work; and restricted leisure activities.

In summary, it is evident that one of the shortcomings of the studies reviewed here is their failure to consider the costs that outages impose on various types of electricity consumers other than industrial users. A few studies attempt to estimate these costs for residential consumers, but, as discussed earlier, these efforts have serious weaknesses. More general weaknesses of the previous analyses are that they fail to view the household as a productive unit and, more specifically, that they ignore the possibility that an outage may make productive household labor idle. This indicates that any study that considers only the cost of idle appliances may underestimate the costs that outages impose on residential consumers. Therefore, an alternative method of measuring outage costs for residential consumers is developed in chapter 5, Residential Outage Costs.

Relation between outage costs and outage duration

One of the most important issues arising from the estimation of outage costs is the relation between outage duration and the resulting cost. If total outage costs are not linearly related to total outage duration, then the studies estimating outage costs as a linear function of total hours or kilowatt-hours of outages—that is, those in Istanbul, Taiwan, Jamaica (Julius), and Chile and those by Kaufman, Priestman, Shipley and others, and Telson—will obtain inaccurate cost estimates.

The study in Sweden is one of the few that explicitly considers the relation between outage cost and duration. Outage costs for industrial, residential, agricultural, rural, and urban users of electricity are divided into fixed and variable components. This study shows that fixed costs are incurred as soon as the outage occurs and are independent of the length of an outage. Variable costs, however, increase with the duration of an outage. Yet, some estimates of fixed costs for outages longer than one-half hour actually consist of the sum of the fixed cost and variable cost components of the shorter outages. In this sense they do not measure truly fixed costs.[7]

---

7. For example, the fixed costs of an outage between one-half and one hour for the total industrial sector was estimated to be $0.21. This cost actually represents the fixed cost of shorter outages, $0.08, plus the (linearly) variable cost of shorter outages, $0.27/hour × 0.5 hour = $0.13.

Conclusion

This review indicates that most previous attempts to estimate outage costs have failed to develop an adequate conceptual framework within which to analyze outage effects and, consequently, outage costs. The costs of purchasing standby sources of energy are ignored, and even the attempts to measure direct outage costs are inadequate. In general, production is not viewed as a process that occurs over several periods. As a result, most existing outage cost estimates come closer to measuring the financial cost of an outage, rather than its true economic cost. Also, most studies fail to consider the costs that outages impose on other types of electricity users besides the commercial-industrial group. Even those that estimate outage costs for residential consumers ignore the opportunity costs of idle time inputs in households affected by outages. Finally, little attention is given to the relation between outage cost and outage duration. These weaknesses in the existing methodology of the estimation of outage costs are discussed further in the following chapters that develop methods of estimating outage costs for different types of electricity consumers.

Specific methods of estimating outage costs for various types of consumers should be micro-oriented and consumer-specific. Their applicability would depend on the availability of detailed information concerning levels of economic activity and the effects of outages. As indicated in the case study analyzed in Part Two, practical experience shows, however, that it may be possible to develop "shortcuts" that would also allow outage costs to be estimated roughly on a regional, provincial, or national basis. This would limit the field work required at the micro-level. For example, the value added for each kilowatt-hour in certain industries may be a good proxy for mean outage costs for each kilowatt-hour lost. Therefore, any macro-economic input-output data relating electricity inputs to industrial outputs by sector could be utilized to estimate outage costs. In other cases, the production process for a given activity may be similar enough in different countries for more readily available outage cost estimates from another country to be used. By using such estimates and also by adopting efficient sampling techniques, the number of field surveys necessary to estimate outage costs for macro-level studies of reliability could be reduced.

Chapter 5

Residential Outage Costs

A household is a productive unit combining resources such as household members' time, electricity, and other inputs to produce outputs, the enjoyment or consumption of which increase the welfare of the members of the household.[1] In the absence of external effects, the value of resources normally used in household production that are ruined or become idle because of an unforeseen outage could serve as an estimate of the welfare loss resulting from the outage. The unpredictability assumption is important because if exact times of outages were known beforehand, consumers would be able to adjust their schedules to minimize outage costs. As discussed in chapter 4, Estimation of Outage Costs, the short-run costs associated with a kilowatt-hour lost because of unexpected outages will, in general, exceed the maximum amount rational consumers would be willing to pay for the same kilowatt-hour, on the basis of their longer-run demand curve for planned electricity consumption.

---

1. See Gary Becker, "A Theory of the Allocation of Time," *Economic Journal*, vol. 75 (September 1965), pp. 493–517; Kevin Lancaster, "A New Approach to Consumer Behavior," *Journal of Political Economy*, vol. 74 (April 1966), pp. 132–57; and Reuben Gronau, "The Intra-Family Allocation of Time: The Value of the Housewives' Time," *American Economic Review*, vol. 63 (September 1973), pp. 634–51; for a more complete discussion of household production theory.

Household Activities

Although the household can be viewed logically as a productive unit, the measurement of residential outage costs is not straightforward. This is because most of the "outputs," such as leisure, are consumed within the household and are not valued in the market. Also, the value of inputs into this production process, especially household members' time, is often not determined in the market. The most important household outputs that use electricity as a principal market input are housekeeping, nutrition, and leisure.

Of particular relevance to housekeeping activities is the possible flexibility of rescheduling household chores, thereby minimizing outage costs. Interruptions in electricity supply usually affect the functioning of household electrical appliances used for ironing, washing, vacuuming, and other chores. Sometimes, however, it is possible that housekeeping activities which do not require electricity may be substituted for those that do. In addition, during any period, nonhousekeeping activities may be substituted for those involving housekeeping activities. Therefore, the outage costs resulting from idle resources used for housekeeping usually will be small. In general, the costs will not be zero because of the psychological costs of disruptions in the normal routine, assuming that household producers rationally allocate their time to various kinds of production before the outage.

Nutrition, defined here as an economic activity, could be hampered by outages occurring when food is being prepared or consumed, particularly in homes that rely on electric cooking appliances or lighting. For interruptions of relatively short duration, the outage costs may involve only the inconvenience of a delayed meal, but during lengthy interruptions, which are much less frequent, meals may have to be purchased, resulting in an unexpected expense. In areas where outage expectation is high, households may incur additional indirect outage-associated expenses by purchasing nonelectric appliances, such as small kerosene stoves for emergencies. When other fuels such as kerosene, gas, or firewood are used exclusively for cooking, outage costs are likely to be small. If the expenses associated with nonelectric cooking facilities exceeded the costs of purchasing and using an electric stove, and if the former was preferred to the latter specifically because of the low reliability of electricity supply, then the difference in costs between the two alternatives would also constitute an indirect outage cost.

Leisure differs from the housekeeping and nutrition activities in ways that make the associated outage costs more important. First, the production and enjoyment of leisure in most households is limited, particularly for wage earners, to a relatively fixed period of time, usually in the evening. It is assumed that housewives are not limited to enjoy leisure only during the evening hours and, therefore, that their outage costs are small. Thus, it is possible to avoid complications arising from having to estimate the value of housewives' time.[2] Second, those leisure activities, such as television viewing and reading at night, which would require electricity have limited substitution possibilities for nonelectricity-using activities during an outage, at least in the short run. Since the loss of leisure activities is likely to be the most significant component of residential outage costs, a model of household activity based on the consumer's labor-leisure choice is developed to estimate the loss of welfare associated with interruptions in electricity supply.

Clearly, many other household activities and outputs—other than the three categories of housekeeping, nutrition, and leisure—depend on at least the partial use of electricity. For example, power outages also will affect the operation of major appliances including refrigerators, air conditioners, and heaters, which are only partially associated with the disruptions of household activities discussed previously. In these cases, the effects of the disruption would be significant only for outages of several hours, which generally occur far less frequently. In addition to the loss of services from such equipment, the damage to and reduced life span of motors and equipment resulting from voltage variations would have to be considered. Households may also incur indirect outage costs by purchasing emergency items such as standby generators, storage batteries, and kerosene lamps. In this respect, the consequences of outages may be inequitably distributed, because wealthier consumers will be better able to afford voltage-boosting devices and alternative energy sources, thereby reducing direct outage costs. Poorer users, however, may be less dependent on electricity and, therefore, less susceptible to outages.

2. See Reuben Gronau, "The Intra-Family Allocation of Time: The Value of the Housewives' Time." The low outage cost does not imply that the activity of housewives is valueless. It reflects the assumption that housewives have greater flexibility in scheduling their leisure, so that the inconvenience imposed by leisure loss resulting from evening outages is less severe than for wage earners.

Value of Foregone Leisure

Consider a typical household that maximizes utility over some period of time (D days). Utility U is expressed as a function of leisure type S that cannot be enjoyed without electricity, leisure type V that is electricity independent, and income I (net of expenses incurred to enjoy the leisure), which represents all other consumption:

$$(5.1) \qquad U = U(S, V, I).$$

Next, leisure type S is specified as a function of the inputs: time t (hours), electricity consumption e (kilowatt-hours), flow of services z from the stock of electricity using equipment (TV), and other inputs represented by x:

$$(5.2a) \qquad S = S(t, e, z, x).$$

Similarly, leisure type V is a function of time θ and other inputs represented by m:

$$(5.2b) \qquad V = V(\theta, m).$$

Furthermore, e and z may be written as functions of the stock of electricity using capital k, the value of appliances annuitized over their useful life, and of time t which is a measure of intensivity of use. Therefore, $e = e(k, t)$ and $z = z(k, t)$.

The household budget constraint may be written:

$$(5.3) \qquad I = w(H - t - \theta) - p \cdot e - b \cdot k - c \cdot x - r \cdot m$$

where w = effective hourly net income earning rate; H = maximum feasible number of hours of work in the time period; p = mean price for each kilowatt-hour of electric energy; b = equivalent income foregone for each unit of k in the time period; c = cost for each unit of other inputs x used; and r = cost for each unit of other inputs m used.

First, the longer-term situation, a period of one year, is examined. Maximizing utility subject to the linear budget constraint is equivalent to unconstrained maximization of the expression:

(5.4) $L = U(S, V, I) - .$

$$\lambda \cdot \left[H - t - \theta - \frac{1}{w}(I + p\cdot e + b\cdot k + c\cdot x + r\cdot m) \right].$$

The following equations indicate the first-order (necessary) conditions.

(5.5a) $\dfrac{\partial L}{\partial t} = \dfrac{\partial U}{\partial S} \cdot \left[\dfrac{\partial S}{\partial t} + \dfrac{\partial S}{\partial e}\cdot\dfrac{\partial e}{\partial t} + \dfrac{\partial S}{\partial z}\cdot\dfrac{\partial z}{\partial t} \right] + \lambda \cdot \left[1 + \dfrac{p}{w}\cdot\dfrac{\partial e}{\partial t} \right] = 0$

(5.5b) $\dfrac{\partial L}{\partial k} = \dfrac{\partial U}{\partial S} \cdot \left[\dfrac{\partial S}{\partial e}\dfrac{\partial e}{\partial k} + \dfrac{\partial S}{\partial z}\cdot\dfrac{\partial z}{\partial k} \right] + \dfrac{\lambda}{w} \cdot \left[p\cdot\dfrac{\partial e}{\partial k} + b \right] = 0$

(5.5c) $\dfrac{\partial L}{\partial x} = \dfrac{\partial U}{\partial S}\cdot\dfrac{\partial S}{\partial x} + \dfrac{\lambda}{w}\cdot c = 0$

(5.5d) $\dfrac{\partial L}{\partial I} = \dfrac{\partial U}{\partial I} + \dfrac{\lambda}{w} = 0$

(5.5e) $\dfrac{\partial L}{\partial \theta} = \dfrac{\partial U}{\partial V}\cdot\dfrac{\partial V}{\partial \theta} + \lambda = 0$

(5.5f) $\dfrac{\partial L}{\partial m} = \dfrac{\partial U}{\partial V}\cdot\dfrac{\partial V}{\partial m} + \dfrac{\lambda}{w}\cdot r = 0$

(5.5g) $\dfrac{\partial L}{\partial \lambda} = -\left[H - t - \theta - \dfrac{1}{w}(I + p\cdot e + b\cdot k + c\cdot x + r\cdot m) \right] = 0.$

Multiplying equations (5.5a), (5.5b), and (5.5c) by dt, dk, and dx respectively, summing the three resulting equations, and rearranging terms yields:

$$\dfrac{\partial U}{\partial S}\left[\left(\dfrac{\partial S}{\partial t} + \dfrac{\partial S}{\partial e}\cdot\dfrac{\partial e}{\partial t} + \dfrac{\partial S}{\partial z}\cdot\dfrac{\partial z}{\partial t} \right)\cdot dt + \left(\dfrac{\partial S}{\partial e}\dfrac{\partial e}{\partial k} + \dfrac{\partial S}{\partial z}\cdot\dfrac{\partial z}{\partial k} \right)\cdot dk + \dfrac{\partial S}{\partial x}\cdot dx \right]$$

$$+ \dfrac{\lambda}{w}\left[\left(w + p\cdot\dfrac{\partial e}{\partial t} \right)\cdot dt + \left(p\cdot\dfrac{\partial e}{\partial k} + b \right)\cdot dk + c\cdot dx \right] = 0.$$

Simplifying further:

(5.6) $\dfrac{\partial U}{\partial S}\cdot dS + \dfrac{\lambda}{w}\cdot (w\cdot dt + p\cdot de + b\cdot dk + c\cdot dx) = 0.$

Dividing equation (5.6) by equation (5.5d) yields an expression involving the marginal rate of substitution of income for electricity-dependent leisure, keeping utility constant as derived from the consumer's long-run decision:

(5.7) $MRS_{I,S}\cdot dS = w\cdot dt + p\cdot de + b\cdot dk + c\cdot dx$

where

$$MRS_{I,S} = \dfrac{\partial U}{\partial S}\Big/\dfrac{\partial U}{\partial I} = -\dfrac{dI}{dS}\bigg]_{U\ constant}$$

by definition. $MRS_{I,S}$ measures the marginal monetary value of electricity-dependent leisure: that is, it is the income increase that will compensate the consumer just enough for this leisure foregone at the margin to remain on the same indifference curve.[3]

Consider the effect of an unexpected outage during the evening when the family is enjoying leisure type S. During the outage, that is, in the short-run, it can be argued that e and z depend only on t. This assumes a putty-clay type of relation between k, e, and z. For example, in the short run, electricity use may be linearly proportional to time. Therefore, it is possible to write:

$$e = \psi(t).$$

Using the above expressions to evaluate equation (5.7), and replacing dS by ΔS, and so on:

(5.8) $MRS_{I,S}\cdot \Delta S = \left(w + p\cdot\dfrac{\partial \psi}{\partial t}\right)\cdot \Delta t + c\cdot \Delta x + b\cdot \Delta k.$

---

3. See Robert D. Willig, "Consumers' Surplus Without Apology," *American Economic Review*, vol. 66 (September 1976), pp. 589–97.

Thus, the left side of equation (5.8) represents the overall welfare decrease because of an incremental loss of leisure ΔS resulting from the unexpected outage of duration Δt; the right side measures the value of the inputs necessary to produce the leisure. The term $(b \cdot \Delta k)$ is interpreted as representing the value of the input of electricity-using equipment that is foregone during the outage. If the income foregone in each period (bk) is uniformly distributed over the leisure period (t) during which the equipment is used, then the average value of appliance input for every unit of leisure time is bk/t, and therefore $b \cdot \Delta k = b \cdot (k/t) \cdot \Delta t$.

The household's electricity bill, however, will also be reduced by the amount $p \cdot (\partial \Psi / \partial t) \cdot \Delta t$ from kilowatt-hours not used during the outage. Therefore, the net incremental welfare loss or outage cost may be written:

$$(5.9) \quad OC^R = MRS_{I,S} \cdot \Delta S - p \cdot \frac{\partial \psi}{\partial t} \cdot \Delta t = w \cdot \Delta t + c \cdot \Delta x + b \cdot \Delta k.$$

Extreme differences that could occur between outage costs estimated for very rich and very poor consumers of electricity, especially in countries where the income distribution is highly inequitable, may not be realistic. As discussed in chapter 9, Shadow Pricing, if there is diminishing marginal utility of income and consumption, then it is possible to weight the outage costs, depending on the average income level of the household. The use of such social weights, which should reflect national income distributional goals, would tend to reduce the disparity between the disutility of outages to low- and to high-income households.

Finally, an expression is derived for the marginal value of electricity-independent leisure. Multiplying equations (5.5e) and (5.5f) by $d\theta$ and dm, respectively, summing the two resulting equations, and rearranging terms as before, yields:

$$\frac{\partial u}{\partial v} \left(\frac{\partial v}{\partial \theta} \cdot d\theta + \frac{\partial v}{\partial m} \cdot dm \right) + \lambda \cdot d\theta + \frac{\lambda}{w} \cdot r \cdot dm = 0.$$

This may be rewritten:

$$(5.10) \quad \frac{\partial U}{\partial V} \cdot dV + \frac{\lambda}{w} \left(w \cdot d\theta + r \cdot dm \right) = 0.$$

Dividing equation (5.10) by equation (5.5d) allows the marginal rate of substitution of income for electricity-independent leisure, keeping utility constant $(MRS_{I,V})$, to be determined:

(5.11) $MRS_{I,V} \cdot \Delta V = w \cdot \Delta \theta + r \cdot \Delta m$:

where ΔV has been used instead of dV, and so on.

Equation (5.11) is analogous to equation (5.8). It measures the welfare change caused by an incremental change in the availability of electricity-independent leisure ΔV, in terms of the value of the inputs: that is, time Δt and other input Δm, which are required to produce this leisure. The relevance of equation (5.11) to outage cost estimation is discussed in the next section.

Empirical Estimation

As mentioned in the earlier discussion dealing with the theoretical model, the empirical estimation of residential outage costs is particularly difficult because of the nonmarketable nature of the household outputs produced by using electricity. From a practical viewpoint, data on wages and income are far easier to obtain than information on the use of appliances and other inputs. Fortunately in most instances the dominant term in equation (5.9) would be the wage element. Take, for example, a television set, one of the more expensive items of electrical equipment commonly used for leisure. Assuming a purchase price of US$250 and a six-year lifetime (independent of usage and outages) and a discount rate of 10 percent, the annuitized value is US$57.50 a year. For a set that is used four hours a day on the average, the corresponding value of $b \cdot \Delta k$ is US$.04 an hour of outage, which is likely to be a negligible amount, even compared with minimum income earning rates for relatively poor households using electricity. Similarly, the term $c \cdot \Delta x$ is also likely to be relatively insignificant. For example, it could represent a snack being eaten while watching television. An outage would interrupt the snack. If the food is wasted, there will be a small welfare loss, but if it is eaten later, there would be no loss.

It may be concluded that the difficulties of obtaining data on ownership of electrical appliances or other inputs used during leisure time will usually far outweigh any resulting refinement to the basic estimate of outage costs that is derived purely on the basis of more readily available income data. Therefore, in practice the following expression may be used as a good approximation to equation (5.9):

$$(5.12) \qquad \frac{\Delta OC^R}{\Delta t} \approx w.$$

Arguing, analogously, that the wage term is likely to dominate the second term on the right side of equation (5.11), it is possible to derive another approximate relation:

$$(5.13) \qquad MRS_{I,V} \cdot \frac{\Delta V}{\Delta \theta} \approx w.$$

Therefore, the incremental monetary values of both electricity-dependent and -independent types of leisure per time unit are roughly equal to the wage or income earning rate.

In practical terms, the theoretically derived link between the two types of leisure and the income earning rate summarized in equations (5.12) and (5.13) is intuitively reassuring, because electricity-dependent leisure and actual working hours may not be direct physical substitutes for each other. For example, the normal workday could extend from 9:00 A.M. to 5:00 P.M., whereas electricity-dependent leisure may begin only after 7:00 P.M. Therefore, the marginal tradeoff between electricity-dependent leisure and extended working hours may have to occur by adjusting the intervening electricity-independent leisure period.

As discussed earlier, a principal practical advantage of using foregone leisure to estimate the outage costs of residential consumers is the availability of easy-to-obtain income data. Often a good correlation between family income and kilowatt-hours of electricity consumption could be obtained for a typical sample of residential consumers from the utility company's billing records and from household budget surveys. The income levels of households that use electricity could then be estimated.

Since the method of estimating residential consumers' outage costs may sometimes lead to incorrect estimates, the discussion must be further clarified.

(a) It is assumed that workers can vary their work hours to equate their wages with the marginal value of their leisure time. Traditional work practices such as the forty-hour week, union restrictions on hours worked, or insufficient employment alternatives might prevent this. If workers are unable to work as much as they wish, then their wage will overestimate the value of lost leisure. A related point is that the daytime wage rate may not be a good proxy for the value of leisure. The marginal wage rate corresponding to the leisure hours may be more appropriate, and in some cases this may be the overtime rate of pay.

(b) The cost to nonwage-earning members of the family is effectively ignored by allowing only the wage earner to represent the household as an income-earning unit. For example, the value of the housewife's time may be estimated as the average earning rate of women who work outside the home, although the corresponding outage cost may not be accurate, because of the greater work-leisure substitution possibilities for housewives as well as differences between the productivity of housewives and women who work outside the home.

(c) Residential consumers may develop outage expectations, presumably because of the frequency of such occurrences in the past, so that the possibility of interruptions in electricity supply will be considered when labor-leisure decisions are made. This indicates that the cost of the outage will be less than when no outages are expected.

(d) If some leisure is enjoyed outside the household that is affected by the outage, then ideally, this case should be treated separately.

(e) Finally, in unusual situations outages may provide some consumption benefits to residential consumers—perhaps the enjoyment of a novel situation.

These difficulties indicate that the estimate of outage costs inferred from consumers' labor-leisure choices should be independently verified. As noted earlier, the short-run outage cost is likely to exceed the maximum willingness to pay for the lost kilowatt-hours, based on the household's longer-run demand curve. Therefore, empirical verification of equation (5.12) must depend on the determination of the consumer's willingness to pay in the short run to avoid an unexpected outage. Any household survey to test this hypothesis must be carefully worded and administered (see the case study for details).

Chapter 6

‎▄▄▄▄▄▄▄▄▄▄▄▄▄▄▄▄▄▄▄▄▄▄▄▄▄▄▄▄▄▄▄▄▄▄▄▄▄

Industrial Outage Costs

A method of estimating the outage costs incurred by electricity users who produce a marketable output is developed in this chapter. Although the chapter focuses on industrial users, the technique described could be applied to a much wider class of commercial consumers whose productive activities may be analyzed within the same general framework. The method proposed for measuring the economic costs of random outages affecting such users of electricity is based on the application of the notion of short-run opportunity costs.

Types of Outage Costs

The effects and direct costs of outages to industries during working hours are classified into two main categories: (a) spoiled material in the process of being produced or in storage and (b) reduced production during the outage and the following restart period: that is, after electricity is restored but before full production resumes.[1] The estimated

---

1. Links could be developed between this framework for outage cost analysis and the recent work on physically based electricity demand models developed to analyze large industrial loads. With the latter technique, the usage patterns of individual items of equipment and the output flow and storage structure of indi-

outage costs resulting from these effects are discussed in the next section, using the most convenient data as parameters: that is, the average frequency and duration of outages in a given service area.

If the reliability level of usual electricity service is poor, certain industrial consumers, especially those who are sensitive to outages, may wish to improve the security of supply by installing standby generators or by reinforcing their links with the public grid. They may also attempt to modify their production processes to reduce outage costs by scheduling critical outage-sensitive operations during the hours of the day when interruptions would be least likely to occur, or by adopting entirely different production techniques. All additional expenses connected to any new facilities or modifications to normal operating procedures would be indirect outage costs as defined in chapter 3. To use this information effectively in the analysis, however, it would be necessary to determine not only the magnitude of such expenditures, but also the exact level of reliability at which industrial consumers would consider additional costs economically justified. In summary, for industrial and commercial firms, the indirect outage cost of adopting less efficient production techniques at a given level of reliability can be measured by determining how much lower production costs would have been if electric power reliability were not a concern.

Yet information on indirect outage costs is not always readily available from the affected firm. Furthermore, although useful data may be gathered from similar firms, it is difficult to ensure that any observed production cost differentials result from a response to observed reliability, rather than to differences in technologies and capital vintage. The costs of obtaining a standby energy source are easier to determine and sometimes provide insights into the magnitude of direct outage costs as well. A consumer's decision to purchase a standby energy source, which for simplicity is assumed to reduce direct outage costs to zero, would depend on whether or not its cost were greater or less than those of the direct outage costs that could have been expected during the lifetime of the back-up source. Thus, the cost of a standby energy source that was already purchased would serve as a lower limit on the estimate of direct outage costs, whereas if the source had not been purchased, its cost would provide an upper limit on the estimate of direct outage costs.

---

vidual productive processes are analyzed to determine the hourly kilowatt load of a given firm. See, for example, Y. Manichaikul and F. C. Schweppe, "Physically Based Industrial Load," *IEEE Transactions on Power Apparatus and Systems*, vol. PAS-98 (July/August 1979), pp. 1439–45.

Spoiled Product Cost

The economic value of spoiled product depends on the extent to which it has been processed and must include the value of all embodied inputs used in its production. Typically, some raw materials and other inputs that are transformed into finished output by the factors of production might be considered. The outage cost should include the value of the raw material and other inputs ruined, as well as the value-added embodied or included in the spoiled output, resulting from partial or complete processing by the primary factors. In some industries, output will be ruined instantly when an outage occurs; in others the outage would have to be of a certain critical duration before any product would be spoiled. Thus, in the first case the value of spoiled product cost (*SPC*) over a given time interval is a function only of outage frequency, whereas in the second case the cost depends on both outage frequency and duration. For interruptions shorter than the critical duration, no product would be spoiled, but for outages exceeding the critical duration, the value of *SPC* could be an increasing function of duration.

For any specific firm over a given year, the economic value of spoiled output can be written:

$$SCP = \sum_{i=1}^{f} \beta(d_i) \cdot \frac{Q}{h}$$

where Q = total annual value added; h = number of hours of plant operation in the bench mark year; f = frequency of outages per year; d_i = duration of the ith outage in hours; and $\beta(d_i)$ = value of spoiled product for an outage of duration d_i as a fraction of average total value added per hour, Q/h. Note that $\beta = o$ if $d_i \leq \alpha$, where α = critical duration of outage beyond which the output is spoiled, and $\partial\beta/\partial d \geq 0$ in general. β itself may be further broken down as follows:

$$\beta(d_i) = [v(d_i) + m(d_i)]$$

where $v(d_i)$ = the lost value added (from capital and labor), which is already included in the spoiled product; and $m(d_i)$ = the value of other inputs lost, such as raw materials. Both v and m are given as fractions of total average hourly value added. When only raw material inputs in stock are spoiled because of the outage, then $v(d_i) = 0$, and conversely, if finished product was ruined, then $\beta(d_i)$ = value of finished output that was spoiled at product prices.

Idle Factor Cost

During the outage period, a certain fraction ϵ (where $0 \leq \epsilon \leq 1$) of normal output will not be produced. There will be no idle resources and, therefore, no reduction in output if the firm does not use electricity in the production process or if managers can substitute those aspects of the production process that do not use electricity for those that do. This same fraction also measures the fraction of time during the outage when productive resources (capital and labor) are idle.

Furthermore, even after the supply of electricity is restored, a certain fraction of normal output $\bar{\epsilon}$ (where $0 \leq \bar{\epsilon} \leq 1$) may not be produced in some firms during a restart period. For instance, motors must be turned on, furnaces reheated, or equipment cleaned before production can resume. Once again there is an opportunity cost in the form of idle resources. For firms that have restart periods, this cost could depend on: (a) the frequency of outages only; (b) both outage frequency and duration, where duration must exceed a "critical" length of time to result in a positive restart time; and (c) both frequency and duration, where restart time is related in a positive, continuous manner to outage duration.

Thus, the annual opportunity cost of slack factors of production or idle factor cost (*IFC*) during the time of the outage and the subsequent restart period is given by:

$$IFC = \sum_{i=1}^{f} [\epsilon \cdot d_i + \bar{\epsilon} \cdot \gamma(d_i)] \cdot \frac{Q}{h}$$

where $\gamma(d_i)$ = restart time for an outage of duration d_i. Note that $\gamma = 0$ if $d_i \leq \delta$, where δ = critical duration of outage beyond which restart time becomes necessary, and $\partial\gamma/\partial d \geq 0$ in general.

Some firms may have a certain amount of built-in slack productive capacity during normal operation. Because of the fixed capital stock, and the possibility of wide fluctuations in the desired level of output, a firm might have excess capital in the short run. Conversely, since labor is usually viewed as a variable input even in the short run, the reason for any excess available labor might be questioned. The notion that firms invest in workers through on-the-job training is one plausible explanation of why it may be economically rational for the firm to maintain excess labor in the short run.[2] In these cases, the opportunity cost of the outage can be reduced by more intensive utilization of resources during normal working hours after the supply of electricity is restored to meet a production target. This more intensive utilization would, in effect, reduce the net amount of idle resources that results from outages. It is assumed that on average a certain fraction of the opportunity cost of the idle resources, λ, during outage and restart periods can be recovered by this more intensive post-outage utilization of resources. More generally, λ should be allowed to vary according to the length of the outage and the time of its occurrence. Knowledge of the average duration of outages and their distribution over time would allow an average value of λ to be determined. This reduction in outage costs over a year's time or the recovered cost (RC) may be written:

$$RC = \lambda \cdot IFC.$$

Thus, allowing for the possibility of excess capacity, the total basic outage cost (OC^B) for a particular firm during a given year will be:

$$OC^B = SPC + IFC - RC = \frac{Q}{h} \cdot \sum_{i=1}^{f} \{\beta(d_i) + [d_i + \gamma(d_i)](1 - \lambda) \cdot \epsilon\}$$

where, for convenience, $\bar{\epsilon} = \epsilon$ is assumed. Alternatively, OC^B may be split into nonfactor (NFC) and factor cost (FC) components as follows:

$$OC^B = NFC + FC$$

where $NFC = Q/h \cdot \sum_{i=1}^{f} m(d_i)$, and

$$FC = Q/h \cdot \sum_{i=1}^{f} \{v(d_i) + [d_i + \gamma(d_i)](1 - \lambda)\epsilon\}.$$

2. See, for instance, Walter Oi, "Labor as a Quasi-Fixed Factor," *Journal of Political Economy* (December 1962), pp. 538–55.

Overtime Production Cost

For firms that operate twenty-four hours a day and cannot work overtime to make up the production lost because of outages, or for firms that decide not to work overtime, oc^B is an appropriate estimate of the costs that result from outages. Other firms, however, might decide to make up some of their lost production by working overtime. Whether this overtime production occurs on the day of the outage or later does not significantly affect the resulting production costs, assuming that overtime wage rates remain the same. In theory, the firm's decision to work overtime would be based on a comparison of the marginal private costs and benefits of overtime production. The sizes of available inventories or contractual obligations would be important factors in this decision. The constraints imposed by contractors could easily be included in the model by introducing a penalty, such as a fine, for an unmet deadline.

Under conditions approaching perfect competition, it is unlikely that firms would have an economic incentive to make up any lost production. Exceptions might occur because of contractual obligations or because of some kind of previously existing production constraint, such as a shortage of materials, that prevented the firms from producing a profit-maximizing level of output. Firms with some market power, such as monopolies, might also have an incentive to work overtime if they could pass on the extra costs to the consumer. Ultimately, firms might make up all lost production by using overtime, but the question of whether or not a firm decides to work overtime is important, since it has a direct effect on outage costs.

To discuss further how the decision to produce overtime affects the costs of outages, the concept of the opportunity cost of using productive resources must be considered in greater detail. Within the short-run production period being considered, labor has alternative uses in market or household production (see chapter 5, Residential Outage Costs). Thus, even if the lost product of labor during the outage and restart periods is recovered by employing labor for overtime production, an opportunity cost still will result from the outage that can be measured as the foregone leisure of overtime workers, rather than the foregone output of the firm (IFC). Within the same short-run framework, suppose that the net lost production of capital caused by the outage is recovered by an equal amount of overtime production using machines outside of normal working hours. Then there will be no cost associated with capital made idle during the outage, assuming that capital is not already used twenty-four hours a day, that depreciation is a function of the actual hours of usage, and that the additional maintenance and other costs for capital incurred during overtime are negligible. No alternative productive use of capital is foregone because of this overtime production, and, thus, there is no net opportunity cost with respect to capital (see also chapter 4, Estimation of Outage Costs).

If a firm wishes to recover a fraction of the output lost because of the outage, then the period of overtime, h_o, during which the primary factors must be employed is defined by the expression:

$$(Q/h)h_o = \rho \cdot FC.$$

Therefore,

$$h_o = \rho \sum_{i=1}^{f} [v(d_i) + \{(d_i + \gamma(d_i)\}(1 - \lambda)\epsilon]$$

where ρ = fraction of FC that is recovered $(0 \leq \rho \leq 1)$.

The value of lost nonfactor inputs does not appear in this expression because that loss is permanent and cannot be recouped by overtime. The term h_o may be interpreted as a measure of the effective lost hours of production resulting from the outage.

The resource cost of such overtime work can be written in the following form:

$$\left(\frac{\bar{w}}{w}\right)\left(\frac{L}{h}\right)h_o$$

where $\bar{w}/w$ = effective wage ratio, which is assumed to reflect the opportunity cost of overtime labor relative to normal labor, and L = the labor component of annual value added. Since overtime wage rates are often institutionally determined, the actual wage ratio may not be the appropriate measure for $\bar{w}/w$. In case of severe distortions in the labor market, shadow wage rates would have to be used to represent the opportunity cost of labor, both during normal and overtime working hours (see chapter 9).

The general expression for outage cost, including the overtime case, is given by:

$$OC = NFC + (1 - \rho) \cdot FC + \left(\frac{\bar{w}}{w}\right)\left(\frac{L}{h}\right)h_o$$

$$= \frac{Q}{h} \sum_{i=1}^{f} \{m(d_i) + [1 - \rho(1 - \frac{\bar{w}}{w} \cdot \frac{L}{Q})] [v(d_i) + \{d_i + \gamma(d_i)\}(1 - \lambda)\epsilon]\}.$$

The two extreme cases may be examined by the following equations. Case I. No lost output is made up; therefore, $\rho = 0$, and $OC^I = OC^B$. Case II. All lost output is made up;[3] therefore, $\rho = 1$, and

$$OC^{II} = OC^B + \left(\frac{\bar{w}}{w} \cdot \frac{L}{Q} - 1\right) FC.$$ Clearly, then, $OC^{II} \gtrless OC^I$ as $\frac{\bar{w}}{w} \gtrless \frac{Q}{L}$.

The intuitive explanation of this equation is that the more labor intensive the production process, that is, the smaller the ratio of total value added to labor costs, Q/L, the more likely an increase in opportunity cost, because overtime wages will be greater than the opportunity cost reduction resulting from the decrease in the period during which capital is idle.

In summary, a range of values for the costs incurred by industrial consumers resulting from outages may be estimated. For a firm that does not produce twenty-four hours a day, if $\bar{w}/w < Q/L$, then OC^{II} and OC^I are minimum and maximum estimates, respectively, of outage costs. Conversely, if $\bar{w}/w > Q/L$, then OC^{II} and OC^I are minimum and maximum estimates, respectively. For firms producing twenty-four hours a day, the resulting opportunity cost of an outage can be estimated as OC^I. In many cases, however, $\lambda = 0$ and $\rho = 0$ so that:

$$OC = (Q/h) \sum_{i=1}^{f} [m(d_i) + v(d_i) + \{d_i + \gamma(d_i)\} \cdot \epsilon].$$

3. The case when available hours of overtime are not sufficient to allow all lost production to be recovered is not considered here but may be derived quite easily. Given typical outage durations, these instances are apt to be rare.

Chapter 7

Other Outage Costs

Outage costs incurred by consumers other than in the residential and industrial categories are described in this chapter. They are commercial, public services, special institutions, and rural users. Much of the discussion that follows refers to outages of less than a few hours duration, especially when making up disrupted activity at a later time is considered. The more widespread effects of prolonged outages are discussed in the final section.

Commercial

The commercial consumer category covers a variety of electricity users. Outage costs suffered by such consumers generally may be analyzed within a framework similar to that described in chapter 6, Industrial Outage Costs. Since much of the commercial activity in this category could be classified in the tertiary or services sector—for example, shops, restaurants, offices, and small businesses—the possibility of making up work interrupted by outages is much greater by using existing manpower and capacity more intensively during normal working hours.

Generally, the more commercial consumers rely on electricity-using equipment, the larger the corresponding outage costs would tend to be. For example, offices where only the lighting is affected may be able to function normally. If electricity-dependent facilities such as reproducing machines, desk calculators, and computer systems are used extensively, work is more likely to be interrupted. In particular, the erasure or loss of stored computer data could have serious longer-term consequences. Similarly, the higher floors of tall buildings may be inaccessible without electricity-using elevators, although staircases may be used to serve the lower floors and also shorter buildings. Electrical heating and air-conditioning, especially in large buildings, however, will only be affected by relatively long outages of several hours. Considerable flexibility may also be built into the usual office routine, enabling employees to finish an interrupted activity without overtime work. For instance, workers may take their tea or coffee break or have their daily chat during an outage-induced work stoppage, instead of at the usual times.

Shops and stores will be similarly affected. Often, sales activity can continue during the day, especially in smaller shops. Even if volume is reduced, it could often be made up during normal hours, after the electricity supply had been restored. Using equipment such as electronic cash registers and demonstrating electrical appliances to potential customers would, however, be severely curtailed. Commercial firms engaged in small-scale production activities not large enough to fall into the industrial category, such as artisans' workshops and family businesses, could be analyzed in terms of the disruption of production and the spoilage of materials. Again, considerable flexibility and slack is likely to be present, and workers, especially self-employed persons, could work more intensively to recoup outage-related losses.

Spoilage costs resulting from outages are likely to be most important to commercial users such as supermarkets, restaurants, and hotels, who use refrigeration to store perishable items. These costs will tend to be small, however, except during lengthy outages, typically lasting several hours. Customers might even enjoy the novelty value of the new situation, for example, dining by candlelight at a restaurant in spite of potentially delayed service.

Commercial establishments that are open at night, such as late-closing shopping centers, movie theatres, and night-clubs, would have to close if the outages were relatively long. Transacting business during outages would be more difficult, and theft and security problems are more likely to arise.

In summary, the outage costs of the large variety of commercial electricity consumers must be examined on a case-by-case basis, especially when considering the recovery of lost activity during normal working hours by using existing slack capacity more intensively.

Public Services

The costs society incurs as a result of electric power outages affecting public sector services are especially difficult to estimate, since no directly related consumption charges exist. Public illumination is seriously affected by electric power outages, because there is little possibility of substituting this output between different hours of the day, or of using nonelectrical inputs to provide the service at short notice. Generally the decision concerning the marginal investment on public illumination is unlikely to be made on the basis of an explicit cost-benefit analysis. Yet, if street lighting is either inadequate, resulting in reduced security for citizens at night, or too extensive, leading to increased costs and municipal taxes, then the public would pressure the local government to change the situation. Therefore, in the absence of a detailed knowledge of the benefits of public illumination, it may be argued that a community has invested in street lighting to the point where the marginal costs and benefits of such lighting are roughly equal.

An outage affecting street lighting will clearly reduce community welfare. From the preceding analysis, it may be deduced that one estimate of this welfare loss would be the value of the capital equipment used for public illumination, annuitized over the total lifetime hours of usage and prorated during the outage period, plus the cost of routine maintenance, which is unaffected by outages. Electricity charges not paid during the outage would be netted out. This estimate of welfare loss would generally be minimal, since the public illumination benefits lost may not be at the margin, thus raising the question of consumers' surplus. (This assumes that the community demand curve for public illumination is downward sloping.) Therefore, as noted, the short-run costs imposed on citizens by an unexpected outage, such as the sudden loss of security, are likely to exceed the willingness-to-pay for public illumination in the longer term. If data are available, the increase in street crimes resulting from decreased street lighting may be used to measure outage costs. The increased risk or incidence of accidents as well as the time wasted because of traffic congestion resulting from nonfunctioning traffic lights could be used to estimate outage costs for this specific type of interruption.

Typical examples of other public sector outputs likely to be disrupted by power outages include sewage and water treatment plants, telephone and mass transport services, and radio and television. An appropriate measure of outage costs may be used for each case, such as foregone output, idle productive capacity, or citizens' willingness to pay more to avoid the effects of outages.

Generalized services in urban centers, such as those provided by the police, fire, and sanitation departments, are likely to be affected by outages to the extent that they depend on electricity for lighting, communications, pumping, transport, and so on. Any consequent loss of security and safety or breakdown of public order will be extremely difficult to estimate in economic terms before the outage. In a given situation, the duration and geographic extent of a blackout may have to exceed certain critical values before such society-wide effects become significant. Beyond this critical point, however, economic and social losses are likely to rise sharply, especially if social conditions, time, and weather combine to aggravate the situation and if the public authorities are unprepared and unable to cope with the crisis. (See the section on secondary effects at the end of this chapter for a discussion of the New York City power failure during the hot summer night of July 13, 1977.)

Special Institutions

Specialized institutions, such as hospitals, health clinics, universities, schools, places of worship, orphanages, and homes for the elderly, are discussed in this section. The economic costs of outages for hospitals are significant enough to merit detailed treatment. Although a hospital essentially provides health services, this output is difficult to measure and furthermore, since little is known about the specific production process, several difficulties arise in estimating outage costs.

If there are no standby facilities, some intermediate products in hospitals, including medicines and blood, will spoil during a long outage, and the value of the spoiled products would be one component of the direct outage costs. Obviously, electrical instruments and equipment are useless without electricity. In some cases, the decrease in the delivery of health services will depend on the time of the outage, for example, the need for lights. In other cases time would not be important, for example, when an artificial respirator is required. If this lost health service cannot be made up easily through more intensive use of such facilities at other times, the annuitized value of the idle equipment would provide a minimum estimate of the outage cost. It is also possible that nonelectric equipment may be useless during an outage, because it is used in a situation that requires electricity as a complementary input; surgical equipment would be one example. The opportunity cost of this idle equipment should also be included.

Another related result of an outage is the loss of human life—an extremely crucial cost. Although the personal, psychological cost to family and friends is likely to be immeasurable, one estimate of the social cost could be the expected earnings or foregone net future output of the deceased person. In general, estimating such costs would be a complex task. Contingencies involving risk to human life, however, are likely to be associated with certain critical facilities, such as operating rooms and intensive care equipment, which will normally have back-up power, for example, batteries. Often, the hospital may have a standby generator, in some cases to meet legal requirements imposed by the community. Whether to impute corresponding, indirect outage costs will depend to some extent on how the need for a back-up source was determined. If the decision to install the equipment had been made only to meet legal requirements and was not made on an economic basis, it would be difficult to infer the corresponding indirect outage cost.

The effectiveness of labor inputs also will be reduced by an outage: that is, some labor may be made idle. The extent of this idle labor and, therefore, the resulting opportunity cost will vary with the time the outage occurred and is likely to be particularly significant during the night. The effect of outages on hospital auxiliary facilities such as kitchens, laundries, heating, and air-conditioning should also be considered.

Many of the outage costs incurred by health clinics are likely to be similar to those experienced by hospitals, although there are differences in the type and scale of operations, such as the lack of inpatients and less electric equipment. The effect of power failures on educational institutions will vary with their dependence on electricity. For example, the activity in night schools and universities with extensive laboratory facilities will be disrupted more than work in day schools and ordinary classrooms. In periods of heavy rain, however, lighting may be essential even during the day. The nature of religious institutions would tend to minimize the costs imposed by outages, unless there is heavy dependence on electric lighting and heating during hours of worship. Electricity interruptions restrict activities in orphanages and homes for the elderly, and, in the latter, increased health risks could be significant.

Rural

This section focuses on outage costs of rural electricity consumers in the agricultural sector. Consumers in small urban areas, often classified in the rural category for other purposes such as billing, can be treated like the various other urban users described earlier.

The distinguishing characteristics of rural grid-supplied electricity systems are the relatively low customer densities and the correspondingly high capital costs of supply. Consequently, supply networks will be weaker and less reliable. Rural electricity users, however, are more likely to compensate for these conditions than their urban counterparts by having alternative or standby sources of power and by generally relying less on electricity. Thus, indirect outage costs may be more significant for rural consumers.

The outage costs of large agro-industries may be analyzed in the same way as industrial electricity consumers. Seasonal availability of agricultural produce for processing and of the rural labor supply has to be considered. Large mechanized farms could also be treated analogously. The drying, milling, extracting, preserving, and storage of vegetables and grain may be affected by outages. Electric motors used to pump water will not function during outages, but adequate water storage facilities could minimize the associated outage costs. In the livestock sector, outages could disrupt milking, egg laying, hatching, ventilation, water supply, feeding, and waste removal, as well as produce refrigeration and storage.

Since the living quarters of farm owners and workers are usually connected to the same electricity supply as the farm's productive facilities, the outage costs to households, as described in chapter 5, Residential Outage Costs, must be added to the foregone output and spoilage costs discussed above. On electrified small farms the household component of outage costs is likely to be in proportion to the disruption of productive activities. In determining income earning rates for such consumers, however, the value of auto-consumption should not be overlooked.

Secondary Effects

In the analysis of outage costs presented thus far, the main emphasis has been on tracing the effect of electricity supply failures on the immediate consumers. In certain instances, however, more widespread effects must be considered.

The disruption of public services could lead to external costs. For example, stopping sanitation services or water and sewerage treatment may have external health diseconomies, such as greater incidence of bowel diseases or susceptibility to epidemics. The outage-delayed production of an industrial firm could be an intermediate input for a second firm at a different time and location. Therefore, secondary costs could be imposed on the latter. That may seem quite unrelated to the original outage. Finally, as discussed earlier, lengthy and widespread outages may lead to a breakdown of law and order, which could have far-reaching consequences and economic costs.

The New York City blackout of July 13, 1977, which lasted twenty-five hours and affected nine million people, is the best documented case of an extensive and long-lasting power failure.[1] The total outage costs have been conservatively estimated at US$350 million, of which about US$155 million was incurred by damaged or looted businesses. Practically all social agencies, including the law enforcement and criminal justice authorities, were reported to have been totally unprepared for the effect of the blackout. There was much uncontrolled looting and collective arson by people without previous arrest records and with higher employment status than experienced criminals. The cascading nature of secondary effects is best exemplified by the outage costs of the New York City Metropolitan Transportation Authority (MTA). The MTA suffered a direct revenue loss of US$2.6 million, outage-related vandalism, and overtime payment losses of US$6.5 million, and recently was forced to initiate a US$11 million program for new equipment to prevent major disruptions caused by future blackouts.

---

1. See Systems Control Inc., "Impact Assessment of the 1977 New York City Blackout" (U.S. Department of Energy Report), no. HCP T5103-01, Arlington, Virginia, July 1978, processed; Robert Sugarman, "New York City's Blackout: A $350 Million Drain," *IEEE Spectrum* (November 1978), pp. 44–46; G. L. Wilson and P. Zarakas, "Anatomy of a Blackout," *IEEE Spectrum* (February 1978), pp. 39–46; and "Blackout '77: Once More with Looting," *Time*, vol. 110 (July 25, 1977), pp. 12–26. For an analysis of the central Illinois power failure of March 1978, which lasted several days, see Gregory C. Kohm, "A Survey of Disruption and Consumer Costs Resulting from a Major Residential Power Outage," Argonne National Laboratory, report no. ANL/EES-TM-29, Argonne, Illinois, June 1978; and Gregory C. Kohm, "Costs of Interruptions of Electrical Service in the Commercial Sector," Argonne National Laboratory, report no. ANL/EES-TM-30, Argonne, Illinois, September 1978.

Chapter 8

~~~~~~

Power System Planning and Supply Costs

The effective application of the reliability level optimization and planning model presented in chapter 3 requires prior estimation of two cost categories: outage costs and electricity supply costs. Since outage costs have been treated in detail in chapters 4 to 7, this chapter analyzes supply costs in depth. First, however, the rationale underlying investment decisions in the energy sector should be discussed, as well as how the new reliability optimization procedure changes the conventional philosophy of power system planning.

The Investment Decision

In chapter 2, Introduction to Reliability, the purpose of a power system was defined simply in relation to its capability to deliver electricity from the source to the consumer. Well before the decision is made to invest in electric power, however, broader issues must be faced involving the total future energy needs, availability of supply, and the optimal mix of different sources to be developed. Although the entire range of national energy sector investment and pricing policies is best analyzed and determined within an explicit economic framework, in practice such decisions are often made by policymakers on an arbitrary or judgmental basis.

Today's societies require increasing amounts of energy for a variety of uses in homes, industries, and businesses as well as for agriculture and transport. Arrayed against these energy needs are the short-term, depletable, fossil fuel supplies—petroleum, coal, and natural gas—in addition to the longer-run energy sources—water, nuclear, solar, geothermal, wind, tidal power, and biomass (that is, organic and often noncommercial fuels such as wood and animal waste.)[1]

At this stage, two basic decisions are required. First, the appropriate level of demand for energy that must be served to achieve social goals such as economic development and growth and basic human needs should be determined. Then, a mix of energy sources must be established that will meet the desired demand, based on several national objectives, such as minimum cost, independence from foreign sources, conservation of resources, environmental considerations, and price stability.[2] The analysis is complicated by uncertainties regarding the future evolution of demand and supply, relative costs and prices, and the lack of compatibility of the different energy sources with all the various energy uses. Furthermore, closely associated with the investment decision is the pricing policy, which will be based on criteria such as economic efficiency in resource allocation, economic second-best considerations, sector financial requirements, social equity considerations, and other political constraints.[3] Pricing decisions may also have feedback effects on investment decisions through demand. (See chapter 3, Method of Optimizing Reliability.)

The electric power sector is usually one of the most important elements within the broader energy framework. Once the major decisions regarding energy policy have been made at the national level, the power sector authorities must perform a similar but more detailed analysis. More specifically, the demand for electricity must be forecast, preferably disaggregated by geographic region and customer category. Then alternative

---

1. Short-term and long-term energy sources are also called renewable and non-renewable, but the distinction is not strictly correct because the second law of thermodynamics forbids isolated, self-regenerating energy sources.

2. See Mohan Munasinghe and Colin J. Warren, "Rural Electrification, Energy Economics, and National Policy in the Developing Countries," *IEE International Conference on Future Energy Concepts, London, January–February 1979*, IEE Conference Publication no. 171.

3. See Mohan Munasinghe and Jeremy J. Warford, "Shadow Pricing and Power Tariff Policy," *Marginal Costing and Pricing of Electrical Energy, Proceedings of the State-of-the-Art International Conference, Montreal, May 1978*, pp. 159–80.

methods of physically meeting these requirements and their corresponding costs must be determined. These steps, which result in the determination of power system costs, are detailed in the following sections.
Again, the procedure involved in selecting an optimal plan and reliability level, described fully in chapter 3, adds an extra dimension to
the conventional technique of system expansion planning in which the
target reliability level is arbitrarily determined. This method considers
as variables, first, the reliability level and, subsequently, if necessary,
also the demand forecast by an iterative technique.

Load Forecast

The major elements of load forecasting that are relevant to the system planning process are reviewed in this section. For greater detail,
the reader is referred to the notes cited in the text.[4] Unlike in the traditional engineering context, where demand is synonymous with capacity
or power, the terms demand and load forecast are used interchangeably
to denote the magnitude as well as the structure of the requirements
of both electrical power and energy (kilowatt and kilowatt-hour, respectively) except when the appropriate distinction is necessary. The structure of demand includes disaggregation by geographic area, by consumer
category, and over time, as well as load and diversity factors and system
losses.

A knowledge of loads at the disaggregate level is important, because
the demand characteristics vary by consumer type, by geographic area,
and with time. Therefore, the properties of the aggregate demand, for
example, at the system level, may be quite different from the characteristics of individual loads. Disaggregate loads are important in the system
planning process. For generation planning, the system may be modeled
as one source feeding a single lumped load but, in designing transmission networks, the characteristics of demand by region and by major
load center, such as a city, become important. Ultimately, for distribu-

---

4. See, for example, Federal Power Commission, *The Methodology of Load
Forecasting*, 1970 National Power Survey (Washington, D.C., 1970); Robert
L. Sullivan, *Power System Planning* (New York: McGraw-Hill International,
1977), chap. 2; and G. E. Huck, "Load Forecast Bibliography—Phase I," *Pro-
ceedings of the IEEE Power Engineering Society Summer Meeting, Vancouver,
July 1979*, paper no. F7950-3.

tion grid planning, a detailed knowledge of demand at each load center is required, as discussed in the next section. Furthermore, the sum of many disaggregate demand forecasts, estimated by using several independent techniques, often can serve as a useful check on an independently made global forecast for the same region.

A discussion of the basic relation between power and energy might be helpful at this point. The commonly used unit of energy in heavy current electricity applications is the kilowatt-hour. The rate of energy flow per unit of time is called power or capacity, which is measured in kilowatts. Therefore, it follows that energy in kilowatt-hours is the product of power in kilowatts and time in hours. More accurately, energy is the integral of instantaneous power flow, over time. The distinction between power and energy is important because the same amount of energy may be delivered quickly at a relatively high rate of power flow or more slowly at a lower power level. This point is best exemplified in nuclear fission by contrasting the practically instantaneous explosion of an atomic bomb with the controlled release of power from a nuclear reactor.

The load factor (LF), which is the ratio of average to maximum, or peak, kilowatts during a given interval may be specified at various levels of aggregation. The LF may be determined for a single customer or for an entire system on a daily or annual basis, and so on. It is important, because the size and, therefore, the cost of power system components are determined to a great extent by their capability to handle peak power flows. Since most customers require their maximum kilowatts only during a relatively short peak period during the day, the LF is also a measure of the utilization of capacity. (See also the discussion of the load duration curve in the next section.) A load forecast could be made either in units of peak power or of total energy consumed during a given period. The LF may be used to convert from one unit to the other, and also to check for mutual consistency when both types of forecasts have been made independently.

In general, the kilowatt peaks of different customers do not occur simultaneously. The diversity factor (DF) of a group of consumers is the ratio of the sum of the individual peak demands to their combined or simultaneous peak demand. Therefore, the DF is a number greater than or equal to unity. It measures the divergence or spreading of individual peak loads over time, and enables a coincident peak load to be computed for the group from the disaggregate peak values. The total amount of both kilowatt and kilowatt-hours generated at source will be greater than the corresponding values consumed because of power and energy losses in the system. Generation losses are usually of the station-use type: that is, involving use of auxiliary equipment at the power plant. Transmission and distribution network losses are basically technical losses, including transformer losses. Theft is a common loss in some countries and must be considered in the demand forecast. Since it is also a type of electricity consumption, ideally, the corresponding user benefits, and outage costs should also be considered in the optimizing process. In practice, this would be extremely difficult to do, because little is likely to be known about these consumers.

Load forecasts are made for different periods.[5] Very short-term demand projections are made on a daily or weekly basis, typically for optimizing system operation and scheduling of hydro units. Short-run forecasts ranging between one and three years are used in hydro-reservoir management, distribution system planning, and so on. The horizon for medium-term demand projections is about four to eight years, which corresponds to the lead times generally required for major transmission and generation projects. These forecasts, therefore, are especially useful in determining the timing and sequencing of such facilities. Some nuclear power stations may, however, take more than ten years to complete. Long-range demand projections, usually of ten to thirty-five years, are extremely important in long-run system expansion planning. Since they are most relevant to the topic addressed in this study, these forecasting methods are discussed next. In general, such long-range demand projections may be developed at various levels of disaggregation, ranging from national forecasts to projections for specific groups of consumers in localized areas.

The earliest approach to long-term load forecasting basically involved trend-line extrapolation. More specifically, a time series of past demand for electricity was analyzed as a function of time, using a variety of techniques ranging from simple graphing to sophisticated mathematical curve fitting. The resulting trend, sometimes expressed as a compound growth rate, was extended into the future. Because this method implicitly assumes that present growth patterns will remain essentially unchanged

5. See Frank D. Galiana, "Short Term Load Forecasting," *Systems Engineering for Power: Status and Prospects, Henniker, New Hampshire, August 1975*, NTIS no. CONF-750867, pp. 105–14; and K. N. Stanton, "Medium Range, Weekly, and Seasonal Peak Demand Forecasting by Probability Methods," *IEEE Transactions on Power Apparatus and Systems*, vol. PAS 71 (May 1971), pp. 1183–89.

into the future, it is often acceptable where stable socioeconomic conditions permit electricity demand to increase steadily for many years. Adjustments based on expert judgment may be made to the trend-line estimates if significant changes are expected in the overall environment, such as economic and demographic shifts, and weather changes. Systematically enumerating and summing of individual loads after considering the effects of diversity is another simple technique that has been used effectively, especially with large consumers, to develop the overall forecast.

Correlation methods of forecasting are more sophisticated than the trend line techniques. The basic rationale underlying the correlation approach is that regional or national electricity load growth could be forecast indirectly by linking it to several other variables whose future evolution would be easier to predict than the demand for electricity itself. The simplest methods include the correlation of electricity demand to some measure of economic activity, for example, per capita gross national or regional product, personal disposal income, or industrial or commercial value added. Demand may also be correlated with electricity price through the price elasticity of demand.[6] Then, projected values of income and price could be used in the estimated equations to forecast future load growth. Both the extrapolation and the correlation approaches require some knowledge of historical data on electricity demand specific to the consumer group and the area or country under consideration. When this information is unavailable, techniques that use appropriate data from other comparable regions may be necessary.[7]

More complex multiple correlation techniques consider several additional variables, such as prices of competing fuels and energy sources, temperature and weather, land usage, and population shifts. These methods often involve fitting nonlinear demand functions. Such econometric methods that explicitly consider the price of electricity as an explanatory

6. The elasticity of the dependent variable y with respect to the independent variable x is given by: $\epsilon_{y.x} = \dfrac{\partial y}{\partial x} \Big/ \dfrac{y}{x}$.

7. See for example H. Aoki, "New Method of Long Range or Very Long Range Demand Forecast of Energy, Including Electricity, Viewed from a Worldwide Standpoint," Electric Power Development Company Ltd., Tokyo, Japan, 1974; in which an attempt is made to correlate the growth rate and the level of per capita gross national product (GNP) and per capita kilowatt-hour electricity consumption for 111 countries.

variable are particularly relevant to this analysis, because in the optimization model presented in chapter 3, price is included in the specification of demand. This allows potential variation in the load forecast to occur through the iterative price feedback loop depicted in figure 1.1 of chapter 1. In a recent review of the topic, it was pointed out that problems encountered to date have been mainly conceptual.[8] These include the difficulties of: (a) modeling multipart (for example, fixed and variable charges) and multiblock (that is, varying prices for different consumption blocks) tariffs, as well as discontinuities in the demand function; (b) distinguishing between short- versus long-term, and static versus dynamic adjustments; and (c) incorporating the resulting changes in the prices of competing fuels. The recent resurgence of interest in marginal cost pricing has resulted in the continued development of econometric models that emphasize isolating the effects of electricity price on the demand level.[9]

All the models discussed so far have been mathematically deterministic, since the uncertainty in the load projections usually is accounted for by parametric shifts in the forecasts to test for sensitivity. Recently, more sophisticated techniques have been developed involving matrix methods, such as input-output matrices that capture the relations between productive sectors, and stochastic processes, such as those representing sectoral growth probabilities in terms of a Markov model. Such methods enable researchers to consider probabilistic effects explicitly.[10] The resulting long-range demand forecasts are still deterministic, however. Again, for sensitivity testing, the basic assumptions may be varied to provide low-, medium-, and high-demand forecasts, covering a range of load growth rates.

To summarize, no single, universally superior approach to load forecasting exists. In general, it is better to use several independent long-

8. See Lester D. Taylor, "The Demand for Electricity: A Survey," *The Bell Journal of Economics*, vol. 6 (Spring 1975), pp. 74–110.

9. See several papers that recently appeared in *Marginal Costing and Pricing of Electric Energy, Proceedings of the State-of-the-Art International Conference, Montreal, May 1978.*

10. See, for example, IAEA, *Nuclear Power Planning Study for Indonesia* (Vienna, 1976); N. R. Prasad, John M. Perkins, and G. Nesgos, "A Markov Process Applied to Forecasting. Part I—Economic Development," *Proceedings of the IEEE Power Engineering Society Summer Meeting, Vancouver, July 1973*; and N. R. Prasad, John M. Perkins, and G. Nesgos, "A Markov Process Applied to Forecasting. Part II—The Demand for Electricity," *Proceedings of the IEEE Power Engineering Society Winter Meeting, New York, January 1974.*

range forecasting methods to cross-check the results and to obtain a probable range within which the demand projection will fall. The more sophisticated techniques tend to obscure the basic methodological assumptions as well as weaknesses in the data, and, therefore, the simpler techniques may be more appropriate if the available information is considered unreliable. The determinants of demand must be selected carefully, because they vary from case to case, and the level of disaggregation chosen should depend on the data, as well as on the ultimate purpose of the projection. Demand forecasting is a dynamic process in the sense that the procedure must be repeated often, in light of improved information and techniques of analysis. Establishing a reliable data bank is invaluable for this constant revision of the demand forecast. Finally, in some cases institutionally imposed constraints that reduce demand, such as peak suppression or not connecting customers, as well as the existence of privately owned or captive generation, may lead to a substantial gap between the potential and the achievable demand.

System Design and Planning

The reliability optimization procedure described in chapter 3 was developed in accordance with alternative power system expansion plans that were designed to meet the projected demand at various levels of reliability. This section deals with the principles by which such alternative systems are designed. Since a very rigorous and highly mathematical treatment of power system design and planning is unnecessary here, the presentation is generally descriptive and focuses on the economic aspects of the various tradeoffs involved.[11] In particular, any references to cost minimization in this section imply that such costs may be readily determined, as described in the next section on costing.

Ideally, the planning of the whole system should be carried out on an integrated basis, as implied in the optimization model described in chapter 3. To make the practical problems of system design tractable, however, it is convenient to break the procedure down into parts associated with the main subsystems: generation, transmission, and distribu-

11. See, for example, Robert L. Sullivan, *Power System Planning*; and Upton G. Knight, *Power System Engineering and Mathematics* (New York: Pergamon Press, 1972).

tion. This type of hierarchical decomposition is logical from several points of view.[12]

First, as mentioned in the previous section on load forecasting, various completion times are associated with the discrete projects that comprise a long-range system expansion plan. These range from five to ten years for the design and construction of a large nuclear generating plant, to one to two years for distribution schemes. Second, the problems and design philosophies associated with the different parts of the total power system are inherently dissimilar. For example, distribution system planners require detailed knowledge of localized geographic areas and, as the case study indicates, must be familiar with thousands of small components, such as distribution transformers, switches, and reclosers, although their analysis may be relatively simple. At the other extreme, however, generation planning is carried out at a more aggregate, system-wide level, and is concerned with several relatively large generating units, generally having modes of interaction that are more complex to analyze. Consequently, the models and criteria currently used to design the various subsystems are also different. These are reviewed briefly here nonmathematically. Although the discussion is cast in the context of traditional system expansion planning, that is, essentially choosing the design that minimizes only system costs while meeting given load and reliability requirements, the basic ideas involved may be readily adapted to the new method in which the reliability level is treated as a parameter to be varied.

Early approaches to system design and planning were rather intuitive and relied heavily on the designer's past experience. In contrast, the more advanced mathematical methods currently used by some utility companies rely on optimization models. The goal is the minimization of an objective function, usually the present discounted value of system costs, subject to constraints, such as meeting the load and reliability targets, and not violating technical and operating requirements.[13] (See, also, chapter 3, Method of Optimizing Reliability.)

12. See David A. Wismer, *Optimization Methods for Large Scale Systems* (New York: McGraw-Hill, 1971).

13. For a more detailed and mathematical treatment, see IEEE, *Application of Optimization Methods in Power System Engineering*, IEEE Tutorial Course Text no. 76CH1107-2-PWR (New York, 1976); and Robert Fischl, "Optimal System Expansion Planning: A Critical Review," *Systems Engineering for Power: Status and Prospects, USERDA Conference, Henniker, New Hampshire, August 1975.* NTIS no. CONF-750867, pp. 233–60.

From a general point of view, if the problem is deterministic and the objective function and constraints are known, then some definitive nominal design may be found. An example of a known objective function would be the best estimates of plant costs, load, and demand in generation planning. Given uncertainty, flexible design strategies are required, such as the worst case concept, in which upper and lower design limits are determined that correspond to maximum and minimum values of the objective function and constraints. Another strategy uses the statistical concept where, given a probabilistic distribution of values of the objective function and constraints, the average design configuration that emerges from among the allowed design variations is found.

The specific solution techniques for the optimization problem may be considered under three categories: programming, search, and other special procedures. The mathematical programming approaches, including linear, nonlinear, integer, mixed-integer, and dynamic programming versions, are most useful when the objective function is simple and well defined. They rely on explicit, computerized algorithms that are used to find the solution after a finite number of steps. Search techniques, used when programming methods would be difficult to apply, for example, with poorly defined, complex, or implicit objective functions, are generally easier to implement. They do not guarantee convergence to the solution within a reasonable time, however. Special procedures are often elegant but, generally, they are applicable only to particular problems.[14]

The basic questions in generation system design relate to the size, timing, type (or mix), and location of generating plants. The economic aspects of each of the choices involved are clarified in the following discussion. The problem of size and timing resulting from the growth of peak megawatt demand over time in a typical capacity-limited system, is depicted in figure 8.1.[15] The installed capacity of existing generating plant (MW_0) will be sufficient to meet the demand in two years' time, after allowing for a suitable reserve margin (see also, chapter 2, Introduction to Reliability.) Two expansion alternatives, which meet all the constraints, are to be considered: in the first one, two medium-sized generating plants will come on-stream in the second and fourth years of the system plan, whereas in the second option, a small plant will be

---

14. See, for example, Lester R. Ford and Delbert R. Fulkerson, *Flows in Networks* (Princeton: Princeton University Press, 1962).

15. 1 megawatt $= 10^3$ kilowatts $= 10^6$ watts.

Figure 8.1. *Size and Timing of Generation Additions to Meet Peak Demand for Power*

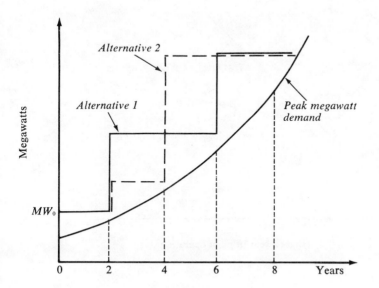

Note: MW_0 = capacity of existing generating plant.

commissioned in the second year, followed by a large power station in the sixth year. The system planner must choose the cheaper alternative. Generally, in a real system the two expansion paths would be compared over a longer period, but in this example, the alternative plans have been made roughly equivalent after the sixth year to highlight the nature of the choice of size and timing of the next two generation additions. Moreover, in predominantly hydroelectric systems, shortages of energy because of limited reservoir storage capability may precede any capacity or power constraints.

The selection of an appropriate plant mix is best discussed in the context of the system's annual load duration curve (LDC). A typical LDC for a given year is shown in the lower half of figure 8.2, a graph of the hourly system megawatt demand plotted against the number of hours in the year during which this demand level is equaled or exceeded. The peak demand ($\overline{MW}$) occurs only over a short period and, since the average level of megawatt demand (that is, the total energy in megawatt-hours or area under the LDC curve divided by 8,760 hours) is less than

Figure 8.2. *Types (or Mix) of Generating Plant Required to Meet the Annual Load Duration Curve* (LDC)

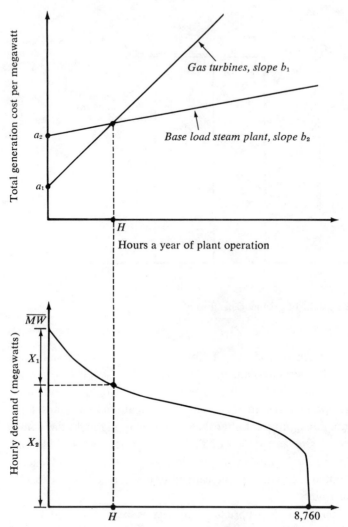

Hours a year during which the given level of demand is equaled or exceeded

Note: Top, cost characteristics of typical thermal plants; *bottom,* system annual load duration curve.

$\overline{MW}$, the load factor will be less than unity. (See the preceding section on load forecast.)

For simplicity, only two kinds of generating units are considered: gas turbines and base load steam plants; the relevant characteristics of both are depicted in the upper part of figure 8.2. The figure is a graph of the total average cost per megawatt of installed capacity, that is, capital cost plus operating cost, plotted as a function of the numbers of hours of operation. Gas turbines have lower capital costs (represented by the intercept a_1, which is the investment cost per megawatt, annuitized over the lifetime of the machine), but higher fuel costs (as indicated by the slope b_1 of the operating cost curve) than the steam plant. The cost characteristics of these units have been simplified for convenience of analysis by assuming fixed values of a_1, a_2, b_1 and b_2. This will not, however, affect the logic of the discussion that follows. Usually, for a given type of generator, the capacity cost for each megawatt installed decreases as the machine size increases, and for a given machine, the operating cost need not increase linearly with hours of usage.

As the upper diagram shows, from the economic point of view gas turbines are more expensive than base load units if they are to be used more than H hours a year and vice versa. This essentially static picture is only illustrative because, actually, the relevant streams of present discounted investment, plus operating costs of the machines, would have to be compared for many years. Pursuing this simplified logic further, however, the lower diagram indicates that it would be economical to serve the bottom X_2 megawatts of load (that is, the base load) with steam units and the upper X_1 megawatts of load (that is, the peak load) with gas turbines, where $X_1 + X_2 = \overline{MW}$. A reserve margin may be included, if necessary.

In practice, many kinds of generating units including nuclear, coal- and oil-fired steam, gas turbine, conventional and pumped-storage hydro, and, more recently, geothermal, tidal, and wind powered units that have characteristics varying by type and by size, would have to be taken into account. When generation additions are being considered to meet future load growth, however, the basic principle of selecting units with lower capital costs but higher operating costs for peaking purposes, and vice versa, generally holds true.

Usually, the choice of generator location affects the design of the transmission system and, therefore, both these problems should be analyzed within a common framework. Transmission planning typically involves the solution of a dynamic network-type problem, in which the basic objective is to select at least cost the type, timing, and location of line additions that would connect the various sources or generating stations to the different sinks or load centers. In addition, the requirements imposed by load, reliability level, technical, and other constraints must be satisfied.

A commonly used network model is the dc-load flow model, which may be used in either a linear or nonlinear framework.[16] In the single-step, essentially static concept, the design optimization procedure is repeated at various points in time when generation and load levels are specified, for example, in the last year of the planning horizon. This is done to provide instantaneous snapshots of the system's evolution. In dynamic methods, large computing times are required to handle transmission line variations over both space and time, as in the analysis of a large interconnected area during each year of the planning period. The time problem may be simplified by preselecting several expansion alternatives according to certain performance criteria. None of these techniques can guarantee a definitive solution, however, given the size of the problem and limits on calculating times.

Transmission system performance criteria, against which the system model is judged, are of two general types: steady state and transient.[17] Steady state performance of the system consists basically of verifying that line and transformer design limits are not exceeded under normal loading and operating conditions or with single contingencies, such as loss of a single line, transformer, or generator. Transient performance criteria are used to test the system model for stability in a variety of situations. One group of tests involves the ability of an interconnected system to maintain steady state stability under normal and contingency conditions when perturbed by a small disturbance, such as the switching on of a minor load. Verifying a system's dynamic stability is also very important. This involves the degree of damping of high amplitude oscillations induced by a large fault, such as failure of a major line resulting from a three-phase fault to ground or loss of a block of generators.

Having examined the transmission system design and planning problem, it is appropriate now to return to the question of generator loca-

16. See B. Stott, "Review of Load-Flow Calculation Methods," *Proceedings of the IEEE*, vol. 62 (July 1974), pp. 916–29.

17. For a more detailed discussion of transmission design criteria, see: Canadian International Development Agency, *Regional Power Systems Engineering Seminar, Kathmandu, Nepal, February–March 1977*.

tion. As discussed in chapter 2, Introduction to Reliability, the reliability analysis of combined generation and transmission system models raises formidable problems. Similar problems arise in system planning and, therefore, although the generation and transmission subsystems are intimately related, separate models are generally used to design each subsystem.

More specifically, a typical large computerized generation planning model would yield the appropriate plant mix, size, and timing. Sometimes the formulation includes a limited, but not very accurate, representation of the transmission network.[18] Then the optimum locations would be chosen from among a variety of potential sites to supply the specific load centers, within the framework of a more detailed transmission planning model. Sometimes, however, site selection is so complicated that it tends to dominate the transmission model. In practice it would be necessary to iterate between the models to converge to the best mutually consistent solution.

Although generation and transmission system planning is an interrelated process, in principle, the distribution grid serving a localized geographic area or load center can be designed independently. Recently, computerized methods have been developed to determine the optimum size, timing, and location of distribution substations and primary feeders, as well as the planning of secondary networks.[19] Sophisticated models and computerized algorithms are not as widely used in distribution system design as in generation and transmission work, however.

In the more conventional approach, forecast loads are imposed on the existing distribution system at specific future times, and the network is systematically strengthened to meet these loads adequately. Meeting consumer demand within acceptable voltage limits would determine the location of new substations and primary feeders and the upgrading of

18. See, for example, Dennis Anderson, "Models for Determining Least Cost Investments in Electricity Supply," *The Bell Journal of Economics and Management Science*, vol. 3 (Spring 1972), pp. 267–301.

19. See Stewart B. Holt, Jr. and Dale M. Crawford, "Distribution Substation Planning Using Optimization Methods," *Application of Optimization Methods in Power System Engineering*, IEEE Tutorial Course Text no. 76CH1107-2-PWR (New York, 1976), pp. 69–76; D. L. Wall, G. L. Thompson, and J. E. D. N. Green, "An Optimization Model for Planning Radial Distribution Networks, *IEEE Transactions on Power Apparatus and Systems*, vol. PAS-98 (May/June 1979), pp. 1061–68; and Yngve Backlund and Janis A. Bubenko, "Computer-Aided Distribution System Planning," *Electrical Power and Energy Systems*, vol. 1 (April 1979), pp. 35–45.

existing ones. Loading under normal and emergency (or fault) conditions, as well as during peak and off-peak periods, would be examined. Flexibility in design would be an important consideration. For example, this would facilitate isolation of faulted sections of feeders and would enable customers to be switched from faulted to functioning feeders.

Often, because of the large numbers of customers and components such as line sections, switches, distribution transformers and so on, only certain representative feeders or circuits would be analyzed in detail to establish general criteria such as maximum kilovolt-amp for a circuit. These criteria could then be applied to other feeders without further study. In general, the larger and more complex the service area, the greater would be the advantage of using even simple computerized techniques for circuit-by-circuit analysis. The distribution system design problem is examined more closely in the case study, chapter 11, Long Range Distribution System Planning.

Costing

The process of costing or estimating the power system supply costs may be broken down into two steps. The first stage involves determining the appropriate model of the physical system to be costed; this could be done in two ways. One obvious candidate, which would correspond very closely to the real physical system, is the model or combination of submodels used in the system design stage described in the previous section.

Recently, several researchers have attempted to take the alternative approach of estimating neoclassical, long-run production functions of electric power systems to determine the cost structure, economies of scale, technical progress, factor substitution possibilities, and so on.[20] These researchers have used the Cobb-Douglas constant elasticity of substitution (CES) and translogarithmic formulations.

20. See, for example, Phoebus J. Dhrymes and Mordecai Kurtz, "Technology and Scale in Electricity Generation," *Econometrica*, vol. 32 (July 1965), pp. 287–315; M. Galatin, *Economies of Scale and Technical Change in Thermal Power Generation* (Amsterdam: North-Holland, 1968); Fred McCoy, "The Production Function Method I," *Marginal Costing and Pricing of Electric Energy, Proceedings of the State-of-the Art International Conference, Montreal, May 1978*; and Laurits Christensen, "The Production Function Method II," *Marginal Costing and Pricing of Electric Energy*, pp. 107–13.

The system design discussed earlier encompasses these issues, however. Furthermore, no generalized production model derived from neoclassical economic theory could hope to capture the detailed information regarding the physical system that is included in an engineering planning model. In particular, sector-wide production functions based on cross-section or pooled—that is, cross-section and time series—data are generally appropriate to determine historical trends in the economics of power sector evolution, rather than to represent a given system accurately. Production functions estimated for a single system using time series data are more specific, but they still remain oriented in the past rather than the future. To summarize, an engineering model used in the design and planning of a system is far more appropriate than an economic production function model for estimating future system supply costs when the reliability level is to be optimized.

Once the model of the physical system has been identified, the next step in estimating the supply costs is to determine the items to be costed and their valuation. Again, two methods are possible. In the first method, commonly used in the United States, the financial viewpoint of a private electric power utility is adopted.[21] The items in the costing exercise are based primarily on accounting concepts. They include physical assets, services, depreciation, interest, and taxes that may be affected by regulatory requirements. The values placed on them are the private financial costs incurred by the utility. These include the purchase cost of assets and services, financing charges, and the cost of raising capital based on the debt-equity mix. The second method is basically economic and more appropriate in the context of the national economy or society as a whole. The goods and services used as physical inputs to the electric power system, such as labor, land, physical capital, and materials, are considered scarce economic resources that could be used in alternative production and valued accordingly. This approach is particularly appropriate where the utility is publicly owned, which frequently occurs in the developing countries.

Since the principal economic criterion for optimizing system reliability is the maximization of the net benefit accruing to society as a whole, rather than to the power utility alone, the second approach discussed above is more relevant to this discussion. The identification and

21. See James Suelflow, *Public Utility Accounting: Theory and Application* (East Lansing: Michigan State University, 1973).

shadow pricing of real economic resources used as inputs into the elec-tric power sector are discussed in detail in the next chapter.

In conclusion, it should be noted that the process of system planning and determining electricity supply costs is usually complicated by several practical difficulties. These include uncertainties in the demand projections as discussed earlier, errors in the cost estimates, technological changes, construction delays, and environmental constraints. Often these problems cannot be analyzed in a general framework and have to be treated on an individual basis. In some cases the uncertainties inherent in load forecasts, cost estimates, and so on may be associated with appropriate probability distributions, permitting statistical decision theory to be applied to long-range system planning.[22] With unreliable data, greater flexibility in system planning is possible by adopting an approach in which several distinct scenarios are simulated to provide the decisionmaker with a range of alternative choices. Most recently, it has been proposed that the theory of fuzzy sets be combined with the criteria used for decisionmaking in long-range system expansion planning; in this type of analysis uncertainties such as demand shifts are represented by unpredictable system states (creating a "fuzzy" environment).[23]

22. See, for example, R. Schlaifer, *Analysis of Decision Under Uncertainty* (New York: McGraw-Hill, 1969); and H. Raiffa, *Decision Analysis: Introductory Lectures on Choices Under Uncertainty* (Reading, Mass.: Addison-Wesley, 1970).

23. S. B. Dhar, "Power System Long-Range Decision Analysis Under Fuzzy Environment," *IEEE Transactions on Power Apparatus and Systems,* vol. PAS-98 (March/April 1979), pp. 585–96.

Chapter 9

Shadow Pricing

This chapter offers a brief introduction to the use of shadow prices that would be relevant to the electricity sector. The discussion on valuing inputs and outputs is developed in the context of a national economy, rather than from the viewpoint of a private power utility company, and, therefore, it is particularly relevant to the developing countries. Generally, when market imperfections occur, shadow prices may be used instead of the distorted market prices to represent the true economic opportunity costs of various goods and services in the economy. Such shadow prices have their roots in the theory of welfare economics and cost-benefit analysis.

General Principles

In the idealized world of perfect competition, the interaction of atomistic profit-maximizing producers and atomistic utility-maximizing consumers yields a situation that is called pareto-optimal. In this state, prices reflect the true marginal social costs, scarce resources are efficiently allocated, and for a given income distribution, no one person can be made better off without making someone else worse off.[1]

1. See Francis J. Bator, "General Equilibrium, Welfare, and Allocation," *American Economic Review* (March 1957), pp. 22–59; and Ezra J. Mishan, *Cost Benefit Analysis* (New York: Praeger, 1976), part vii.

Conditions are likely to be far from ideal in the real world, however. Distortions resulting from monopoly practices, external economics and diseconomies not internalized in the private market, interventions in the market process through taxes, duties, and subsidies result in market prices for goods and services that may diverge substantially from their shadow prices or true economic values. Moreover, if there are large income disparities, the passive acceptance of the existing skewed income distribution, which is implied by the reliance on strict efficiency criteria for determining economic welfare, may be socially and politically unacceptable. These considerations suggest the use of appropriate shadow prices instead of market prices for economic analysis, especially in the developing countries where market distortions are more prevalent.[2]

The relevance of shadow prices is illustrated in figure 9.1, which is derived from figure 3.3. The curves of marginal supply costs (MSC_{ns}) and negative outage costs ($-MOC_{ns}$) without shadow pricing, yield the apparent "optimal" reliability level R_{ns}^m. But this result is inappropriate, because both system and outage costs have been valued in terms of the nominal private financial costs incurred by the utility and consumers. The corresponding shadow-priced marginal supply and negative outage costs (MSC_s and $-MOC_s$) intersect at the reliability level R_s^m, which is the correct optimal value from the national viewpoint. In general, R_s^m and R_{ns}^m will not coincide, because each of the two shadow-priced marginal cost curves may lie above or below the corresponding nonshadow-priced curves, depending on the distortions in the economy.

Consider a general equilibrium model of the economy in which the national goal is embodied in some acceptable objective function such as aggregate consumption. Consumption is to be maximized subject to constraints such as limits on resource availabilities and distortions in the economy.[3] Then the shadow price of a given scarce economic resource represents the change in the value of the objective function caused by a marginal change in the availability of that resource.[4] In the more specific context of a mathematical programming macroeconomic model, the op-

2. For a discussion of the limitations of shadow pricing see: Richard S. Weckstein, "Shadow Prices and Project Evaluation in Less Developed Countries," *Economic Development and Cultural Change* (April 1972), pp. 474–94.

3. See Stephen A. Marglin, *Public Investment Criteria* (London: George, Allen, and Unwin, 1967).

4. See Partha Dasgupta and Joseph Stiglitz, "Benefit Cost Analysis and Trade Policies," *Journal of Political Economy*, vol. 82 (January–February 1974), pp.

Figure 9.1. *Effect of Shadow Pricing*
on the Optimal Reliability Level

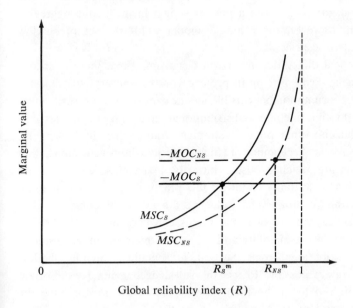

Global reliability index (R)

Note: MSC_{NS}, $-MOC_{NS}$, and $R_{NS}{}^m$ are, respectively, the marginal supply costs, negative marginal outage costs, and apparent optimal reliability level without shadow pricing. MSC_S, $-MOC_S$, and $R_S{}^m$ are the corresponding shadow-priced quantities.

timal values of the dual variables that correspond to the binding resource availability constraints in the primal problem have the dimensions of price and could be interpreted as shadow prices.[5]

Two basic types of shadow prices may be distinguished, which involve a society's concern with or indifference to income distributional considerations. To illustrate this point, consider the simple national goal of maximizing the present value of aggregate consumption over a given period. If the consumption of different individuals is added directly without considering their income levels, then the shadow prices desirable

1–33; and Peter Warr, "On the Shadow Pricing of Traded Commodities," *Journal of Political Economy*, vol. 85 (1977), pp. 865–72.

5. See David G. Luenberger, *Introduction to Linear and Non-Linear Programming* (Reading: Addison-Wesley, 1973), chap. 4; and Peter G. Sassone, "Shadow Pricing in CBA: Mathematical Programming and Economic Theory," *The Engineering Economist*, vol. 22 (Spring 1977), pp. 219–33.

from such a model are called efficiency prices because they reflect the pure efficiency of resource allocation. When the consumption of the lower income groups is given a greater weight in evaluating aggregate consumption, however, the resultant model yields the set of shadow prices called social prices.[6]

Two practical difficulties are worth discussing. First, there is an objection to using social pricing in project work on the grounds that the weighting of consumption benefits by income category is necessarily quite arbitrary, and that income redistributional goals are better realized through fiscal and other policy instruments rather than by biasing investment decisions. Acceptance of efficiency prices, however, implies that equal weights are attached, also arbitrarily, to benefits accruing to all individuals.[7] Also in many countries few practical policy tools may be available to the government to influence the existing income distribution.[8] In practice, the use of social versus efficiency prices depends on factors such as data availability and the commitment of the government to income distributional goals. Second, in actually estimating shadow prices, it is rarely possible to use the full-fledged general equilibrium approach referred to in the theory. Many countries do not have the requisite data, and it would be wasteful and time-consuming to reanalyze such a large model whenever new investment decisions were required. Instead, partial equilibrium techniques are used to evaluate the effect of the change in the availability of a given resource by its effect on a few key areas, rather than throughout the economy.

The partial equilibrium method has been criticized on the basis of nonmarginality, for its lack of simultaneity, and because of the judgmental element involved in choosing which linkages will be analyzed when the effect of some disturbance is to be evaluated. In principle, however, these objections can be overcome by using an iterative process of successive, convergent approximations and by considering a sufficient number of linkages, so that the partial equilibrium shadow prices closely approximate the corresponding general equilibrium values.

6. See Lyn Squire and Herman G. van der Tak, *Economic Analysis of Projects* (Baltimore: Johns Hopkins University Press for the World Bank, 1975), chap. 6.

7. However, Ezra J. Mishan, *Cost Benefit Analysis,* chap. 61, argues that the only implication is that of a potential pareto improvement rather than uniform weighting of benefits.

8. See Partha Dasgupta, Amartya Sen, and Stephen Marglin, *Guidelines for Project Evaluation* (UNIDO) (New York: United Nations, 1972), chap. 7; and Ian M. D. Little and Jan A. Mirrlees, *Project Appraisal and Planning for Developing Countries* (New York: Basic Books, 1974), chap. 4.

Numeraire

To derive a consistent set of economic prices for goods and services it is necessary to adopt a common yardstick or numeraire to measure value, as the following example illustrates.

If bananas are to be compared with pineapples, it may be argued that the equivalent units should be either one banana for one pineapple or 1 kilo of bananas for 1 kilo of pineapples. In the first case the common yardstick is one fruit; in the second it is the unit of weight. Clearly, if the weights of the two types of fruits are not identical, the result of the comparison will depend on the yardstick used.

Unfortunately, the situation is more complicated with a unit of account, or numeraire for economic value, because the same nominal unit of currency may have a different value depending on the economic circumstances in which it is used. For example, a rupee's or a dollar's worth of a certain good purchased in a duty-free shop is likely to be more than the physical quantity of the same good obtained for one rupee or one dollar from a retail store, after import duties and taxes have been levied. Therefore, it is possible to distinguish intuitively between a border-priced rupee used in international markets free of import tariffs and a domestic-priced rupee used in the domestic market subject to various distortions. A more sophisticated example of the value differences of a currency unit in various uses often arises in countries where there is inadequate aggregate savings and investment, and therefore the rate of economic growth is low. In this case, a rupee of savings, which could be invested to increase the level of future consumption, may be considered more valuable than a rupee devoted to current consumption.

The choice of the numeraire, like the choice of a currency unit, should not influence the economic criteria for decisionmaking except in magnitude, provided the same consistent framework and assumptions are used in the analysis.[9] For example, only one difference exists between two studies using as units rupees and rupiyal (ten rupees). All monetary quantities in rupees will be numerically ten times as large as those in

---

9. For a discussion of the different assumptions used in various approaches to shadow pricing, see Hugh Schwartz and Richard Berney (eds.), *Social and Economic Dimensions of Project Evaluation* (Washington, D.C.: Inter-American Development Bank, 1977); and Deepak Lal, *Methods of Project Analysis*, World Bank Staff Occasional Papers, no. 16 (Baltimore: Johns Hopkins University Press, 1974).

rupiyal. Therefore, one numeraire may be selected instead of another because it is easier to apply.

One numeraire that has proved to be most appropriate in many instances is a unit of uncommitted public income at border prices. This is essentially the same as freely disposable foreign exchange available to the government, but is expressed in units of local currency converted at the official exchange rate.[10] The discussion in the next section uses this particular yardstick of value. The border-priced numeraire is particularly relevant for the foreign-exchange-scarce developing countries, and represents the set of opportunities available to a country to purchase goods and services on the international market. Unless otherwise specified, all values referred to in the following discussions are in real terms: that is, net of inflation.

Application of Shadow Prices

The estimation and use of shadow prices is facilitated by dividing economic resources into tradable and nontradable items. The values of directly imported or exported goods and services are already known in border prices: that is, the foreign exchange costs converted at the official exchange rate. Locally purchased items whose values are known only in domestic market prices, however, must be converted to border prices by multiplying the domestic prices by appropriate conversion factors (CF). Therefore, the treatment of tradables and nontradables is somewhat different, as the following discussion indicates.

When tradables with infinite elasticities are involved, the cost, insurance, and freight (c.i.f.) border price for imports and the free-on-board (f.o.b.) border price for exports may be used with a suitable adjustment for the marketing margin.[11] If the relevant elasticities are finite, then the change in import costs or export revenues, which will be the dominant component, as well as any shifts in other domestic consump-

10. See Ian M. D. Little and Jan A. Mirrlees, *Project Appraisal and Planning for Developing Countries*, chap. 9, and Lyn Squire and Herman van der Tak, *Economic Analysis of Projects*, chap. 3. A numeraire based on private consumption is advocated in Partha Dasgupta, Amartya Sen, and Stephen Marglin, *Guidelines for Project Evaluation* (UNIDO).

11. Infinite elasticities of world supply for imports, and world demand for exports.

tion and production, and income transfers should be considered. (See appendix B for details.) The free trade assumption is not required to justify the use of border prices, since domestic price distortions are adjusted, in effect, by subtracting all taxes, duties, and subsidies.

The discussion may be clarified by the following example. Imagine a household in which a child is given an allowance of ten rupees a month as pocket money. The youngster may purchase a bag of candy from the grocery store for two rupees. Since the parents want to discourage consumption of sweets, however, they impose a fine of one rupee on each bag of candy. The fine is exactly like an import duty, and the child must surrender three rupees for every bag of candy (valued at its domestic price, inside the household). From the point of view of the whole family unit, however, the total external payment for the item is only two rupees because the one rupee fine is a net transfer within the household. Therefore, the true economic cost, or shadow price, of the bag of candy (valued at its border price) is two rupees, when the effect of the fine on the distribution of income between parent and child is ignored.

Next, nontradable economic resources are considered. This category includes both the conventional definition of a nontradable as a commodity whose domestic supply price over some given range of output lies between the f.o.b. and c.i.f. prices for export and import, respectively, and also items that are not traded at the margin because of prohibitive trade barriers, such as bans or rigid quotas. If the increased demand for a given nontradable good or service is met by the expansion of domestic supply or imports, then the associated border-priced marginal social cost (MSC) of this increased supply is the relevant resource cost. If the input is supplied through the decreased consumption of other domestic or foreign users, then the border-priced marginal social benefit (MSB) of this foregone domestic consumption, or reduced export earnings, would be a more appropriate measure of social costs. The socially optimal level of total consumption for the given input (Q_{opt}) would be at the point where the curves of MSC and MSB intersect. The differences between MSB and MSC arise from price and other distortions that lead to nonoptimal levels of consumption $Q \neq Q_{opt}$. More generally, if both effects are present, a weighted average of MSC and MSB should be used. The MSB would tend to dominate in the short-run, supply-constrained situation, and the MSC should be more important in the longer run, when expansion of output is possible (see appendix B).

A correspondingly similar analysis may be used when the supply of a nontradable is increased. The MSC of composite goods may be determined by successively decomposing the nontradable into its constituent inputs. This should be done until only the ultimate tradable inputs, which can be valued at border prices, and nontraded primary factors, such as labor and land, remain. The MSB for intermediate and final consumption should be evaluated by the foregone social profit and consumers' surplus, respectively; the income transfer effects of any price changes should be added to these. In practice the MSC is often used instead of the MSB because of data constraints.

As noted earlier, the MSC of nontradable goods and services from many sectors can be determined through appropriate decomposition. For example, suppose one rupee's worth, in domestic prices, of the output of the domestic construction sector may be broken down successively into n components, such as capital, labor, and materials. These are valued at rupees $a_1, a_2, \ldots, a_n$, in border prices. Since the conversion factor of any good is defined as the ratio of the border price to the

domestic price, the construction conversion factor equals $\sum\limits_{i=1}^{n} a_i$.

With nontradables that are not important enough to merit individual attention or that lack sufficient data, the standard conversion factor (*SCF*) may be used. The *SCF* is equal to the official exchange rate (*OER*) divided by the more familiar shadow exchange rate (*SER*). Conversion of domestic-priced values into border price equivalents by application of the *SCF* to the former is conceptually the opposite of the traditional practice of multiplying foreign currency costs by the *SER* to convert to the domestic price equivalent. A convenient approximation to the standard conversion factor is the ratio of the official exchange rate to the free trade exchange rate (*FTER*), when the country is moving toward a freer trade regime:[12]

$$SCF = \frac{OER}{FTER} = \frac{\epsilon X + \eta M}{\epsilon X (1 - t_x) + \eta M (1 + t_m)}$$

where X = f.o.b. value of exports; M = c.i.f. value of imports; ϵ = elasticity of export supply; η = elasticity of import demand; t_x =

12. For a more detailed discussion of alternative interpretations of the *SCF* and *SER*, see Lyn Squire and Herman G. van der Tak, *Economic Analysis of Projects*, and Bela Balassa, "Estimating the Shadow Price of Foreign Exchange in Project Appraisal," *Oxford Economic Papers*, vol. 26 (July 1974), pp. 147–68.

average tax rate on exports (negative for subsidy); and t_m = average tax rate on imports.

The most important tradable inputs used in the electric power sector are capital goods and petroleum-based fuels; world market prices may be used for both where appropriate. In some countries fuels, such as coal, are available that have no clear-cut alternative uses. In these cases the MSC of production may be used. The most important nontradable primary factor inputs are labor and land, which complete the discussion on shadow price applications. In particular, the procedure outlined for estimating the shadow wage rate (SWR) also illustrates the effect of income distributional considerations. Other important nontradable inputs, such as the services of the domestic construction sector, may be broken down into tradables and primary factors, as discussed earlier.

Consider a typical case of unskilled labor in a labor surplus country, for example, rural workers employed for dam construction. The foregone output of workers used in the electric power sector is the dominant component of the SWR. Complications arise because the original income earned may not reflect the marginal product of agricultural labor and, furthermore, for every new job created, more than one rural worker may give up former employment.[13] Allowance must also be made for seasonal activities such as harvesting. In theory, if the laborer has to work harder in a new job than before, then the disutility of foregone leisure should be included in the SWR, but in practice this component is ignored. Overhead costs, such as transport expenses, should also be considered. These concepts may be summarized by the following basic equation for the efficiency shadow wage rate (in efficiency prices):

$$ESWR = a \cdot m + c \cdot u$$

where m and u are the foregone marginal output and overhead costs of labor in domestic prices, and a and c are corresponding conversion factors to convert these values into border prices.

The effect of these changes on consumption patterns is important to consider. Suppose a worker receives a wage W_n in a new job and that the income foregone is W_o, both in domestic prices; W_o may not necessarily be equal to the marginal product foregone m. It could be assumed, quite

13. See John R. Harris and Michael P. Todaro, "Migration, Unemployment, and Development," *American Economic Review*, vol. 60 (March 1970), pp. 126–42.

114   THEORY

plausibly, that low-income workers consume all their increase in income
(W_n W_o). Then this increase in consumption will result in a resource
cost to the economy of $b \cdot (W_n - W_o)$, where b is the border-priced
MSC of increasing private consumption, in domestic prices, by one unit.
The increased consumption also provides a benefit given by $w \cdot (W_n -
W_o)$, where w represents the MSB, in border prices, of increasing domestic-
priced private sector consumption by one unit. Therefore:

$$SWR = a \cdot m + c \cdot u + (b - w)(W_n - W_o).$$

The consumption term $(b - w)$ disappears if at the margin (a) society is indifferent to the distribution of income or consumption, so that
everyone's consumption has equivalent value; and (b) private consumption is considered to be as socially valuable as uncommitted public
savings, the numeraire. (See appendix B for a more detailed explanation
of b and w).

Regarding land, the appropriate shadow value placed on this primary
factor depends on its location. In most cases, the market price of urban
land is assumed to be a good indicator of its economic value in domestic
prices, and the application of an appropriate conversion factor, the SCF,
to this domestic price will yield the border-priced cost of urban land
inputs. Rural land that can be used for agriculture may be valued at
its opportunity cost: that is, the net benefit of foregone agricultural
output. The marginal social cost of other rural land is usually assumed
to be negligible, unless there is a specific reason to the contrary. If a
hydroelectric dam floods virgin jungle, however, loss of valuable timber
or spoilage of a recreational area with commercial potential might be
involved.

The shadow price of capital is usually reflected in the discount rate
or accounting rate of interest (ARI), which is defined as the rate of
decline in the value of the numeraire over time. Although there has been
much discussion concerning the choice of an appropriate discount rate,
in practice the opportunity cost of capital (OCC) may be used as a proxy
for the ARI, in the pure efficiency price regime.[14] The OCC is defined as
the expected value of the annual stream of consumption in border prices,

14. See, for example, Stephen A. Marglin, "The Social Rate of Discount and
the Optimal Rate of Investment," *Quarterly Journal of Economics* (1963); Ezra
J. Mishan, *Cost Benefit Analysis*, chap. 31–34; and Arnold C. Harberger, *Project
Evaluation* (London: Macmillan and Co., 1972).

net of replacement, which is yielded by the investment of one unit of public income at the margin. A simple formula for ARI, which also includes consumption effects, is:

$$ARI = OCC\,[s + (1 - s)w/b]$$

where s is the fraction of the yield from the original investment that will be saved and reinvested.[15]

The objective of this section has been to facilitate the application of shadow pricing in power sector economic analysis. A word of caution is necessary, however. Although the principles underlying the use of shadow prices are relatively straightforward, usually the estimation of shadow prices on a rigorous basis is a long and complex task.[16] Therefore, the electric power sector analyst is advised to use shadow prices that have already been calculated by other specialists. Alternatively, perhaps the analyst could make simple estimates of a few important items, such as the standard conversion factor, opportunity cost of capital, and shadow wage rate. When the data are not precise enough, sensitivity studies may be necessary over a range of values of such key national parameters.

15. Lyn Squire and Herman G. van der Tak, *Economic Analysis of Projects*, chap. 10.

16. See Colin Bruce, "Social Cost-Benefit Analysis: A Guide for Country and Project Economists to the Derivation and Application of Economic and Social Accounting Prices," World Bank Staff Working Paper, no. 239 (Washington, D.C.: World Bank, August 1976).

Part Two

▬▬

Case Study

The objective of the case study is to test and to evaluate the reliability and system optimization theory developed in Part One. The parameters of this study were determined on the basis of the following three criteria.

First, the study was implemented in a developing country because the World Bank is particularly concerned with the needs of the Third World for economic development. In a developing country, the application of the theoretical methodology can be examined critically under conditions of data scarcity compared with the industrialized countries. In this context, shadow pricing concepts must also be applied.

Second, a distribution study was selected because it afforded greater opportunities for advancing the state-of-the-art in engineering. This supply side consideration paralleled the major demand side effort in economics to measure outage costs. The engineering component is especially relevant, because generation and transmission system models and planning techniques tend to be much more sophisticated and better investigated than those generally used in distribution network studies, although usually distribution failures account for most consumer outages.[1] (See chapter 8, Power System Supply Costs.) Furthermore, it is possible to compute load-point outage frequency and duration indexes,

---

1. See, for example, R. N. Allan, E. N. Dialynas, and I. R. Homer, "Modelling and Evaluating the Reliability of Distribution Systems," *IEEE Transactions on Power Apparatus and Systems*, vol. PAS-98 (May–June 1979).

117

which are appropriate for estimating consumer outage costs more accurately for distribution systems than for generation and transmission systems. Third, the choice of Cascavel, in southern Brazil, as the city for study was influenced by the need to collaborate with a local electric power utility that was willing and able to assist in the study.[2] Other considerations that affected the decision included the importance of having a representative mix of consumer types, as described in chapter 10, and the requirement of implementing the methodology within a reasonably compact, medium-sized urban area, for example, a population of 100,000.

The techniques described in Part One were applied in a relatively straightforward fashion, by following the sequence of steps summarized in the flow chart depicted in figure 1.1 of chapter 1. A highly disaggregate load forecast was prepared using correlation techniques in conjunction with urban land use and socioeconomic data. The design and costing of alternative distribution system expansion paths was detailed and developed over a longer period than is common in most distribution planning studies. Expected outage frequency and average duration indexes were computed at the point of consumption using a relatively simple technique. Outage costs were estimated by using information on local economic activity, as well as several consumer surveys that were based on the theoretical models developed earlier. Finally, the cost-benefit analysis and fine-tuning of the system optimization procedure led to the innovative step of designing so-called "hybrid" distribution networks or grids. The reliability level of these hybrid grids was varied in different neighborhoods, depending on their sensitivity to outages.

The methodology was implemented primarily by employing three computerized models that were used specifically to determine the demand forecast, the alternative distribution system designs, and the outage costs and system costs. Despite their potential complexity and size, these computer programs were adapted especially to be implemented on compact mini-micro-computer systems.

2. Compania Paranaense de Energía Eléctrica (COPEL), Parana, Brazil.

Chapter 10

Demand Forecast

The load forecast developed in this chapter is specifically for the purpose of long-range distribution system planning. Therefore, as discussed in chapter 8, Power System Planning and Supply Costs, a computerized approach was used to make these demand projections, which are both long term and highly disaggregate:[1] (a) by type of consumer—twenty-four categories; (b) geographically—247 cells, each 500 × 500 meters square; and (c) in time—annually over twenty years.

Straightforward correlation techniques were combined with land use and socioeconomic information to obtain the desired results. First, the intensity of energy consumption by consumer category was estimated by relating the kilowatt-hour use to convenient measures of customer magnitude, for example, kilowatt-hours for each household, each unit of industrial value added, each hospital bed, and so on, in any given year. Then, land use, demographic, and other socioeconomic data were used to determine the customer magnitudes incident in each geographic cell and over time. For example, the number of households, total industrial value added, and number of hospital beds in each cell were examined for each year.

The product of the intensity of energy use and the customer magnitude yielded the total disaggregate energy demand by consumer category, by

1. Details of the computation are provided in appendix C.

119

geographic cell, and by year. Throughout the analysis a neutral price assumption was used. that is, the price of electricity would be constant in real terms. This pricing assumption was the most safe and reasonable choice, since the Brazilian federal government, which regulates electricity tariffs, has adopted a policy of nominal price increases equal to the annual rate of inflation during the past few years.

Electricity consumers were divided into six major categories to determine the demand forecast and to estimate outage costs. Each major category was also divided into the following subcategories:

(1) Residential—lower, lower-middle, upper-middle, and upper income groups;

(2) Main industrial—metallurgy and mechanical,[2] nonmetallic minerals, wood, vegetable oils, food and beverages, and other;

(3) Service industrial—telephone, water and sewage treatment, metallurgy and mechanical, and other;

(4) Commercial—light, medium, and heavy;

(5) Public illumination—express, important, main, normal, and secondary roads;

(6) Special institutions—hospitals and schools.

Land Use and Occupancy by Geographic Cell

The future geographic distribution of the various consumers was based upon the long-range urban development plan adopted by the Cascavel city authorities.[3] This plan included a map, figure 10.1, detailing the location of the following land classifications:

ZR1—Residential area surrounding the core of the business district, an area predominantly occupied by families in the upper and upper-middle income groups;

ZR2—Inner suburban area for families in the upper-middle and lower-middle income groups;

ZR3—Outer suburban area for families in the lower income group;

2. The output of this type of industry was divided equally between the main and service industrial sectors.

3. Prefeitura Municipal de Cascavel, *Plano Diretor de Desenvolvimento* (Parana, Brazil, 1975).

ZC and ZCR—Heavy commercial area and high-rise apartments for upper and upper-middle income families in the center of the city;

SC and SL—Medium commercial area and medium-sized apartment buildings for upper-middle and lower-middle income families;

ZI—Main industrial area where no residential buildings are permitted;

SI—Service industrial area along the main highways and some residential buildings for lower income families;

SV—Green areas for recreation;

ZM—Military area.

A comprehensive set of zoning regulations describes the uses permitted for each class of land, the amount of land that may be occupied, the ratio of floor area to land area, minimum lot sizes, setback from lot lines, and so on. These regulations were used to determine future occupancy levels in dwelling units, population, and commercial floor space. For example, in ZR3, only single-story residences will be permitted on a minimum lot size of 450 square meters. Streets, walkways, and playgrounds will require about 15 percent of the land. An additional 10 percent will be required for service commercial establishments, such as groceries, laundry, and drugstores.

Therefore, for a typical square kilometer of ZR3 land, the following mix might be found:

Streets   = 15 percent of 1 square kilometer = 0.15 square
                     kilometer
Commercial   = 10 percent of 1 square kilometer = 0.10 square
                     kilometer
Residential   = 75 percent of 1 square kilometer = 0.75 square
                     kilometer
Number of houses   = 750,000 square meters per square kilometer/
                     450 square meters per home
                   = 1,666 homes per square kilometer

Assuming five persons in each family, one square kilometer of ZR3 could contain a maximum of 8,333 people if it were 100-percent saturated and each family had a house on a minimum-sized lot.

Since distribution planning requires a knowledge of loads by small geographic areas to locate future substations and primary feeders advantageously, the individual load areas or cells should be sized so that the maximum demand is well within planning limitations. A load of 5,000

Figure 10.1 *Cascavel Urban Zoning Classification*

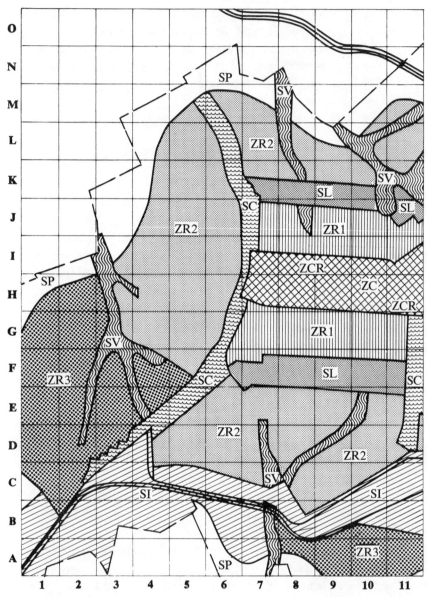

Note: ZR1 ⫼ = residential (upper and upper-middle income); ZR2 ▦ = residential (upper-middle and lower-middle income); ZR3 ▩ = residential (lower income); ZC ⧆ ZCR ⧅ = heavy commercial and residential (upper and upper-middle income); SC ▨ SL ▦ = medium commercial and residential (upper-

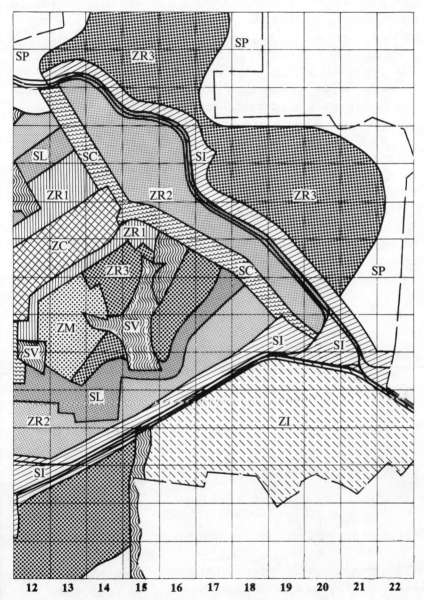

middle and lower-middle income); ZI ◳ = main industrial; SI ▨ = service industrial and residential (lower income); SV ▧ = recreational; SP ☐ = peripheral; and ZM ▣ = military zone.

kilowatts would be appropriate when planning 15-kilovolt primary systems, for example. This usually results in cell sizes ranging from 0.1 square kilometer for the centers of large cities to 1.0 square kilometer for rural areas.

For this study, a single cell size of 0.25 square kilometer (500 meters × 500 meters) was selected. The location of the cells corresponded to COPEL's coordinate system, which simplified the correlation of existing load levels with forecast demands. The selected grid was superimposed onto a map containing the various land classifications. As an illustration, a similar but larger 1-kilometer square grid is shown in figure 10.2.

The fractional area, in square meters, of each cell within the various zoning classifications was derived from the map and entered into a computerized data base used for load forecasting.[4]

The future land use was then used to compute the probable mix of consumers for each cell. For example, a cell might contain 0.15 square kilometer of ZR3 land and 0.1 square kilometer of recreation land (SV). Maintaining the same assumptions as in the earlier numerical example, the land uses within this cell would be:

Residential area $= 0.75 \times 0.150 = 0.1125$ square kilometer

Maximum number of houses $= 1660 \times 0.1125 = 250$ homes

Street area $= 0.15 \times 0.150 = 0.0225$ square kilometer

Light commercial area $= 0.10 \times 0.150 = 0.0150$ square kilometer

Recreational area $= 1.0 \times 0.100 = 0.100$ square kilometer

Residential Electricity Consumption

The basic unit for analyzing residential consumption was the average household of five persons. This mean household size of five persons was approximately constant over all income classes and was also assumed

4. See Walter G. Scott, "Computer Model Forecasts Future Loads," *Electrical World* (September 15, 1972), pp. 114–16.

to remain unchanged in the future. Using COPEL's billing data, as well as income and other data from a 1975–76 household survey, it was possible to plot the curve of average annual household kilowatt-hour consumption against income net of taxes (by income class), as figure 10.3 shows.[5] Assuming that this relation between kilowatt-hours and real income remains unchanged in the future, and estimating the average annual rate of growth of gross household income in real terms to be 4 percent on the basis of past growth rates and long-run economic projections, the corresponding future annual kilowatt-hour consumption of households in each income class could be determined, as summarized in table 10.1. It was also assumed that the real electricity price and the tax structure with resepect to real income would remain essentially the same.

Next, a forecast was made of overall population, as well as the fraction of population served with electricity, on the basis of the most recent demographic information and discussions with city planners, as shown in table 10.1. The distribution of population by income class was 20 percent lower, 45 percent lower-middle, 27 percent upper-middle, and 8 percent upper in 1976, and it was estimated that this income structure would remain basically unchanged during the forecast period. The mean real income level of each income class, however, was assumed to grow at 4 percent annually, as previously mentioned.

The forecast population was distributed throughout the city as follows: the 1976 distribution of residential consumers by level of kilowatt-hour consumption, and therefore by income class, was known on a cell-by-cell basis from COPEL billing records. For the future years, the city was divided into the three saturation regions—high, medium, and low—based on population density, as shown in figure 10.2. A 100-percent saturation level implied that the land was carrying the maximum residential population permitted under the applicable zoning regulations. The forecast population by income class was allocated across the residential zones on the basis of reasonable estimates of saturation factors and numbers of single and multifamily dwellings per cell. (See appendix C for details.)

Kilowatt-hour consumption figures for each residential class may be obtained on a cell-by-cell basis from the forecast of the number of households and each household's kilowatt-hour consumption.

5. CURA, "Pesquisa Fisico-Socio-Economica" (prepared for the Cascavel City Government) (1975–76).

Figure 10.2. *Cascavel Cell Grid, Saturations 1, 2, 3,*
and Layout of Principal Roads

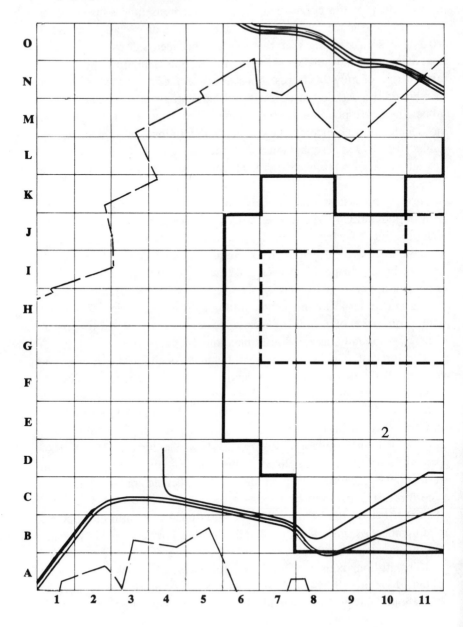

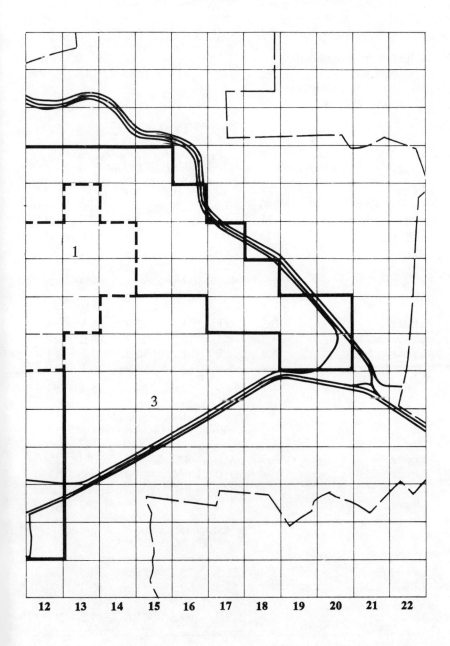

Table 10.1. *Forecast of the Cascavel Urban Population,*
Electricity Service, Electricity Consumption, and Income

		1976	1980	1984	1988	1992	1998
Population (thousands of persons)		90	146	214	281	341	399
Average annual growth rate (percentage)		18	13	10	7	5	4
Income group	Percent-age of total population	*Percentage of income class served by electricity*					
Lower	20	25	40	50	60	70	80
Lower-middle	45	50	60	70	80	90	90
Upper-middle	27	75	85	90	95	100	100
Upper	8	100	100	100	100	100	100
Total		55.8	66.0	73.8	81.7	89.5	91.5
		Total annual electricity consumption (gigawatt-hour)					
Lower		0.3	0.8	1.8	2.9	5.5	8.6
Lower-middle		3.5	8.1	16.2	25.7	38.2	50.7
Upper-middle		5.9	12.0	21.2	32.8	47.6	61.7
Upper		4.4	8.0	12.8	17.9	24.1	30.8
Total		14.1	28.9	52.0	79.3	115.4	151.8
		Average annual household electricity consumption (kilowatt-hour)					
Lower		307	360	430	500	580	680
Lower-middle		794	910	1,060	1,210	1,380	1,570
Upper-middle		1,631	1,840	2,060	2,310	2,580	2,860
Upper		3,283	3,520	3,760	4,040	4,400	4,820
		Average annual household net income (1976 Cr\$ $\times$ 10^3)[a]					
Lower		18.4	21.5	25.2	29.5	34.5	40.3
Lower-middle		47.7	54.3	62.3	71.6	82.3	94.7
Upper-middle		97.5	111.8	128.0	146.8	167.8	191.1
Upper		228.6	249.7	269.5	301.6	341.2	386.3

a. US\$1 = Cr\$12.35 (end 1976).

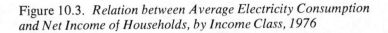

Figure 10.3. *Relation between Average Electricity Consumption and Net Income of Households, by Income Class, 1976*

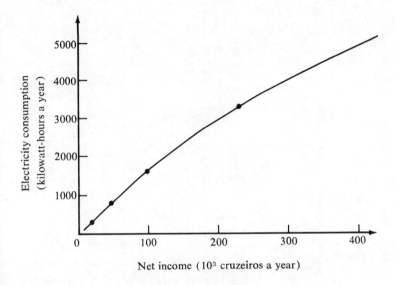

Industrial Electricity Consumption

The growth of value added in each of the six main industrial sectors was forecast for the 1976–96 period, based on the most recent data on industrial activity and discussions with local firms, government officials, and so on. Past data on value added for each kilowatt-hour consumed were analyzed for each type of industry. These data made it possible to estimate future industrial loads.

Electricity consumption for telephone service and water and sewage treatment in the service industrial group could be forecast by analyzing population growth and from information obtained from public officials. Other service industrial needs were determined by estimating energy usage per square meter of land for this kind of activity, chiefly on the basis of trends in their past relation with population. The industrial load forecast is summarized in table 10.2.

The industrial loads were known on a cell-by-cell basis for 1976 from COPEL billing data. These loads were allowed to grow in their existing locations at the given rates until 1980, after which they were gradually

Table 10.2. Industrial Electricity Consumption

Sector	Value added (1976 Cr$) per kWh	Load factor	Annual megawatt-hour consumption						Average annual growth rate over 20 years
			1976	1980	1984	1988	1992	1996	
Main industrial									
Metallurgy and mechanical	23.5	0.15	255	446	780	1,364	2,386	4,173	15
Nonmetallic minerals	14.9	0.123	804	1,407	2,460	4,303	7,525	13,162	15
Wood	32.3	0.204	4,338	5,477	6,914	8,729	11,020	13,913	6
Vegetable oils	19.6	0.435	5,420	8,529	13,419	21,117	33,227	52,283	12
Food and beverages	19.9	0.183	3,267	5,141	8,089	12,729	20,029	31,515	12
Other	14.1	0.46	1,239	1,949	3,067	4,825	7,593	11,948	12
Subtotal	22.6	0.25	15,323	22,949	34,729	53,067	81,780	126,994	11.15
Service industrial									
Telephone	25.5	0.46	470	767	1,251	2,039	3,324	5,420	13
Water and sewage treatment	5.1	0.25	2,800	4,251	6,453	9,756	14,871	22,574	11
Metallurgy and mechanical	23.5	0.15	255	446	780	1,364	2,386	4,173	15
Other	—	0.24	3,500	6,121	10,707	18,726	32,752	57,283	15
Subtotal	—	0.25	7,025	11,585	19,191	31,885	53,333	89,450	13.56
Total	—	0.25	22,348	34,534	53,920	84,952	135,113	216,444	12.02

130

allocated to the main industrial (ZI) and service industrial (SI) areas. By 1984, all industrial activity would be confined to ZI and SI zones, as the urban authorities planned.

Other Electricity Consumption

For commercial electricity use, a survey was made to determine the floor area and electrical equipment in a variety of commercial establishments. The survey results and recent data on the growth of energy consumption were used to determine the future energy requirements for light, medium, and heavy commercial consumers. These projections were adjusted to correlate commercial load growth with population increases in each area.

For street lighting, energy requirements were based on five types of streets and their associated lighting standards: that is, express, important, main, normal, and secondary. The street lighting load was increased with the growing population, industrial, and commercial saturation of each zone.

For schools, energy requirements during the forecast period were based on recent trends of energy use: that is, averaging approximately 4 kilowatt-hours for each student year. Also, it was assumed that the percentage of students in the population would increase steadily from about 9 percent in 1976 to 20 percent in 1996.

For hospitals, future energy requirements were based on recent trends in energy use for each hospital bed: that is, approximately 1,000 kilowatt-hours for a bed annually. A constant ratio of six beds to every 1,000 persons was assumed based on information provided by local authorities on future hospital construction.

Summary of Demand Forecast

The demand for electric energy was estimated annually over the entire twenty-year forecast period, in each of the 247 geographic cells, and for each of the twenty-four consumer categories by using a variety of

Table 10.3. *Summary of Demand Forecast*

Consumer category	1976 GWh	1976 MW	1980 GWh	1980 MW	1984 GWh	1984 MW	1988 GWh	1988 MW	1992 GWh	1992 MW	1996 GWh	1996 MW	Load factor[a]
Residential	14.1	4.4	28.9	8.9	51.0	15.7	80.2	24.7	115.9	35.8	152.1	46.9	0.37
Main industrial	15.3	7.0	23.0	10.5	34.7	15.8	53.1	24.2	81.8	37.4	127.0	58.2	0.25
Service industrial	7.0	3.2	11.6	5.3	19.2	8.8	31.9	14.6	53.3	24.3	89.5	40.9	0.25
Commercial	13.5	4.8	28.3	10.1	51.4	18.3	82.8	29.5	122.5	43.7	164.5	58.7	0.32
Public lighting	3.0	0.8	4.9	1.3	7.2	2.0	9.4	2.6	11.5	3.1	13.5	3.7	0.42
Hospitals and schools	0.6	0.1	1.0	0.3	1.4	0.4	1.9	0.5	2.4	0.6	2.8	0.7	0.46
Total	53.5	20.3	97.6	36.4	164.9	61.0	259.3	96.1	387.4	144.9	549.3	209.1	

Note: GWh = gigawatt-hour; MW = megawatt.
a. The load factor for each consumer category is a weighted average that includes the effect of diversity.

correlation techniques, in conjunction with land use, saturation, and socioeconomic data.

Electricity consumption data were examined by consumer category, for the period 1970 to 1975 inclusive, to determine the evolution of the load factor(LF). With this information, appropriate constant values of LF were estimated for the forecast period, incorporating the effects of diversity among consumers. These values were used to project the disaggregate demand for power on the basis of the corresponding kilowatt-hour load forecast made earlier. The global demand forecast for the entire city at four-year intervals and by major consumer categories is summarized in table 10.3.

Chapter 11

━━

Long-Range Distribution
System Planning

This chapter is concerned with the development of alternative system plans that were designed to achieve different levels of reliability. Again, the main purpose of the illustrative case study, described in part 2, was to test the new methodology of optimizing power system reliability levels, with special emphasis on the empirical estimation of outage costs. A comprehensive distribution system planning study was not intended. Therefore each of the alternative system designs is based upon the same voltage criteria and constructed with similar materials and equipment in accordance with the same engineering standards. In this study the reliability level among the different expansion alternatives usually was varied by providing different substation and feeder capacities, as well as several interconnection possibilities between distribution circuits. In addition, this adjustment made it possible to limit the innumerable and time-consuming variations in system design that could have been generated by minor alterations in the types of equipment and configurations used. The points at which such further fine-tuning of the system design could be carried out are indicated in the text.

Stages of Distribution System Development

Before examining the system design criteria, it is pertinent to discuss the three basic engineering stages in the development of a distribution system: the design of equipment and components; the determination of general construction standards based on the available equipment and components; and the selection of the types of construction standards to be applied in a specific situation.

Manufacturers have the major responsibility for the first stage, the design of distribution equipment and components such as transformers, insulators, and switches. Overall, the efficiency, dependability, and compactness of these components have steadily improved. Since most of them have been standardized for use in the industrialized countries, the developing countries could lower costs by adapting component designs to local conditions, especially for rural electrification.

Utility or consulting engineers are largely responsible for the second stage: the development of general construction standards. Usually these consist of drawings and materials lists to accomplish specific functions, such as a pole with a cross arm, insulators, and hardware to support a three-phase primary line. In general, construction design standards in the industrialized countries have reflected successfully the increases in construction labor costs and advances in equipment design. Again, developing countries that accept these design standards without modification could be using their scarce resources inefficiently.

In the third stage, engineers select and merge construction standards to build facilities to carry out specific tasks. For example, a substation may be built to serve an area, or primary lines laid to serve a factory or a residential area. This final stage, which predominantly involves planning, is most relevant to the case study.

In many countries where capital is in short supply, it is not unusual to find similar facilities being constructed to serve all classes of consumers. When this happens, customers are rarely satisfied. A uniformly low service level probably will not provide industries with the quality of service they require to be competitive with manufacturers from neighboring countries. Remote farmers and villagers will be dissatisfied with the high electricity tariffs associated with a service level above their simple needs. Therefore, the principle of varying the reliability level according to the needs of specific groups of consumers should be considered whenever possible.

Definitions and Design Criteria

This section defines and describes distribution systems and their voltage standards, reliability criteria, and construction design criteria.

Distribution systems

As described in chapter 2, Introduction to Reliability, an electric power system may be broken down into three segments: generation, transmission, and distribution. Transmission and distribution facilities, both of which help to transport power from the generating source to the ultimate user, are usually distinguished from one another on the basis of their operating voltage. Installations operated at voltages higher than 45 kilovolts may be considered definitely transmission whereas lines operated at voltages lower than 25 kilovolts are distribution related. Facilities operating in the intervening range are more difficult to classify. For example, it is common to find a 34.5-kilovolt line being used to transmit power from a central station to many small towns where the voltage is stepped down to 12 or 6 kilovolts. This is definitely a transmission function. The same line, however, may serve several small industrial consumers and even some farms along the way, which may be considered a distribution function.

For this study, primary feeders were designed to operate only at 13.8 kilovolts, to keep the variability in the design within practical limits. It may well be more economical to serve certain parts of the city at 34.5 kilovolts in the future although such fine-tuning of the system was not considered to be within the scope of this study.

The major components of the Cascavel network, a typical distribution system, are shown in figure 11.1 and are described below.

    (a) The distribution substation includes the transformer, which steps down the transmission voltage from 138 kilovolts to the distribution primary voltage of 13.8 kilovolts, and other facilities such as switch gear, busses, and fuses.

    (b) The distribution primary system, that is, circuits or feeders, consist of the conductors and associated facilities that carry electricity from the substations to the distribution transformers.

    (c) The distribution transformer reduces the voltage from the primary level—for example 13.8 kilovolts—to the utilization level.

    (d) The secondary system and service line consist of conductors and associated hardware to deliver power to the consumer's service inlet.

    (e) The service inlet receives power from the secondary system, connects the supplier and the user, and measures electricity use.

Figure 11.1. *Major Components of a Typical Distribution Network*

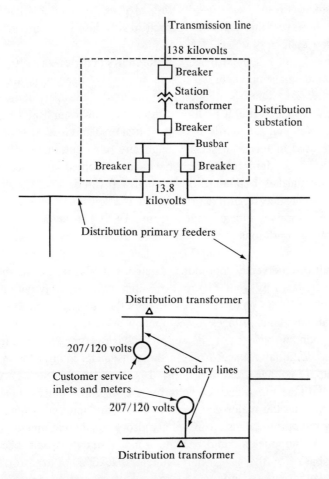

Voltage standards for distribution systems

All power distribution systems experience voltage drops caused by the flow of current. If the delivered voltage is too low, equipment performance will be poor; if it is too high, equipment may fail prematurely. Therefore, an acceptable range of supply voltage must be established, and the voltage ratings of customer equipment must be standardized to correspond to the supply voltage. In general, frequency variations are not as serious as voltage fluctuations, but they can still affect electric timing devices, synchronous motors, and other mechanisms. Since frequency changes result from overloading of generation rather than distribution, however, this aspect is ignored in this case study involving a distribution system.

Although voltage standards vary in different countries, the principles used in matching equipment ratings to supply voltage levels are universal. In Brazil, there is no national standard, but many individual utilities use voltage criteria patterned after the ones established by the American National Standards Institute (ANSI).[1] Therefore ANSI standards were used in this analysis, although any other internationally accepted set of standards could also have been adopted. In brief, with the ANSI standards for standard or nominal 120-volt service, the power supplier is obligated to provide voltage at the consumer's service inlet within the favorable voltage ranging from 114 to 126 volts under normal operating conditions. These conditions are somewhat relaxed in the tolerable voltage ranging from 110 to 127 volts, which is applicable under fault or emergency conditions. The consumer's equipment should perform satisfactorily from 110 to 126 volts and acceptably within the wider limits of from 106 to 127 volts. In both the favorable and tolerable ranges, the minimum voltages for equipment use are 4 volts lower than the corresponding values for the supply voltage at the service inlet to allow for additional voltage drops in the consumer's internal wiring.

The supply voltage variations allowed by the ANSI criteria—12 volts for the favorable range and 17 volts for the tolerable range—must be allocated among the major components of the distribution system. Determining the optimal division of voltage drops for the various distribution system components could become a major study in itself, because it is the basis for the sizing of conductors, loading of transformers, choosing lengths of secondaries, placement of capacitors, and so on.[2] For the purposes of this study, however, the following allocation of voltage variations was selected, based on existing COPEL criteria and on engineering judgment.

    (a) *Service line.* A 1-volt drop can be expected under normal conditions.

    (b) *Secondary system.* Analysis of the COPEL secondary system indi-

1. See ANSI, Publication no. C84.1, 1970, and appendix C for further details.

2. For details, see, for example, *Westinghouse Distribution Systems Reference Book* (East Pittsburgh: Westinghouse Corp., 1959).

cated that the voltage drop varies from 1 to 3 volts, and therefore an average value of 2 volts was used in the study.

(c) *Distribution transformer.* COPEL distribution transformers have an average loading of approximately 60 percent, with a consequent drop of about 2 volts.

(d) *Station regulator.* A 2-volt band width spread is the normally accepted value.

(e) *Primary system.* The primary system was allocated the remainder of the voltage ranges.

Favorable voltage range: $12 - (2 + 1 + 2 + 2) = 5$ volts

Tolerable voltage range: $17 - (2 + 1 + 2 + 2) = 10$ volts

These results are summarized in table 11.1.

Reliability criteria for distribution systems

As stated previously, the reliability standards traditionally used in designing electric power systems do not appear to have been derived from explicit cost-benefit studies but, instead, have been based on rule-of-thumb, general desirability, and affordability. In reliability modeling, some sophisticated distribution reliability models have been proposed only recently (see chapter 2, Introduction to Reliability). Traditionally, the main emphasis has been on analysis of generation and transmission systems. Although many utilities gather outage statistics, however, these

Table 11.1. *Division of Voltage Variation over the Distribution System Components*

Components	Favorable range		Tolerable range	
	Volts	Percentage nominal	Volts	Percentage nominal
Station regulator band width	2.0	1.67	2.0	1.67
Primary system	5.0	4.17	10.0	8.33
Distribution transformers	2.0	1.67	2.0	1.67
Secondary system	2.0	1.67	2.0	1.67
Service line	1.0	0.82	1.0	0.82
Total distribution system	12.0	10.00	17.0	14.16

Note: Based on nominal 120-volt service.

Table 11.2. Alternative Distribution System Characteristics

	High-reliability system	Medium-reliability system	Low-reliability system
Service under normal conditions	Voltage within favorable range during peak hours	Voltage within favorable range during peak hours	Voltage within tolerable range during peak hours
Service under emergency conditions, for example, with circuit B1 faulted (see schematic below)[a]	Substation A, circuit A1, and interconnection have sufficient capacity to pick up all loads of circuit B1 during peak hours and to deliver power within the tolerable voltage range.	Substation A, circuit A1, and interconnection have sufficient capacity to pick up all loads of circuit B1 only during off-peak hours and to deliver power within the tolerable voltage range.	None, no interconnection provided
Design considerations and costs dictated by	Emergency conditions	Normal conditions	Normal conditions
Outage duration determined by	Time to switch	Time to repair during peak hours, and time to switch during off-peak hours	Time to repair

a. Corresponding reasoning applies if circuit A1 is undergoing an outage.

data are rarely analyzed fully, translated into meaningful probabilities, and used systematically to improve system performance.[3]

The system in Cascavel is currently designed with sufficient capacity to withstand the loss of a station transformer or a feeder at peak load. For this study the system was considered highly reliable. In addition, medium- and low-reliability systems were defined and modeled for the study, as described below and summarized in table 11.2 and in the accompanying circuit diagram.

(1) *High-reliability system.* Under normal conditions, the system will have sufficient capacity to deliver power at peak load within the favorable voltage range. In emergencies, the system will have sufficient capacity and interconnections between circuits to pick up the load of a faulted circuit during the peak, after appropriate switching to isolate the fault, and to deliver power within the tolerable voltage range. The duration of an outage will be determined by the time it takes to despatch a trouble lineman to the area, locate the problem, isolate the fault, and restore service by appropriate switching. The design and costs of a high-reliability system are basically dictated by the system's emergency capabilities.

(2) *Medium-reliability system.* Under normal conditions, the system will have sufficient capacity to deliver power at peak load within the favorable voltage range. Interconnections between circuits are provided so that loads can be picked up from a faulted circuit under off-peak load conditions and so that power can be delivered within the tolerable voltage range. The duration of an outage will vary between the corresponding values for the high- and low-reliability systems, depending on the loading. System design and costs are basically dictated by capabilities under normal conditions: that is, favorable supply voltage at peak.

3. In practice, the design of most distribution systems is based on one or more of the following rules-of-thumb.
  (a) Sufficient capacity to withstand the loss of a specific portion of the system, such as a substation transformer, at peak;
  (b) Limiting the load on a circuit (for example, 5,000 kilovolt-amps on a 13.8 kilovolt feeder);
  (c) Limiting the length of primary mains (for example, 5.0 kilometers for a 13.8 kilovolt feeder);
  (d) Installation of reclosers based upon length of line or connected kilovolt-amps or number of customers, and so on;
  (e) Installation of fuses at every branch point; and
  (f) Installation of remote-controlled, motor-operated switches.

(3) *Low-reliability system.* Under normal conditions, the system will have sufficient capacity to deliver power at peak load within the tolerable voltage range. No connections between circuits are provided for this system. The duration of an outage will be determined by the time it takes to despatch a trouble lineman to the area, locate the problem, isolate the fault, and restore service. Service is restored by switching or repair, depending on the location of the fault, as well as the switches. Again, the design and costs of the system are basically dictated by its capabilities under normal conditions; in this instance, tolerable supply voltage at peak.

A large number of variations of these three basic designs could have been generated by selecting different system components, configurations, and operating practices. These would include, for example, covered, insulated, or underground primary conductors, reclosers, switches, standby crews, more frequent maintenance, and so on. As discussed at the beginning of this chapter, however, these variations were not considered, since they were not relevant to the study.

Even without using these additional components and configurations, it would have been possible to design other basic system configurations with higher and lower reliability levels than those considered. The physical characteristics of Cascavel, however, made this unnecessary. For example, a spot network system with automatic or centrally dispatched switching might have been justified for the downtown area of a much larger city. In many small towns or rural areas, however, it would have been more sensible to build a distribution network that did not have sufficient capacity to meet all peak period requirements. For example, a system that relied on planned and rotating power cuts during the peak may have been more appropriate.

Construction design criteria for distribution systems

Several engineering considerations were included in the planning and design of the alternative distribution primary systems. The systems each were designed to meet a distinct level of reliability; they differed in regard to normal and emergency conductor loading and voltage regulation. Each plan, however, had the same final year substation configuration, quantity and location of substations, and standard overhead primary conductors. Differences in costs and losses among the systems arose from the variations in the capacity and number of circuits, as well as the timing of these investments in each plan.

COPEL's distribution design criteria were reviewed, and in general they were found to be reasonably adequate and convenient. A more comprehensive distribution system planning study may have included an extensive evaluation of such criteria, requiring a major effort beyond the scope of this study.

The basic COPEL distribution substation layout used in the study are shown in figure 11.2. These substations had ring main busbars on the high voltage sides (138 kilovolts), Y (138 kilovolts) to delta (13.8-kilovolt) transformers, main-transfer busbars on the low voltage sides, and used oil or airblast circuit breakers depending on location and availability. The low- and medium-reliability systems modeled had 20-megavolt-amp transformers, whereas the high-reliability system used 10-megavolt-amp transformers. This was the least-cost solution imposed by the requirement that there must always be spare capacity equivalent to one transformer. COPEL distribution primaries were constructed with precast concrete poles and crossarms, 15-kilovolt class insulators, and the following bare all-aluminum conductors: sizes 2/0 AWG, 4/0 AWG, 336 MCM, and 477 MCM; having capacities of 7.08, 10.64, 12.9, and 16.66 megavolt amps, respectively, at 13.8 kilovolts.[4]

Table 11.3 summarizes the main criteria used in designing the three systems. The conductor loadings for the low- and high-reliability systems were based on reserve requirements. Two different levels of maximum conductor loading were used to derive the two variants A and B of the basic medium-reliability system.

In general, distribution transformers and secondary systems are designed at a minimum level of reliability. Unlike the primary feeders, secondary systems rarely contain interconnecting sections and surplus capacity for shifting loads. Also, they are constructed with covered or insulated wire to minimize faults—an acceptable practice at secondary voltage levels. An in-depth investigation of the transformer and secondary system was not within the scope of this study, although this is an area for potential savings. Further studies could result in changes in construction practices, especially in electrifying areas of low consumer density.

When an outage does occur on the secondary system, the consumers are without service until repairs are completed. The number of con-

---

4. AWG = American Wire Gauge; MCM = thousands of circular mils; 1 circular mil = 0.7854×10^{-6} square inches.

Figure 11.2. *Typical Distribution Substation Layout*

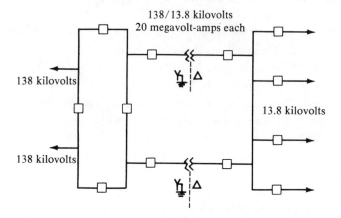

138/13.8 kilovolts
20 megavolt-amps each

138 kilovolts

13.8 kilovolts

138 kilovolts

High-reliability system: 40 megavolt-amp substation

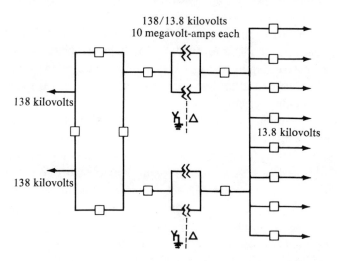

138/13.8 kilovolts
10 megavolt-amps each

138 kilovolts

13.8 kilovolts

138 kilovolts

Note: Substation components: ☐ oil or air blast circuit breaker; ⟨⟨ transformer—Y (center grounded) to delta.

Table 11.3. *System Reserve Requirements, Voltage Drops, and Conductor Loading*

System plan	Station transformer reserve capacity	Circuit switching reserve capacity	Maximum voltage drop (percentage)		Maximum conductor loading (percentage of rated capacity)	
			Normal	*Switched*	*Normal*	*Switched*
Low-reliability	None	None	8.33	—	100	—
Medium-reliability	None	Off-peak switching only	8.33	8.33	95 (type A) 65 (type B)	100
High-reliability	One transformer (10 megavolt-amps)	Switching at any time	4.17	8.33	50	100

145

sumers out of service for any one outage is small, however, and outages are generally rare. For example, the failure rate of COPEL distribution transformers is approximately 3.4 percent a year. Although it appears high, an average consumer will face only one such failure every 29.4 years. Thus, the differences in the rate of secondary system failures between the three alternative system designs would be small compared with the differences in the primary system failure rate.

Outage Parameters

Outage records for the Cascavel distribution system were analyzed to determine outage statistics for the primary system, transformers, and secondaries. The load pattern for the system was also studied to determine the relation between annual peak demand and demands during various periods.

Analysis of past outage data

In the subsequent analysis, outages refer to supply interruptions caused by faults in the distribution network, rather than at the generation or transmission level. For convenience, outages were divided into two categories: temporary ones usually lasting less than five minutes and permanent outages, where field switching or repairs were required.

Generally, the type of power system design, as well as the operating practices, would affect the characteristics of both temporary and permanent outages. In this study, however, the basic design of the system has negligible influence on temporary outages: that is, the availability of interconnections between circuits and extra capacity in the substations does not affect the frequency or the duration of these faults. Thus, the effects of temporary faults, which will be small anyway, may be ignored, because they do not change with alternative system designs and therefore do not affect the comparative analysis of outage costs. In contrast, the frequency and duration of permanent outages are greatly affected by the basic design of the system, as described earlier in the section on reliability criteria. Therefore, circuit interconnections and extra substation and feeder capacity limits the duration of permanent outages to only the isolation and switching time. With limited interconnections or no interconnections, outage duration will be determined by both the switching and the repair times.

Data on permanent outages in the Cascavel distribution grid in 1975 and 1976 were analyzed to determine outage frequency and duration during three specific intervals of the day: 0001 to 0800, 0801 to 1800, and 1801 to 2400 hours. These daily time intervals were chosen for convenience of analysis, as well as to distinguish among periods usually devoted to sleep, economic activity, and leisure, as well as between off-peak and peak periods. The results summarized in table 11.4 indicate that the percentages of total minutes of outage time during the three daily periods were quite stable during the two years, although there were greater variations in the annual outage frequencies and average durations. These outage data were combined with the information on the physical characteristics of the distribution network. The data were used with the total length of primary feeders to derive both the average annual

Table 11.4. *Analysis of Permanent Faults during 1975 and 1976*

Year and daily period	Annual frequency	Duration (minutes)		Percentage of total
		Average	Total	
1975				
0001–0800	24	72	1,732	46
0801–1800	45	23	1,013	27
1801–2400	24	43	1,043	27
All 24 hours	93	41	3,788	100
1976				
0001–0800	89	39	3,572	45
0801–1800	245	8	2,632	33
1801–2400	131	12	1,767	22
All 24 hours	465	17	7,971	100
1975 and 1976 (Biannual totals and averages)				
0001–0800	113	47	5,304	45
0801–1800	290	13	3,645	31
1801–2400	155	18	2,810	24
All 24 hours	558	21	11,759	100

frequency and the average annual probability for each kilometer of feeder that an outage would occur during each of the three daily periods. Table 11.5 summarizes the exposure of feeder lines to random accidents, such as a car hitting a utility pole or a tree falling on a line.

Load duration analysis

A load duration analysis provides the relation between demand and energy that is vital to an in-depth study of the effect of outages on the system. The basic data for this analysis were the hourly demands during 1976 for the representative feeders 1 and 2, which served about 80 percent of the total Cascavel load. The 8,760 hourly demands on each feeder were analyzed monthly and annually by the three daily periods to provide the results presented in table 11.6.

The Cascavel annual load duration information over all periods is summarized in table 11.7 and figure 11.3. The curves in the figure indicate the percentage of time during the year in which the given level of power demand is equaled or exceeded, and the energy supplied at or above that power level. For example, the generation and transmission facilities providing the top 10 percent of demand are only needed 1.45 percent, or 127 hours, of the year, although they supply only 0.08 percent of the total energy.

Table 11.5. *Outage Statistics Based on 1975–1976 Data*

Daily period	Outage frequency[a] (frequency/ kilometer/ year)	Outage duration (minutes/ outage)	Outage probability (probability/ kilometer/ year)[b]
0001–0800	0.717	47	0.000192
0801–1800	1.840	13	0.000106
1801–2400	0.984	18	0.000136
All 24 hours	3.541	21	0.000142

a. Outage frequency = [(freq$_{75}$ + freq$_{76}$)/2 ÷ (78.8 kilometer of primaries)].

b. Outage probability = [(total minutes$_{75}$ + total minutes$_{76}$)/2 ÷ (hours per year in the time period × 60 × kilometers of line)].

Frequency and duration factors

The past outage statistics and the results of the load duration analysis were used to determine the outage frequency and duration factors for the three systems. The average outage frequency for each kilometer of primary feeder given in table 11.5 was assumed to remain the same in the future for all the basic system designs.

The present Cascavel system has the configuration and capacity to be considered a high-reliability system. Therefore the 1975–76 outage duration factors (table 11.5) were used throughout the study to represent the time taken for a "trouble" lineman to be despatched, to locate and

Table 11.6 *Loading, by Period*

Feeder and daily time period	Demand		Energy	
	Kilowatts	Percentage of peak	Megawatt-hours	Percentage of total
Feeder 1 (Serving predominantly residential and commercial consumers)				
0001–0800	2,700	67.5	3,971	23.3
0801–1800	3,750	93.8	7,377	43.3
1801–2400	4,000	100.0	5,688	33.4
Feeder 3 (Serving predominantly residential and industrial consumers)				
0001–0800	3,700	82.2	4,974	23.7
0801–1800	4,400	97.8	9,717	46.3
1801–2400	4,500	100.0	6,275	30.0
Feeders 1 and 3 (Serving about 80 percent of total city load)[a]				
0001–0800	6,100	73.1	8,944	23.5
0801–1800	7,750	92.8	17,094	45.0
1801–2400	8,350	100.0	11,963	31.5

a. The loading of feeders 2 and 4, that represented the remaining 20 percent of the demand, was unavailable.

Table 11.7. *Load Duration Analysis*

Load as a percent- age of peak	Percentage of time given load is equaled or exceeded for feeder			Percentage of energy supplied above the given load for feeder		
	1	*3*	*1 + 3*	*1*	*3*	*1 + 3*
100.0	0.25	0.08	0.02	—	—	—
95.0	0.28	0.30	0.33	0.03	0.02	0.02
90.0	1.36	0.68	1.45	0.13	0.05	0.08
85.0	3.70	3.17	3.49	0.38	0.26	0.32
80.0	6.35	9.10	6.07	0.84	0.78	0.73
75.0	9.73	13.42	10.10	1.51	1.63	1.49
70.0	10.37	20.88	14.79	2.52	3.31	2.61
60.0	24.38	38.65	36.86	5.78	8.72	7.35
50.0	51.59	52.52	53.44	12.33	17.25	15.94
40.0	61.24	71.83	67.69	23.68	28.54	27.41
30.0	93.94	93.23	96.28	38.72	43.83	43.05
20.0	99.92	99.89	99.98	58.76	62.30	60.71
10.0	99.99	99.99	100.00	79.38	81.50	100.00[a]
0.0	100.00	100.00	100.00	100.00	100.00	100.00

Feeder	Loss factor (percentage)	Load factor (percentage)
1	26.24	48.48
3	31.22	53.03
1 + 3	30.23	52.44

a. Minimum demand was 18.18 percent of peak.

isolate the fault, and to restore service by switching. This represented the high-reliability situation.

For the low-reliability system, consumers are faced with the time it takes to despatch the lineman to locate the fault, isolate the problem, if possible, repair the damage, and restore service. All of the consumers on a circuit do not have to wait until repairs are completed if feeders are designed with a switch halfway between the substation and the end of a circuit. If the trouble is near the substation, the substation breaker is opened, and all consumers will be without service until repairs are made. If the problem is beyond the midpoint switch, then the trouble lineman can open the switch, and only the consumers on the further half will not have service until the damages are repaired. Assuming a uniform density of consumers, as well as a constant outage probability

Figure 11.3. *Cascavel Distribution System:*
Load Duration Analysis

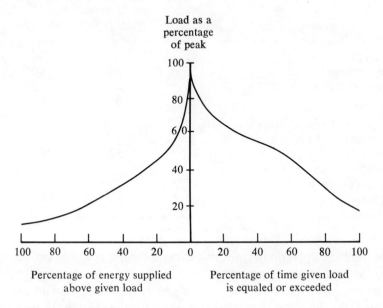

Note: For feeders 1 and 3, serving 80 percent of the urban load.

along the length of a feeder, the average percentage of waiting time
during an outage may be estimated. For example, when the problem is
in the first half of the feeder, all the consumers it serves will be without
electricity the entire time of the outage. If the second half of the feeder
is affected, only 50 percent of the customers will be without service until
repairs are made. The average customer waiting period is, therefore, 75
percent of the average time needed to restore service.

These data on the high- and low-reliability cases were combined with
average repair times based on data supplied by COPEL to estimate the
outage durations for the low-reliability system presented in table 11.8.

The medium-reliability system incorporates aspects of both the low-
and high-reliability designs. The system is designed to deliver power at
peak load, at least within the tolerable voltage range.

If an outage occurs when the actual load is less than some critical
value, for example, x percent of the peak load, then the customers on
the faulted line can be switched to another line and supplied within
the tolerable voltage range. Customers must wait only until the fault is

Table 11.8. *Outage Durations for the Low-Reliability System*

Activity	Time required (minutes) by daily period		
	0001–0800	0801–1800	1801–2400
Obtain crew	45	15	30
Repair damage	120	60	90
Restore service	30	—	15
Subtotal	195	75	135
Average time to repair faced by consumers (75 percent of subtotal)	146	57	101
Despatch lineman and locate and isolate fault	47	13	18
Total time	193	70	119

isolated and the appropriate switching is performed, a situation equivalent to the high-reliability case.

If an outage occurs when the load is greater than x percent of the peak load, the other lines are incapable of picking up the faulted load, and these consumers must wait until the fault is isolated and repaired. This is equivalent to the low-reliability case. For a given medium-reliability system design, switching studies are performed to determine the percentage x. The load duration curve indicates the load level at any given time during the day, and these data may be used with the value of x to compute the average fault duration for the system for different periods of the day.

The final parameters used to forecast the future frequencies and durations of outages for the basic system design are summarized in table 11.9.

System Design

A computerized primary system model consisting of a digital data base and a package of analytical programs was used to design the alternative systems.[5] (See appendix C for details.)

5. See Walter G. Scott, "Rural System Engineering and Computer Models" (no. C76408-OIA) (paper presented at the IEEE National Rural Electric Conference, April 1976, Atlanta, Georgia; processed).

Table 11.9. *Outage Frequency and Duration Parameters
for the Three System Designs*

| | Outage frequency (frequency/ kilometer/ year)[a] | Mean outage duration (hours), by system reliability level and period | | | |
| Daily period | | High relia- bility[b] | Medium- reliability[d] | | Low relia- bility[c] |
			Off- Peak[b]	Peak[c]	
0001–0800	0.717	0.8	0.8	3.2	3.2
0801–1800	1.840	0.2	0.2	1.2	1.2
1801–2400	0.984	0.3	0.3	2.0	1.0

a. Exposure factor is assumed to be the same as in 1975–76, see table 11.5.
b. Switching time only, see table 11.5.
c. Switching time plus 75 percent of repair time, see table 11.5.
d. Forecast outage duration = (mean duration during off-peak × fraction of off-peak time) + (mean duration during peak × fraction of peak time).

The data base contained all the pertinent physical and electrical characteristics of the distribution primary system, including the relations among the principal subdivisions of each feeder: that is, nodes, sections, and branches. The major analytical programs computed the voltage levels, conductor loadings, and line losses for any feeder. Other analytical programs estimated the fault currents and optimized the location of capacitors. A third set of programs was used to simulate operating conditions, such as the switching of loads between feeders, addition of new loads, and changing of load levels.

The data bases of the load forecast and the primary system model were correlated through the coordinates placed in the node file.[6] The 1996 loads were then imposed upon the existing system, and an analysis of the voltage, load, and loss was run. This pointed out where the existing system would be weak in meeting 1996 load levels.

The system was now expanded to alleviate the weaknesses pinpointed in the above analysis. For each alternative design, additions included new substations, primary branches, and interties in accordance with the corresponding target reliability level. As each group of additions was entered into the data base, the resultant circuits were analyzed for voltage, conductor loading, and losses. This iterative process of making

6. See chapter 10 and appendix C.

additions, analyzing, and making further changes was continued until the system met the desired reliability criteria within voltage and loading limits. The final product of this process was a primary system that could meet the end-year (1996) load levels within prescribed boundaries. This long-range plan became the guide or target for the interim four-year plans.

During the development of the load forecast, load levels had also been established for the interim years (1980, 1984, 1988, and 1992), based on the growth of demand over the forecast period, 1976 to 1996. At each of these interim years, appropriate additions to the distribution network were determined by the iterative process described earlier. These additions enable the system to meet the load levels for that year within operating and design criteria.

The above process was used to develop the three basic plans (low-, medium-, and high-reliability), as well as an additional alternative medium-reliability plan, Medium B, whose chief characteristics are summarized below. All the designs ultimately required the same seven substations shown in figure 11.4. The sequence and sizing of the substations for the various plans are presented in table 11.10 and figure 11.5.

The number of feeders and the length of line in service for the alternative plans, for selected years, are shown in table 11.11.

Reliability, Losses, and System Costs

The expected long-range reliability levels, such as outage frequencies and durations for the alternative distribution system designs are estimated

Table 11.10. *Substation Capacities*
(megavolt-amps)

| Study period (years) | Plan reliability level | | | |
| | Low and medium | | High | |
	Additions	*Total*	*Additions*	*Total*
1976–80	20	40	40	60
1981–84	40	80	20	80
1985–88	40	120	40	120
1989–92	80	200	70	190
1992–96	20	220	50	240

in this section. Supply interruptions caused by failures at the generation and transmission level were assumed to be essentially the same for all the distribution network designs, and, therefore, their effects could be ignored in the comparative analysis of outage costs. In this case study, the outage frequency for a distribution system was assumed to depend on the following factors:

(a) exposure—length of primary feeders serving a consumer;
(b) equipment and design—choice of overhead versus an underground system, or type of transformer, and so on;
(c) placement—choice of installing lines along the street versus behind the property, for example; and
(d) maintenance—effectiveness in patroling and repairing lines, checking transformers, and similar duties.

Changing the exposure was the most clear-cut and convenient, but not necessarily the most cost-effective, method of generating the variations in outage frequency for this case study. The other factors could also have been varied and tested according to the proposed methodology,

Table 11.11. *Number of Feeders and Length of Lines*

| | Plan reliability level | | |
| | | Medium | |
Year	Low	(A and B)	High
	Number of feeders		
1976	4	4	4
1980	6	6	10
1984	10	10	13
1988	14	14	21
1992	20	20	25
1996	24	24	37
	Length of line in service (kilometers)		
1976	70.6	70.6	70.6
1980	91.0	92.15	95.2
1984	104.9	108.9	110.8
1988	124.8	136.6	138.4
1992	142.3	159.9	154.5
1996	157.2	181.8	179.7

Figure 11.4. *Substation Locations, 1996*

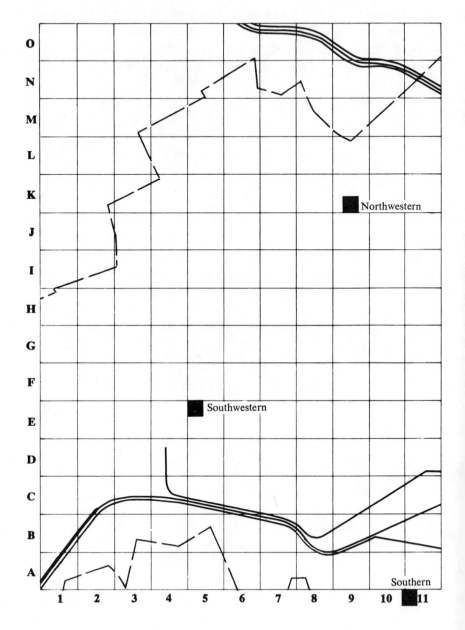

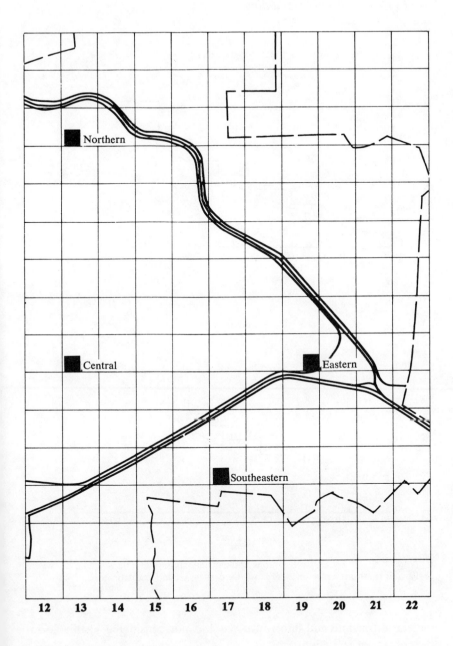

Figure 11.5. *Substation Additions*

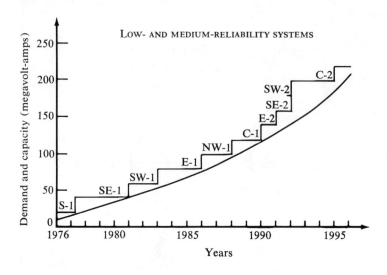

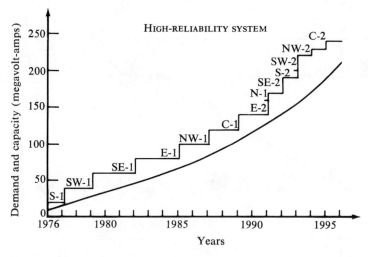

Note: The letters in both graphs indicate substation locations given in figure 11.4, and the numbers 1 or 2 refer to the first or second transformers.

but the extra time and effort involved was not considered justifiable in the context of this study.

The annual frequencies of outages for the different plans are given in table 11.12. (See appendix C for details.)

Table 11.12. *Average Annual Frequency of Outages*

	Plan reliability level					
	Low and medium (A and B)			High		
	Daily period (hours)			Daily period (hours)		
Year	0001–0800	0801–1800	1801–2400	0001–0800	0801–1800	1801–2400
1976	13	34	18	13	34	18
1980	11	29	16	7	18	10
1984	8	20	11	6	16	9
1988	7	17	9	5	12	6
1992	5	13	7	5	11	6
1996	5	12	6	4	9	5

Table 11.13. *Maximum Outage Duration*
(hours)

| Daily period (hours) | Plan reliability level | | | |
	Low	Medium A	Medium B	High
0001–0800	3.2	1.0	0.8	0.8
0801–1800	1.2	0.7	0.2	0.2
1801–2400	2.0	1.3	0.6	0.3

For a given plan, the average number of outages on the system decreased each year because the exposure, or average line length, decreased. The maximum outage duration was constant over the twenty years, however, assuming that the present durations would be typical. Table 11.13 shows the maximum outage durations for the basic system plans.

Loss levels are a measure of the efficiency of design and management of reactive volt-amps or VAR. High losses indicate that the system has been poorly designed because capacity is insufficient and VAR flows have been ignored. Very low losses also signal poor design because of excess capacity and perhaps too much VAR control. Overall kilowatt demand losses for the different system designs were determined at the time of system peak, using the primary system analysis program, whereas annual kilowatt-hour energy losses were estimated from the peak demand loss and annual loss factors (derived in the load duration analysis). These losses are summarized in table 11.14.

Table 11.14. *Energy and Demand Losses*

	Plan reliability level					
	Energy losses (megawatt-hours)			Demand losses (kilowatts)		
Year	Low and me- dium A	Me- dium B	High	Low and me- dium A	Me- dium B	High
1976	1,480	1,480	1,480	560	560	560
1980	3,380	2,740	1,120	1,380	1,110	420
1984	3,870	3,130	1,950	1,460	1,180	740
1988	3,300	2,670	1,940	1,240	1,010	730
1992	4,680	3,790	3,460	1,760	1,430	1,310
1996	6,340	5,130	4,510	2,390	1,940	1,700

Table 11.15. *Substation Construction Costs*
(Cr\$ $\times$ 10^3)

Item	Labor	Materials	Adminis- tration	Total
High-reliability				
New 20 megavolt-amps	2,835	14,165	1,890	18,890
Additional 10 megavolt- amps	700	3,505	470	4,675
Low- and medium-reliability				
New 20 megavolt-amps	2,325	11,635	1,555	15,515
Additional 20 megavolt- amps	895	4,480	600	5,975

The construction and annual recurrent costs provided by COPEL were reviewed and compared with similar data from other utility companies, and in general they appeared to be reasonable. The basic items of expenditure used to estimate the alternative distribution system supply costs are summarized in tables 11.15 to 11.18.

Recurrent annual expenses consisted of replacements, operation and maintenance (O&M), and administrative and general (A&G) costs. Replacements are required for major components that fail and are not

Table 11.16. *Line Construction Costs*
(Cr$ × 10³)

| Type | Cost per kilometer | | | |
	Labor	Materials	Adminis-tration	Total
New construction				
2/0 AWG	55	95	15	165
4/0 AWG	60	110	20	190
336 MCM	70	130	20	220
477 MCM	85	145	25	255
Reconductoring				
2/0 AWG	20	35	10	65
4/0 AWG	30	50	10	90
336 MCM	40	75	15	130
477 MCM	50	90	15	155

Note: AWG = American wire gauge; MCM = thousands of circular mils.

Table 11.17. *Street Light Costs*
(Cr$)

Type	Cost per unit
400 watt sodium vapor (includes pole)	7,195
700 watt mercury vapor (includes pole)	6,320
400 watt mercury vapor (includes pole)	5,620
250 watt mercury vapor (pole not included)	1,575
125 watt mercury vapor (pole not included)	870

covered by routine operation and maintenance. Operation and maintenance costs generally are the labor and materials required to keep the system in good working order. Administrative and general costs include the managerial functions, buildings, and so on, associated with the operation and maintenance of the system.

The annual costs for each plan consisted of the construction costs for that year plus the annual recurrent costs for the entire system. These costs were determined by system plan for each study year for the substations, primary feeders, and street lights. Items that were common to the different plans, such as the 1976 existing plant, primary laterals, distribution transformers, secondaries, service inlets, and meters, have

Table 11.18. *Annual Recurrent Costs*

Item	Substations	Lines
Replacements (percentage of investment)	0.6	0.20
Operation and maintenance		
20 megavolt-amps substation (Cr$/kilovolt-amp)	19.5	—
30 megavolt-amps substation (Cr$/kilovolt-amp)	13.8	—
40 megavolt-amps substation (Cr$/kilovolt-amp)	13.8	—
Lines (Cr$/kilometer)	—	1,850
Administration and general (percent of O&M)	32.0	34.0

Table 11.19. *Cumulative Annual Costs*
(Cr$ $\times$ 10^3)

| Year | Plan reliability level | | | |
	Low	Medium A	Medium B	High
1976	0	0	0	0
1980	4,390	4,640	4,640	28,670
1984	42,330	43,040	43,770	55,760
1988	85,080	87,100	87,970	109,100
1992	135,170	138,280	139,550	170,450
1996	161,090	165,570	167,030	219,400
Percentage of high-reliability plan costs	73.4	75.5	76.1	100

been excluded, because they would be effectively netted out in the analysis of comparative costs.

The annual costs for the plans are summarized in table 11.19. (See appendix C for details.)

Chapter 12

~~~~~~

Outage Cost Measurement

The empirical investigation of outage costs borne by Cascavel electricity consumers is described in this chapter. The theoretical concepts and models developed in chapters 5 to 7 were used as the bases for field surveys of different kinds of electricity consumers to estimate their outage costs. Residential and industrial consumer categories incurred the greatest outage costs, whereas these costs for the other types of consumers were relatively small.

Residential Consumers

A random sample of twenty-seven residential customers was selected from the 1976 list of approximately 9,000 electricity-using households in Cascavel. These consumers answered an in-depth survey designed to determine their opinion of the quality and value of electrical services, electricity consumption, income, leisure-time habit patterns, and the value they placed on foregone leisure during an outage. The complete questionnaire is given in appendix F.

Unfortunately, the sample size was limited by the time and manpower resources available to carry out the survey. In view of the difficulty of obtaining meaningful answers to questions on outage costs involving hypothetical willingness to pay, considerable time had to be devoted to explaining the problem to consumers and putting them at ease. Care had to be taken also to avoid giving the impression that the interviewers wanted to increase or decrease their electric supply reliability, increase or decrease their electricity bill, obtain income information for tax purposes, and so on. At least two adult members of each home were required to be present to obtain replies that were representative of the household. Consequently, a team of three persons (including a translator) took one week to complete the twenty-seven interviews.

All households in the sample indicated that electricity was an essential service in their daily lives; in general, the poorer consumers felt that they were getting good value for money, whereas some of the higher income households thought that the price of electricity services was too great. A direct estimate of outage costs was obtained by asking consumers how much extra they would be willing to pay to avoid outages of different durations at various times during the day (questions 4 and 5). Customers indicated no willingness to pay extra to avoid daytime outages. The direct amounts that consumers were willing to pay to avoid evening outages was found to be linearly proportional to outage duration, on average, over the range of three to eighty minutes, and the estimate of outage cost is based on values in this range. For outages of less than a few minutes many people indicated that they would sit out the inconvenience rather than pay, and for outages over one-and-a-half hours the outage cost for each time unit tended to also fall off quite rapidly, as households were unwilling to pay large sums of money: that is, the impact on income became important. Indirect estimates of outage costs were obtained by determining what additional amounts each household considered reasonable for payment to the utility company if the current incidence of outages was halved and as a compensatory refund on their electricity bill if the existing outage rate was doubled (questions 3, 9, and 12).[1] The evening time outage cost estimates given in table 12.1 are average values of the direct and the two indirect estimates for each household. Although related, questions 4, 9, and 12 were not asked consecutively. This reduced the possibility of consumers giving answers to a later question by merely extrapolating from one of the earlier questions. In fact, good agreement was obtained between the various estimates of outage costs for each household, and

---

1. The terms direct and indirect used in this chapter refer to the nature of the questions asked during the survey to estimate outage costs. They have no relation to the direct and indirect outage costs discussed in chapter 4, Estimation of Outage Costs.

this was taken as an added sign of reliability of the estimates. As expected, however, the indirect estimate of outage costs from question 9 generally tended to be lower than the estimate from question 12. These two estimates most often straddled the value of the direct estimate of outage costs.

The daily leisure period during which electricity was considered essential had a fairly uniform duration of about one-and-a-half hours (standard error = twelve minutes) and occurred somewhere within the broader time interval of 1930 to 2230 hours. Approximately 60 percent of the latter interval was devoted to television watching, 25 percent to dining, and the remainder to other activities such as reading and conversing. The differences between households were minor; for example, the standard error for the television watching period was only about 10 percent of the mean. Only one of the households in the sample did not possess a television set; however, in this case about 50 percent of their leisure time was spent listening to the radio, and special television programs such as football games were watched on the neighbor's set. Thus, these results confirmed the view expressed by local municipal authorities, that practically all electricity-using homes owned a television set. The mean household size was 5.1 persons, with a standard error of 1.4 persons, and the average time at which families went to sleep was about 2300 hours, with a standard error of forty-five minutes.

After having verified the importance of the loss of leisure incurred by evening power supply interruptions, the survey data were used to test the following null hypothesis developed theoretically in chapter 5, Residential Outage Costs (equation 5.12).

H_0 : Outage cost per hour of electricity-dependent leisure
   = net income earning rate[2]

H_1 : H_0 untrue.

The basic household data on outage costs are given in table 12.1, and are plotted against the net income earning rate in figure 12.1. The best-fit-ordinary-least-square ((OLSQ) regression line and the 45-degree line

---

2. Net income earning rate = gross earning rate minus income tax, estimated from known tax rates. Total household income was, in most cases, the earnings of a single wage earner.

Table 12.1. *Residential Consumer Survey Results*

Observation number	Net income earning rate (Cr$ per hour)[a]	Outage cost (Cr$ per hour)
1	7.4	6
2	7.4	7
3	7.4	13
4	10.5	12
5	11.1	15
6	14.2	10
7	15.4	20
8	18.5	25
9	18.5	35
10	19.7	20
11	21.5	15
12	21.5	25
13	24.6	15
14	24.6	40
15	27.7	20
16	30.8	35
17	40.3	30
18	40.3	30
19	45.5	50
20	48.0	60
21	55.1	45
22	64.6	55
23	64.6	60
24	73.9	85
25	99.1	60
26	116.3	133
27	166.2	150

a. US$1 $=$ Cr$12.35 (end 1976).

indicated by the hypothesis to be tested are shown by the broken and solid lines, respectively. The numerical results of the regression are presented in table 12.2.

The basic unrestricted fitted equation is:

(12.1) $$OC^R = \beta_1 + \beta_2\, Y + U$$

where $OC^R = (n \times 1)$ vector of outage costs per hour; β_1, $\beta_2 =$ coefficients to be estimated; $Y = (n \times 1)$ vector of net income earning

Figure 12.1. *Relation between Outage Cost
and Net Income Earning Rate for Residential Customers*

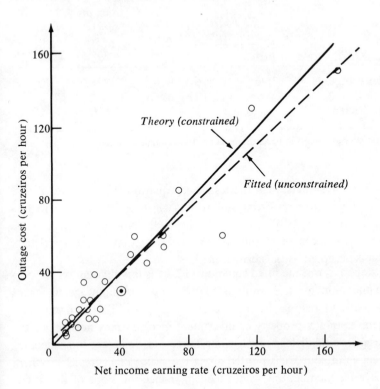

rates per hour; $U = (n \times 1)$ vector of disturbances; and $n = 27 =$ number of observations.

The usual assumptions regarding the OLSQ model are considered valid.[3] Since the null hypothesis to be tested is that $\beta_1 = 0$ and $\beta_2 = 1$, this yields the restricted model:

$$(12.2) \qquad\qquad OC^R = Y + U.$$

A Chow test for homogeneous linear restrictions on the coefficients, was performed to ascertain whether the unrestricted equation (12.1) fitted the observed values significantly better in terms of the sum of

3. See J. Johnston, *Econometric Methods* (New York: McGraw-Hill, 1972), chap. 5, pp. 121–75.

Table 12.2. *Analysis of Regression Results*

Equation	Estimated coefficients[a]		Cor-rected R^2	Sum of squares of re-siduals	Degrees of freedom
	$\hat{\beta}_1$	$\hat{\beta}_2$			
E. 1 (unrestricted)	3.355	0.896 (15.12)	0.901	3,228.2	25
E. 2 (restricted)	0	1	—	3,650.2	27

a. *t*-statistics are given in parentheses under the coefficient value.

squares of the residuals, than the restricted equation (12.2) derived from the theoretical model.[4] From the results of table 12.2, $F = 1.634$. Therefore, since F_{25}^2 $(0.20) = 1.72$, the null hypothesis, $H_0:\beta_1 = 0$ and $\beta_2 = 1$, is accepted at the 20 percent level: that is, the restricted equation is accepted as the correct one.[5]

The slope $(\hat{\beta}_2)$ of the fitted equation (12.1) is less than unity. A possible explanation for this result is that the ratio of nonwage to wage income tends to rise as the income level increases. This nonwage income (for example, property or investment income) may not enter into the consumer's labor-leisure decision. Therefore, since net total income (irrespective of source) is plotted along the x-axis of figure 12.1 rather than net wage income, this would tend to reduce the slope of the fitted line, especially for the higher income levels. Unfortunately, it was very difficult to obtain further information about the breakdown of income by source from the respondents. Saturation effects could also occur at high income levels, which would tend to impose a ceiling on the willingness to pay. Similarly, at the low end of the income scale, there could be a minimum level of outage costs (greater than zero), although

4. See Gregory C. Chow, "Tests of Equality Between Subsets of Coefficients in Two Linear Regressions," *Econometrica*, vol. 28 (July 1960), pp. 591–605; and Franklin M. Fisher, "Tests of Equality Between Sets of Coefficients in Two Linear Regressions: An Expository Note," *Econometrica*, vol. 38 (March 1970), pp. 361–66.

5. This statistic is distributed as F with 2 and 25 degrees of freedom:

$$F = \frac{(3650.2 - 3228.2)}{2} \Big/ \frac{3228.2}{25} = 1.634.$$

Acceptance at the 20 percent level implies acceptance at all lower levels: that is, 10 percent, 5 percent, 1 percent, and so on, for a right tail test.

it is doubtful whether such poor households would have electricity service. Both of the above effects would tend to reduce the slope $\hat{\beta}_2$. The effect of the other neglected terms in the equation from chapter 5 would be to increase slightly the slope of the solid line.

The results of the Cascavel residential electricity consumer survey confirm that the chief outage cost imposed on this category of users is the loss of leisure during the evening hours. This occurs approximately during a one-and-a-half-hour period when electricity is considered essential. Furthermore, it may be concluded that during this critical period, the mean income earning rate for a household is an acceptable measure of the monetary value of marginal leisure lost resulting from outages. The willingness of residential consumers to pay the equivalent of their net income earning rate to avoid evening-time outages is not surprising, given the absolute amounts of money involved. For example, on this basis, in 1976 a typical electricity-using household in Cascavel with an annual income of Cr$60,000 (US$4,860) (Cr$28.5 a working hour) would have to pay only Cr$85.5 (US$6.92) more to halve the incidence of outages from six to three hours a year. This represents approximately 9 percent of their annual electricity bill of Cr$920.

The total residential outage costs were estimated from survey results. The number of residential consumers, by income category, in each geographic cell is known from the load forecast data discussed in chapter 10, whereas the frequency and duration of outages suffered by them during different periods was computed in chapter 11. The aggregate outage costs imposed on such a group over a given time interval is equal to the number of households, times the mean income earning rate for each, times the product of the frequency and the duration of outages expected to occur during the critical evening hours when electricity is considered essential. If income distributional goals are to be considered, these residential outage costs may be multiplied by appropriate social weights, as described in chapters 9 and 13.

Industrial Consumers

A survey of twenty-two industrial firms in Cascavel was conducted in 1976 to determine the effect of outages on these firms and to collect other data to estimate the resulting outage costs. (See questionnaire, appendix F.) Some time was spent explaining to the officials the basic purpose of the research and why their particular firm had been chosen.

Questions focused on the market value of the firm's yearly output, its yearly value added, its normal hours of operation, and overtime pay rates as a multiple of normal pay rates. Also, an attempt was made to learn about the company's expansion plans and potential for growth over the next twenty years. Finally, the officials were questioned concerning the effects of outages. Would outages disrupt production? Would they result in spoiled products or factors? Could production restart immediately after the supply of electricity was restored? In addition, they were asked if any actions had been taken to reduce outage costs, such as purchasing alternative sources of energy or adopting production techniques that would make them less susceptible to outage-induced work disruptions.

On the basis of the survey information, outage cost functions were estimated for nine types of industries, each one consisting of a group of related but separate firms. These functions relate outage costs as defined in chapter 4, Estimation of Outage Costs, to outage duration.[6] More specifically, an outage cost function (OCF) was estimated for each industry type:

$$OCF = a + b \cdot d$$

where OCF = outage cost measured as a fraction of annual value added; d = outage duration in hours; and a and b = coefficients to be estimated.

For some industrial groups, step functions were estimated, that is, if $d < d^*$, then $OCF_1 = a_1 + b_1 d$, and if $d \geq d^*$, then $OCF_2 = a_2 + b_2 d$. This was usually the case when large spoilage costs were incurred, because of an outage of duration d^* or longer. For some industry types, the outage cost function varied during different periods. For example, only a few of the firms in the group operated normally at night, and thus, the OCF during the night would be different than that estimated for daytime periods.

Consider a soy oil producer belonging to the vegetable oils industry group, who could not produce during outages. The restart time for the plant varied between twenty minutes—following an outage that lasted only five minutes—and five hours, after an outage of five or more hours. In addition, this firm incurred spoiled product costs, equal to approxi-

---

6. Although attempts were made to estimate both direct and indirect outage costs, the latter were found to be negligible.

mately Cr$30,000, if the outage exceeded one-half hour. Therefore, during the outage and restart periods, spoiled product costs as well as idle factor costs were incurred for outages of sufficiently long duration.

Next, a set of observations was determined to relate outage durations and costs. The oil-producing firm planned to operate twenty-four hours a day, or 8,760 hours a year. Thus, one hour of average production accounted for about 0.00011 of annual value added. Consider an outage of one hour that involves a restart time of one hour. Idle factor and restart costs for such an outage amounted to 0.00022 of annual value added. However, spoiled product costs must be considered also. Since spoiled costs equaled Cr$30,000 and the firm's annual value added was approximately Cr$112,200 $\times$ 10^3, these costs amounted to about 0.00027 of annual value added. Therefore, total outage costs for an outage of one hour duration was estimated as 0.00049 of annual value added.

Following the same procedure for outages of different durations, a set of observations relating outage cost to duration were determined for the soy oil industry. The outage costs were weighted by the share of soy oil in the value added for the vegetable oils industry group. Next, all the other industries belonging to the same group, such as soy storage firms, were treated the same way. Finally, the outage costs of all the industries in the group corresponding to a given outage duration were added together to obtain a set of observations relating outage cost to duration for the whole vegetable oils group. The *OCF* was fitted to these data points.

Outage cost functions were estimated for various periods: that is, day, evening, or twenty-four hours, and for nine industrial groups. The results are summarized in table 12.3. Six of these functions are linear and therefore indicate that for these sectors outage costs increase with outage duration in a fairly smooth, continuous manner. For four of these industry types—mechanical and metallurgy, nonmetallic minerals, wood, and water treatment—outage costs were incurred only during the day period: 0801 to 1800 hours. For the telephone group, the same outage costs were incurred at any time of the day or night. For the food and beverages group, outage costs were linearly related to outage duration only during the evening period from 1801 to 2400 hours. Outage cost functions were piecewise-linear at all times for the vegetable oils group and only during the day for the food and beverage group. These functions reflected the fact that large spoilage costs occurred when the length of the outage exceeded a certain critical duration.

Table 12.3. *Industrial Outage Cost Functions*

Number	Industry	OC function type[b]	Estimated coefficients[a] ($\times 10^{-4}$)[a]	($\times 10^{-4}$)[b]	Remarks[c]
A.1, B.3	Mechanical and met-allurgy	linear	0.0013	3.9	D
A.2	Nonmetallic minerals	linear	0.077	3.5	D
A.3	Wood	linear	0.94	3.9	D
A.4	Vegetable oils	piece-wise-linear	0.037	2.1	$d < 0.5$ hours, A
			3.6	1.9	$d \geq 0.5$ hours, A
A.5	Food and beverages	piece-wise-linear	1.22	2.30	$d < 0.5$ hours, D
			7.07	2.02	$d \geq 0.5$ hours, D
		linear	0.66	0.72	N
A.6	Other	log	7.2	2.9	$d \geq 0.01$ hours, D
B.2	Telephone	linear	0.002	1.1	A
B.3	Water treatment	linear	−0.27	1.1	$d \geq 2$ hours, D

a. $\overline{R^2} > 0.95$ for all estimations.

b. Linear and log refer to functions of the type $C/Q = (a + b \cdot d)$ and $C/Q = (A + b \cdot \log_{10} d)$, respectively, where C = outage cost, Q = annual value added, and d = outage duration (hours).

c. D = daytime operation; N = night-time operation; A = 24-hour operation.

The outage cost function estimate for an industrial group was used with estimates of expected outage frequencies and durations to determine estimates of total costs resulting from outages affecting that sector during a given period of the day in a specific year. This was done by following a four-step procedure. First, the expected duration of outages, in hours, was substituted into the outage cost function. The result was an estimate of the average cost of an outage, as a percentage of annual value added during this period.[7] Second, this estimate was multiplied by the annual

7. As discussed at the end of chapter 2, Introduction to Reliability, some errors are caused by neglecting the effect of the probable spread of outage durations around their mean values on the nonlinear outage cost functions. These inaccuracies would be small, however, compared with the errors arising from uncertainty in the estimates of the outage cost functions themselves, the mean values of outage frequency and duration, and so on.

value added for the industry type to determine the average cost of an outage for the group. Third, this group cost was multiplied by the expected average frequency of outages for that year to estimate the total annual cost of outages for the group. Fourth, this estimate was adjusted to allow for the fact that some of the firms in the group may not have operated every day of the week during the given period: that is, the estimate of total pecuniary costs of outages was multiplied by a factor equal to the fraction of total hours in this period over the year during which the various firms in the industry type normally operated.

Working through another example will help to clarify the procedure. Consider the metals sector. The outage cost function for this sector is:

$$OCF = 0.00000013 + 0.00039\ D.$$

In 1976 the average duration of outages for the low-reliability system from 0800 to 1800 hours was 0.2 hours. Thus, the average cost of an outage that affected the metals group during this period in 1976, measured as a fraction of annual sectoral value added in that group of industries, is given by:

$$0.00007813 = 0.00000013 + 0.00039 \times (0.2).$$

Value added in the metals group in 1976 was Cr\$4.5 $\times$ 10^6, and therefore, the average cost of an outage was:

$$Cr\$351.6 = Cr\$(4.5 \times 10^6) \times 0.00007813.$$

Multiplying this average cost times the average frequency of outages during this period, 33.8, provided an estimate of the total outage costs for the metals group between 0801 and 1800 hours during 1976:

$$Cr\$11,884 = Cr\$351.6 \times 33.8.$$

The estimates of outage costs determined in this way, however, had to be adjusted to allow for the fact that most firms did not operate every day of the week between 0801 and 1800 hours. Typically, firms worked only half a day on Saturday and none on Sundays; also, holidays reduced annual working hours. To account for this, the outage cost estimates were adjusted by multiplying by a factor equaling the fraction of hours in this period during the year when this particular industry type normally planned to operate. In the case of the metals group, this factor approximately equaled 0.62. Thus, total outage costs in 1976 were:

$$Cr\$7,300 = Cr\$11,884 \times 0.62.$$

After summing these costs over the three periods and all the different industry groups, estimates were obtained for the costs of outages affecting total industrial production in a given year.

Other Consumers

The discussion in this section is presented in the context of the general considerations described in chapter 7, Other Outage Costs. The outage costs of commercial consumers, including government offices, were generally found to be minimal, because, almost universally, work could continue by daylight. These customers were not very dependent on electricity-using equipment, such as copying machines, electric type-writers, calculators and cash registers, air conditioners, elevators, and so on. Furthermore there appeared to be a considerable degree of sub-stitutability between electricity-using and nonelectricity-using commercial activities during outages. There was also sufficient slack during normal working hours so that jobs delayed by outages could be made up without overtime. Supermarkets, hotels, and restaurants reported minor amounts of food spoilage, but these were unlikely to be significant, except in extremely rare outages lasting up to five hours.

It was more convenient to analyze the outage costs of public services, such as telephone and water and sewage treatment, within the framework used for industrial consumers. For public illumination, a minimum estimate of outage costs was determined as the net supply cost that the community would have incurred for public illumination during the outage period. On this basis, the dominant component of the net hourly outage cost in a given geographic cell and year was equal to the value of the stock of capital equipment (estimated in Cr$ to be about 3.5 times the annual kilowatt-hours actually required for public illumination), annuitized over a thirty-year lifetime at the appropriate discount rate, and divided by the annual number of hours of operation. That would be, for example, twelve hours a day for 365 days, for a total of 4,380 hours. Payments for electricity were not included in this calculation, since they would not be incurred during outages, whereas routine maintenance expenditures on public illumination were found to be negligible.

Two hospitals of 80 and 200 beds were surveyed to estimate the opportunity costs of productive factors that would be made idle, such as electricity-using equipment and intermediate products, including blood and medicines, that might spoil because of outages. The principal outage costs occurred during the night, from 1900 to 0600 hours approximately, from idle labor and capital, and the average cost was estimated at Cr$0.67 or about US¢5.5 a hospital bed for every hour of outage. There was sufficient slack time during the day, for labor and for machines such as X-ray units, so that delayed activities could be made up during normal working hours. The hospitals did not have private back-up electricity-generating units, because the existing level of supply reliability was considered adequate. Vital facilities such as the operating rooms and intensive care units had relatively inexpensive standby batteries, however, minimizing the possibility of loss of human life.

The outage costs associated with the remaining consumer types were found to be negligible, because they constituted a minor fraction of the total load or because they were relatively insensitive to the effects of outages. For example, the kilowatt-hour consumption of rural consumers in the vicinity of Cascavel was about 1 percent of the total in 1976, and their share of demand would be unlikely to exceed 3 percent of the total even by 1996. Day-school activities were hardly affected by outages.

Chapter 13

*Distribution System
Optimization and Conclusions*

This chapter focuses on the analysis and comparison of distribution system costs and customer outage costs, and the optimization of the system
expansion plan. Six alternative distribution system plans are analyzed.
Basic plans 1 to 3—including two variants of the medium-reliability
system, Plans 2A and 2B—correspond to the low-, medium-, and high-
reliability systems discussed in chapter 11. Plans 4 to 6 are hybrids,
derived from the basic plans.

Modified Framework for Cost-Benefit Analysis

The Cascavel urban area has experienced dynamic economic and
demographic growth over the past two decades, averaging an annual
population increase of more than 20 percent during this period. This
growth is likely to be sustained at a reduced rate in the future, because
of the rich agricultural potential of the land surrounding Cascavel and
because of the development close to the city of the major Itaipu hydroelectric site, with a planned capacity of 12,000 megawatts during the
next ten years. Furthermore, the state government plans to make the city
a regional growth pole. Current conditions, such as a buoyant economy
and low unemployment rates, are also likely to continue.

176

All costs and benefits were evaluated in efficiency (shadow) prices: that is, ignoring income distributional considerations. Use of shadow prices could be kept to a minimum, however, because economic distortions would not be as severe as in most other developing countries, given the buoyant local economy. The 1976 domestic-priced cruzeiro (Cr$)[1] was adopted as the numeraire or unit of account, because, in monetary terms, more than 99 percent of the items to be considered were domestically produced goods and services.

Therefore, the shadow pricing was done in a relatively straightforward way. All the domestically produced equipment and materials were valued directly in terms of their domestic market prices, but net of local taxes where applicable.[2] An opportunity cost of capital (OCC) of 12 percent was selected as the discount rate, based on the most recent information on Brazil. The shadow wage rate (SWR) applied to labor costs was the same as the market wage rate, given the low unemployment rates in the Cascavel area, and the skilled nature of much of the work involved. This simplified procedure eliminated the need for time-consuming estimation of conversion factors for many domestic inputs to convert the values of these items to border prices. (See chapter 9, Shadow Pricing, for details.) Even if the estimates had been made, such an exercise would have had a negligible effect on the final results.

Incremental kilowatt losses in the distribution system which contributed to the peak load were considered as additional costs. Hydroelectric generating capacity costs were assumed to be US$400 to US$450 a kilowatt, annuitized over a thirty to thirty-five-year lifetime, at a discount rate corresponding to the occ. Incremental kilowatt-hour system losses were considered costless, because the Parana state system serving Cascavel was basically 100 percent hydroelectric and is likely to remain so into the future.

Finally, to illustrate the use of social weights, the optimization procedure was repeated using social (shadow) prices. The base case, which used efficiency prices without social weighting, is presented in the next two sections, followed by the results when social weights were applied. The latter had negligible effects on the base case results.

---

1. US$1 = Cr$ 12.35 (end 1976).
2. The prices of the few imported items, less than 1 percent of the total costs, were known in cruzeiros converted at the official exchange rate. These nominal prices were multiplied by a factor of 1.25, representing the ratio of the shadow exchange rate (SER) to the official exchange rate (OER).

Table 13.1. *Global Characteristics of the Four Basic Alternative Distribution System Plans*

System plan	Reliability index ($\Re$)	Outage rate, OR (percentage)[a]	Outage costs, OC (10^6 Cr$)[b]	Supply costs, SC (10^6 Cr$)	Total costs, OC + SC (10^6 Cr$)	Outage costs/ kilowatt-hour lost, OCK (Cr$/kilowatt-hour)
1 (Low-reliability)	0.9935	0.650	150.1	57.5	207.6	14.0
2A (Medium-reliability)	0.9969	0.314	77.2	58.6	135.8	14.9
2B (Medium-reliability)	0.9981	0.191	49.5	57.8	107.3	15.7
3 (High-reliability)	0.9988	0.116	28.4	76.9	105.3	14.8

Note: Present discounted values of quantities from 1976 to 2006 as defined in the text; discount rate = 12 percent.

a. $OR = 100 \cdot (1 - \Re) = 100 \cdot OE/TE$.

b. US$1 = Cr$12.35 (end 1976).

General Characteristics of Outage and Supply Costs

In this section, the relations between the global or city-wide reliability levels, outage costs, and system costs are discussed. These aggregate values are derived by summing the underlying disaggregate results
based on the frequencies and durations of outages at the geographic
cell level. (See chapters 11, 12, and appendix D.) The chief global characteristics of the basic alternative system plans are summarized in table
13.1.[3] As the overall reliability level (R) increased, outage costs (OC)
declined steadily; supply costs (SC) remained fairly stable until there
was a sharp rise in SC between the medium type B and the high-reliability
plans: that is, between Plans 2B and 3. Outage costs for each kilowatt-
hour lost (OCK) or not consumed because of outages, which is a
measure of consumer sensitivity to power supply interruptions, were
highest for system Plan 2B. The scalar global reliability index $\Re$ was
always greater than 0.99, and therefore its variations were not readily
apparent. Therefore it was more convenient to use a new measure of
reliability, the outage rate, OR, which decreases as the reliability level increases and may be defined as: $OR = 100 \cdot (1 - \Re) = 100 \cdot (OE/TE)$.

As discussed in the previous chapter, the four types of electricity use
for which outage costs were significant include residential, industrial,
public lighting, and hospitals. Table 13.2 indicates that the first two
categories were the dominant ones in relation to total energy (TE) use
and outage costs. For the range of reliability levels considered in this
study, the main industrial category appeared to be the one most affected
by outages, in relation to OCK, followed by residential, service industrial,
hospitals, and public illumination. Outage costs for each kilowatt-hour
lost for the main industrial category tended to increase as reliability
increased and as the average outage duration decreased, but OCK did not
vary much with system reliability for the other categories of users.

A more detailed breakdown of outage costs for the two dominant
categories, residential and main industrial, is presented in table 13.3.
As expected, OC increased as the outage rate (OR) increased for all
consumer types. For any given class of residential consumer, the outage

---

3. Unless otherwise stated, all quantities discussed in this chapter are given in
1976 present value terms, discounted at 12 percent, over the thirty-year horizon,
1976 to 2006. Details of the outage and supply cost calculations and typical computer printouts of outage cost results, by cell, by year, and by consumer type may
be found in appendix D.

Table 13.2. Energy Use and Outage Costs, by Major Consumer Category

Consumer category	Total energy, TE (gigawatt-hours)	Outage costs, OC (10⁶ Cr$)ᵃ				Outage costs/kilowatt-hour lost, OCK (Cr$/kilowatt-hour)			
		Plan 1	Plan 2A	Plan 2B	Plan 3	Plan 1	Plan 2A	Plan 2B	Plan 3
Residential	484.1	68.2	34.8	20.5	9.9	17.9	18.2	18.6	17.5
Main industrial	371.8	77.4	40.6	27.8	17.8	31.4	33.5	30.0	26.5
Service industrial	224.7	4.1	1.6	1.0	0.6	3.4	3.2	3.8	3.6
Public lighting	60.4	0.2	0.1	—	—	0.4	0.4	0.4	0.4
Hospitals	11.7	0.3	0.1	—	—	5.9	5.9	5.9	5.9

Note: Present discounted values of quantities from 1976 to 2006 as defined in the text; discount rate = 12 percent.
a. US$1 = Cr$12.35 (end 1976).

Table 13.3. Disaggregate Energy Use and Outage Costs of Residential and Main Industrial Consumers

Consumer category	Total energy, TE (gigawatt-hours)	Outage costs, OC (10⁶ Cr$)[a] Plan				Outage costs/kilowatt-hour lost, OCK (Cr$/kilowatt-hour) Plan				Outage rate, OR (percentage) Plan			
		1	2A	2B	3	1	2A	2B	3	1	2A	2B	3
Residential[b]													
Lower	19.9	2.85	1.36	0.83	0.38	16.5	16.8	17.2	16.2	0.870	0.406	0.243	0.117
Lower-middle	152.3	20.11	10.02	5.98	2.87	16.6	16.8	17.3	16.2	0.798	0.391	0.228	0.117
Upper-middle	198.9	27.47	14.00	8.27	4.01	17.6	17.9	18.3	17.2	0.783	0.394	0.227	0.117
Upper	113.1	17.72	9.43	5.46	2.65	20.6	20.8	21.4	20.0	0.760	0.401	0.226	0.117
Main industrial[b]													
A.1	9.7	0.61	0.26	0.14	0.10	24.9	24.9	24.9	25.0	0.269	0.106	0.056	0.041
A.2	30.5	1.11	0.48	0.27	0.19	13.6	12.8	11.9	11.8	0.251	0.124	0.074	0.054
A.3	63.9	9.45	5.29	3.92	2.84	36.7	48.0	73.1	75.5	0.403	0.173	0.084	0.059
A.4	146.2	44.13	22.18	15.54	8.73	31.8	35.2	31.9	25.2	0.948	0.431	0.334	0.237
A.5	88.1	19.40	10.07	5.92	4.40	35.0	32.0	21.9	22.1	0.630	0.357	0.306	0.226
A.6	33.4	26.70	2.28	2.03	1.52	16.6	21.2	22.8	22.8	0.482	0.322	0.267	0.200

Note: Present discounted values of quantities from 1976 to 2006 as defined in the text; discount rate = 12 percent.
a. U.S.$1 = Cr$12.35 (end 1976).
b. Residential and main industrial subcategories as described in chapter 10.

cost for each kilowatt-hour lost was relatively unaffected by the reliability level but, for any given system plan, residential OCK rose a little
with income level. These results were predictable, given that $OCK =$
OC/OE, and both outage costs and outage energy are linearly proportional to outage duration for a given income class. For a given reliability level, however, OC is linearly proportional to net income, but OE
increases less rapidly.[4]

The values of industrial OCK reflected the nature of the respective
outage cost functions given in table 12.3. For industry types A.1 and
A.2, the intercept term was small so that the linear outage function
(OCF) practically passed through the origin. Therefore, since both OC
and OE are linearly proportional to outage duration, their ratio OCK was
constant and unaffected by the reliability level. Furthermore, these values
of OCK were also quite similar to the corresponding figures for value
added per kilowatt-hour. (See table 10.2 in chapter 10.) For industry
types A.3 and A.6, the respective OC functions had large intercepts and a
logarithmic form, leading to increasing values of OCK as OR and the
mean outage duration decreased. The discontinuities in the OC functions
for A.4 and A.5, resulting from the large spoilage costs, for outages of
duration $d > 0.5$ hours, tended to dictate the behavior of OCK.

In summary, residential consumers suffer outage costs of about Cr$16
to 21 (U.S.$1.30 to 1.70) for each kilowatt-hour lost, over the range
of reliability levels considered. Industrial group A.3 (wood) was the
most sensitive (approximate range Cr$35 to 75 [U.S.$2.80 to 6.10] for
each kilowatt-hour lost), especially to outages of shorter duration,
whereas OCK was lower for the other groups (Cr$12 to 35 [US$1 to
2.80] for each kilowatt-hour lost). The above industrial outage cost
results are consistent with the results of previous studies, given the wide
variation in methodologies, countries of application, and timing of the
different studies. The residential outage costs presented here, however,
are significantly higher because, except in one case (Sweden, 1969),

---

4. Household OC are the costs incurred because of outages during the critical
leisure period, since outages at other times are assumed to have negligible costs.
OE, however, is the quantity of kilowatt-hours lost due to outages throughout the
twenty-four hours of the day. Therefore their ratio, OCK, is smaller, say, by a
factor g, than the outage cost for each kilowatt-hour lost during the critical leisure
hours alone. Assuming that 38 to 40 percent of the daily household electricity
consumption occurs during the one-and-a-half-hour leisure period, and using the
existing distribution of outages at different times of the day, g is approximately 2.3.

previous studies ignored the cost of foregone leisure. (See appendix E for details.)

Within the four income classes of the residential consumer category and for a given system plan, OR was quite stable. There were significant differences among values of OR for the different industrial sectors, however, because of different working hours and wide variations in restart times.

Hybrid Systems and Optimum Reliability Levels

The results of the distribution system optimization procedure described in chapter 3 are summarized in table 13.4 and figure 13.1 on a city-wide basis. Focusing attention on the efficiency priced results in progressing from Plan 1 to Plan 3, there was a steady improvement in overall reliability, a corresponding decrease in global outage costs (OC), and a sharp increase in the distribution system supply costs (SC) between Plans 2B and 3.[5] As a first approximation, the minimum value of the total economic cost to society, that is, the combined outage and distribution supply costs ($OC + SC$), would most probably occur close to Plans 2B and 3.

In the next stage of optimization, the procedure was refined by examining outage and supply costs for specific areas of the city and by using this information as feedback to revise and improve the system design. Typical computer printouts of total outage costs and outage cost for each kilowatt-hour lost and for each geographic cell are shown in figures 13.2 and 13.3. This information and the outage cost results disaggregated by consumer category (tables 13.2 and 13.3) indicated that the areas of high population density in the city center and the main industrial area (ZI) suffered the highest outage costs. Therefore several hybrid distribution system designs were considered by varying the levels of reliability for different neighborhoods.

---

5. Plan 2B is more reliable as well as slightly cheaper than Plan 2A. This is because the strengthened feeder configuration of Plan 2B reduces losses more than enough to compensate for the increase in investment costs relative to Plan 2A. The results for both plans are retained, however, to show that over this range of reliability, SC is essentially constant.

Table 13.4. *Data for Optimization of the Distribution System*

System plan	Outage rate, OR (percentage)[a]	Supply costs, SC (10^6 Cr\$)[b]	Efficiency prices		Social prices	
			Outage costs, OC (10^6 Cr\$)	Total costs, TC (10^6 Cr\$)	Outage costs, OC (10^6 Cr\$)	Total costs, TC (10^6 Cr\$)
1 (Low-reliability)	0.650	57.5	150.1	207.6	145.3	202.8
2A (Medium-reliability)	0.314	58.6	77.2	135.8	74.2	132.7
2B (Medium-reliability)	0.191	57.8	49.5	107.3	47.9	105.7
3 (High-reliability)	0.116	76.9	28.4	105.3	27.6	104.5
4 (Hybrid A)	0.184	59.9	44.5	104.4	42.9	102.8
5 (Hybrid B)	0.166	65.2	44.3	109.5	44.1	109.3
6 (Hybrid C)	0.159	67.4	39.3	106.7	39.1	106.5

Note: Present discounted values of quantities from 1976 to 2006 as defined in the text; discount rate = 12 percent.

a. $OR = 100 \cdot (1 - \Re) = 100 \cdot OE/TE$.

b. US\$1 = Cr\$12.35 (end 1976).

184

Figure 13.1. *Optimization of the Outage System: Costs Versus Outage Rate*

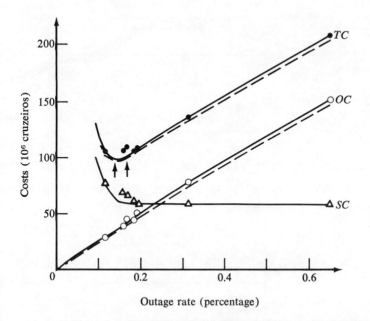

Note: SC = distribution system supply costs; *OC* = global outage costs; and *TC* = total costs. The plotted data points and solid lines refer to efficiency priced costs; the broken lines indicate the costs in terms of social prices.

In hybrid Plan 4, the reliability of service to the main industrial zone (*ZI* of figure 10.1) was maintained at the same level as in the high-reliability Plan 3. The distribution system for all other areas was designed according to the medium-reliability Plan 2B. Plans 1 and 2A were ruled out as viable alternatives for any specific area, because the potential saving in reducing *SC* by changing from a higher reliability design to either of these two plans was generally much smaller than the corresponding increase in *OC*. In Plan 5 the city center areas, *ZC, ZCR,* and *ZR*1 were provided with a high-reliability distribution system; the rest of the city received medium-reliability type B service. Finally, in

Figure 13.2. *Medium-Reliability Plan B:*
Present Discounted Value of Outage Costs, by Cell
(thousands of Cr $)

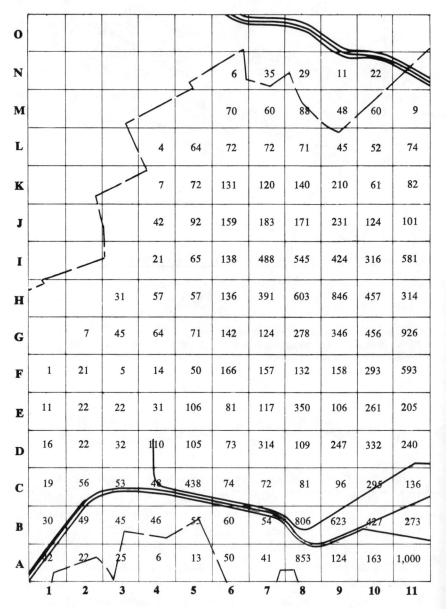

	1	2	3	4	5	6	7	8	9	10	11
O											
N						6	35	29	11	22	
M						70	60	88	48	60	9
L				4	64	72	72	71	45	52	74
K				7	72	131	120	140	210	61	82
J				42	92	159	183	171	231	124	101
I				21	65	138	488	545	424	316	581
H			31	57	57	136	391	603	846	457	314
G		7	45	64	71	142	124	278	346	456	926
F	1	21	5	14	50	166	157	132	158	293	593
E	11	22	22	31	106	81	117	350	106	261	205
D	16	22	32	110	105	73	314	109	247	332	240
C	19	56	53	48	438	74	72	81	96	295	136
B	30	49	45	46	55	60	54	806	623	427	273
A	22	22	25	6	13	50	41	853	124	163	1,000

Note: Discount rate = 12 percent.

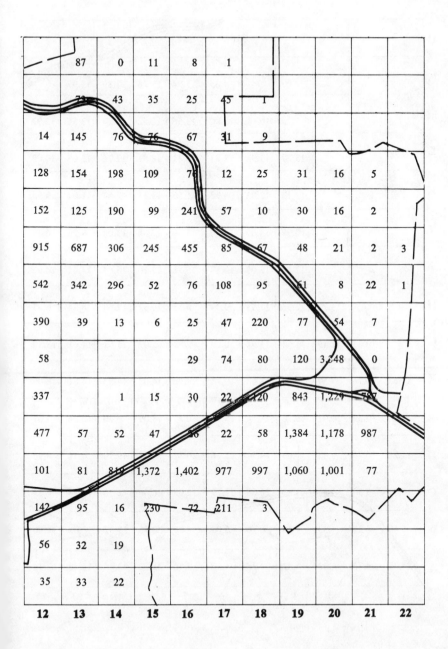

12	13	14	15	16	17	18	19	20	21	22
	87	0	11	8	1					
		43	35	25	45	1				
14	145	76	76	67	31	9				
128	154	198	109	7	12	25	31	16	5	
152	125	190	99	241	57	10	30	16	2	
915	687	306	245	455	85	67	48	21	2	3
542	342	296	52	76	108	95	61	8	22	1
390	39	13	6	25	47	220	77	54	7	
58				29	74	80	120	3,348	0	
337		1	15	30	22	420	843	1,229		
477	57	52	47	76	22	58	1,384	1,178	987	
101	81	810	1,372	1,402	977	997	1,060	1,001	77	
142	95	16	230	72	211	3				
56	32	19								
35	33	22								

Figure 13.3. *Medium-Reliability Plan B:*
Outage Cost per Kilowatt-hour Lost, by Cell

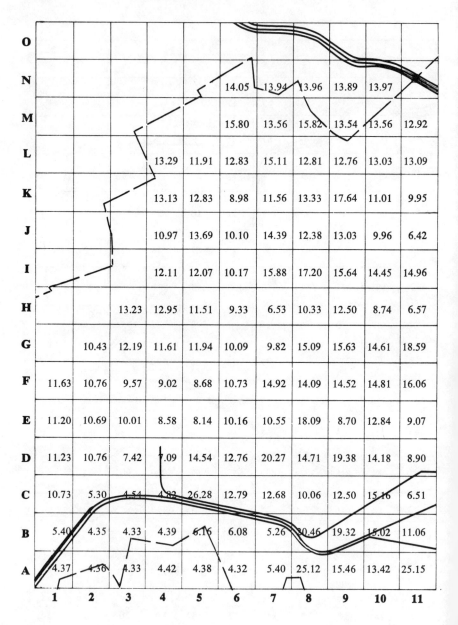

	1	2	3	4	5	6	7	8	9	10	11
O											
N						14.05	13.94	13.96	13.89	13.97	
M						15.80	13.56	15.82	13.54	13.56	12.92
L					13.29	11.91	12.83	15.11	12.81	12.76	13.03	13.09
K					13.13	12.83	8.98	11.56	13.33	17.64	11.01	9.95
J					10.97	13.69	10.10	14.39	12.38	13.03	9.96	6.42
I					12.11	12.07	10.17	15.88	17.20	15.64	14.45	14.96
H				13.23	12.95	11.51	9.33	6.53	10.33	12.50	8.74	6.57
G			10.43	12.19	11.61	11.94	10.09	9.82	15.09	15.63	14.61	18.59
F	11.63	10.76	9.57	9.02	8.68	10.73	14.92	14.09	14.52	14.81	16.06
E	11.20	10.69	10.01	8.58	8.14	10.16	10.55	18.09	8.70	12.84	9.07
D	11.23	10.76	7.42	7.09	14.54	12.76	20.27	14.71	19.38	14.18	8.90
C	10.73	5.30	4.54	4.82	26.28	12.79	12.68	10.06	12.50	15.16	6.51
B	5.40	4.35	4.33	4.39	6.16	6.08	5.26	30.46	19.32	15.02	11.06
A	4.37	4.36	4.33	4.42	4.38	4.32	5.40	25.12	15.46	13.42	25.15

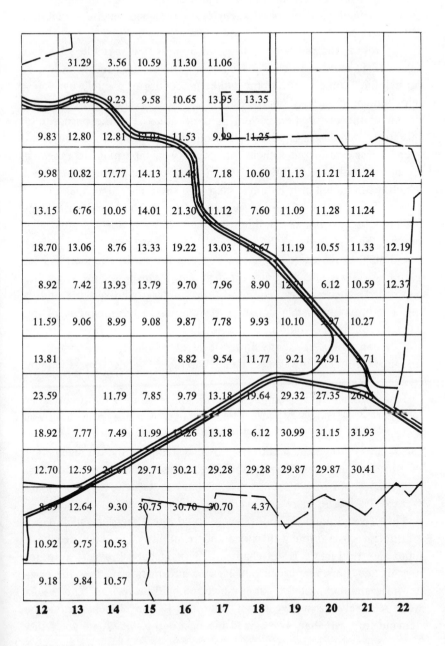

12	13	14	15	16	17	18	19	20	21	22
	31.29	3.56	10.59	11.30	11.06					
		9.23	9.58	10.65	13.95	13.35				
9.83	12.80	12.81		11.53	9.99	11.25				
9.98	10.82	17.77	14.13	11.4	7.18	10.60	11.13	11.21	11.24	
13.15	6.76	10.05	14.01	21.30	11.12	7.60	11.09	11.28	11.24	
18.70	13.06	8.76	13.33	19.22	13.03	8.67	11.19	10.55	11.33	12.19
8.92	7.42	13.93	13.79	9.70	7.96	8.90	12.01	6.12	10.59	12.37
11.59	9.06	8.99	9.08	9.87	7.78	9.93	10.10	8.97	10.27	
13.81				8.82	9.54	11.77	9.21	24.91	4.71	
23.59		11.79	7.85	9.79	13.18	19.64	29.32	27.35	26.0	
18.92	7.77	7.49	11.99	13.26	13.18	6.12	30.99	31.15	31.93	
12.70	12.59	28.81	29.71	30.21	29.28	29.28	29.87	29.87	30.41	
8.59	12.64	9.30	30.75	30.70	30.70	4.37				
10.92	9.75	10.53								
9.18	9.84	10.57								

Plan 6 both the city center and the main industrial zone were supplied at high reliability, whereas all other areas obtained medium-reliability type B service.

The results for the hybrid plans, also presented in table 13.4 and figure 13.1, indicated that Plan 4 had the lowest total costs.[6] Clearly, further fine-tuning of the optimization procedure is possible by examining different parts of the city in greater detail and by varying the design of the distribution system in these areas. For the purposes of this study, demonstrating the application of the new methodology, however, it was considered sufficient to identify an approximate range of reliability levels $0.125 < OR < 0.16$ (see arrows in figure 13.1) within which the optimum distribution system plan should lie. Since the greatest potential savings in OC would be realized by the main industrial consumers, the possibilities for improving reliability in the ZI area even beyond the high level of Plan 3 could have been examined by further fine-tuning, as discussed in chapter 2, Long-Range Distribution System Planning. This could be done, for example, by using reclosers, remote controlled switches, more line inspections, underground systems, and so on. The optimum system design corresponding to the minimum of the TC curve probably would have provided very high-reliability service for the ZI consumers, a slightly lower level of reliability (between Plans 2B and 3) for the city center, and reliability of service corresponding to Plan 2B elsewhere in the city.

It was interesting to examine the variation of $\mathfrak{R}_t$ over the twenty-year plan period, as shown in figure 13.4. For a given system plan there was a steady improvement in reliability with time. As loads increased, more substations and feeders had to be provided, reducing the average length of a feeder. Therefore the probability of outages and the annual outage frequency, both of which are proportional to feeder length, also decreased, leading to increased overall reliability.

The new optimum reliability levels could affect the demand forecast and outage costs through the price and reliability expectation feedback loops shown in figure 1.1 of chapter 1. These feedback effects were not investigated, however, because of lack of information on how the original prices and expected reliability levels should be revised. The results were relatively insensitive to an arbitrary 10 percent change in the demand forecast; Plan 4 remained the best one tested. A range of dis-

6. The plotted data points for hybrid Plans 5 and 6 are off the trend line of TC for optimally designed systems.

Figure 13.4. *Evolution of Outage Rate over Time*

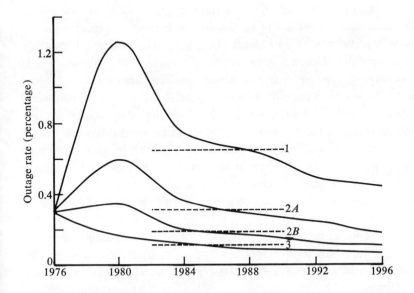

Note: Broken lines indicate the discounted aggregate value of outage rate.

count rates from 10 to 14 percent were tried, but these changes also did not have much effect on the results, with the exception of different values of PDV. Finally, the results were hardly affected by variations of (a) the shadow of wage rate, in the range 0.8 to 1.0 times the market wage rate, and (b) the ratio of overtime to normal wage rates, in the range of $1.5 \geq \bar{w}/w^s \geq 1$. (See appendix D for details.)

Effects of Social Weighting

In the earlier discussion, the optimization analysis was concerned exclusively with efficiency prices. This section considers the effect of social pricing on the earlier results. The question is particularly relevant for residential consumers, whose outage costs for each hour of outage differed widely, because of differences in hourly income earning rates ranging from Cr$8.7 to 108 in 1976. The outage costs for each energy unit lost were more stable across the different income classes, varying from about Cr$16 to 21 for each kilowatt-hour lost.

These results on hourly costs of outages, which followed directly from the theoretical model presented in chapter 5, Residential Outage Costs, seem to argue in favor of high-reliability service for high-income neighborhoods and low-reliability service in low-income neighborhoods. As a first impression, such an interpretation could be considered inequitable on income distributional grounds. As discussed in the Summary and Conclusions, however, better reliability levels should also imply higher electricity prices. Also, outage costs may be interpreted in the economic sense as a reduction in earnings. Therefore the outage costs of low-income groups could be assigned a higher social weight than the outage costs of high-income groups, based on the economic principle of diminishing marginal utility of income consumption. This type of weighting procedure would help to reduce the effects of income disparities on outage costs and on the resultant optimal reliability levels in different geographic areas.

The outage costs of residential consumers were adjusted directly by dividing the mean level of net earnings in each income class by the average net income of the total urban population. This yields the weighting factors 3.679, 1.419, 0.694, and 0.296 for the lower, lower-middle, upper-middle, and upper income groups, respectively. (See appendix B for details.) The effect of this social pricing procedure was to standardize the outage costs during each hour of outage for all income groups at the average net income earning rate—about Cr$32 for every working hour in 1976. In this new situation, however, the outage costs for each unit of energy lost exhibited large differences, varying from Cr$6 to 60 for every kilowatt-hour lost for the high- and low-income groups, respectively. These results may be contrasted with the earlier results using efficiency pricing alone, when the outage costs for every hour of outage varied widely according to the income level, whereas the outage costs for each kilowatt-hour lost were practically constant.[7]

It is not clear how outage costs incurred by nonresidential consumers would affect the incomes of various groups in the economy. For example, owners of industries may absorb losses in reduced profits or may pass them on to the consumer through increased product prices. Allocating outage costs that affect public illumination and hospitals by income group would be equally difficult. Therefore these types of outage costs were assigned a weight of unity in the subsequent analysis, which

7. See also, Mohan Munasinghe, "Costs Incurred by Residential Electricity Consumers Due to Power Failures," *Journal of Consumer Research* (March 1980).

was equivalent to making the neutral assumption that, on the average, the income distributional effect of all such costs would be borne by those whose income is close to the societal average. The same argument applied to the treatment of system supply costs.

The results of the social pricing exercise are summarized in table 13.4 and figure 13.1. The major effect was a small overall reduction in residential outage costs and, consequently, total costs. Consumers with above average income had social weights less than unity and suffered greater (unweighted) outage costs than those at lower income levels, where the weights were larger than unity. Neither the ranking of the alternative expansion plans by total costs, nor the general conclusions regarding the optimal range of global reliability levels, however, were altered. Yet, if the model had been fine-tuned at a more detailed level, social weighting would have had an effect on distribution network optimization by small areas, especially if specific neighborhoods tended to be dominated by particular income groups. This could be quite helpful in analyzing outage costs in low-income or slum areas, provided the social weights were estimated and applied sensibly.

Summary and Conclusions

Since it was to be used for distribution network planning, the demand forecast developed in the case study is highly disaggregated: (a) by twenty-four categories of consumers, (b) by 247 geographic cells, each 0.25 square kilometers; and (c) by year, over a twenty-year period. Other variables and parameters of the problem were also estimated at the same level of detail and then were aggregated in various ways: that is, over the different customer types, geographic areas, or time. In particular, estimating the frequency and duration of outages during three different periods of the day—0001 to 0800, 0801 to 1800, and 1801 to 2400 hours—and distinguishing between working and nonworking days emphasized the degree of detail required to determine outage costs accurately.

The results of the residential outage cost survey and analysis showed that (a) the chief effect of unexpected outages on electricity-using households was the loss of a critical ninety-minute period of leisure during the evening hours when electricity was considered essential by consumers, whereas domestic activities interrupted during the day could be rescheduled with relatively little inconvenience; and (b) over this one-

and-a-half-hour period, the monetary value of lost leisure could be measured by the net wage or income earning rate of affected households, as confirmed by their willingness to pay to avoid outages in the short term.

Industrial outage costs were estimated on the basis of a detailed study of spoilage, factors of production made idle, and recovery of lost production during both normal working hours and overtime. The results of the analysis indicated that there were wide variations in the effects of outages on industrial consumers, depending on the type of industry, the duration of the outage, and the time of day during which it occurred. This approach would be helpful to rank industries by their sensitivity to outages, for example, for emergency load shedding.

The outage costs of other types of electricity users were also estimated but found to be relatively small, since their activities were not greatly affected by outages, or their consumption of electricity was a negligibly small fraction of the total load.

The distribution network was designed and supply costs were determined by using a computerized simulation approach. Using feedback information from the cost-benefit module on disaggregate outage costs and system costs to improve the design of the distribution grid was the most noteworthy feature of the optimization procedure.

The initial alternative system expansion paths each were designed on the basis of a different target reliability criterion that could be applied uniformly over the whole city. The cost-benefit comparison of the resulting outage costs and system costs indicated that as global reliability improved, outage costs decreased fairly steadily. Supply costs, however, were practically constant until a critical level of reliability was reached, after which these costs increased sharply. Next, several mixed or hybrid network expansion plans were designed, based on the principle of providing the highest reliability service to areas with the highest outage costs, and so on. This feedback procedure yielded the optimum system expansion plan in which the city center with high population densities and the main industrial zone received high-reliability service, whereas other areas of the city were served at a lower reliability level.

The optimum system expansion plan and reliability levels were relatively unaffected over a range of variations in the demand forecast, discount rate, and shadow prices considered in the study. In particular, the application of social shadow prices or social weights to reflect income distributional consideration did not have much effect on the final results.

The principal conclusion of the case study is that the long-range expansion plan of a typical urban distribution system may be optimized, with respect to reliability, by using a new economic criterion for system planning, in which the sum of both outage and system costs is minimized. In particular, fine-tuning the procedure permitted the level of distribution reliability to be varied by small areas to yield a more optimal network design. The same basic methodology could be used to optimize a total system plan—for example, at the generation and transmission level—provided appropriate reliability indexes were used.

If the optimum expansion plan—corresponding to the minimum point of the total costs curve in figure 13.1 and involving about Cr$97.5 million—had been adopted, it would have resulted in a net saving to Cascavel of about Cr$8 million (US$0.65 million) in present discounted value terms during the next thirty years. This assumes that the conventional choice would have been the alternative Plan 3. Of this net saving, the reduction in system costs would have amounted to Cr$15 million, whereas the corresponding outage costs would have increased by Cr$7 million. As noted earlier, however, since only the distribution network was optimized, it is possible that an equivalent reduction in total costs may have been achieved at lower supply cost, by varying the reliability level of the generation and transmission system.

If the lower supply costs implied by the optimum expansion plan were distributed uniformly among all consumers, the average electricity price would have decreased by less than Cr$0.01 a kilowatt-hour, which is negligible compared with the 1976 average residential tariff of Cr$0.82 a kilowatt-hour. The approach used here, however, indicates that the optimum reliability level would tend to be higher for areas in which outage costs are greater and, therefore, on the basis of the pricing objectives of economic efficiency and fairness, electricity tariffs should also be higher in such neighborhoods. Allocation of the decreased supply costs only to those consumers receiving lower reliability service outside the ZI area would have resulted in an average price decrease of only Cr$0.011 a kilowatt-hour, which is still very small. The cost allocation would be somewhat different with a marginal cost-based tariff, but in this case, also, the increase in the price level is not likely to be very significant.

Because of the wide variation in electricty consumption patterns, power system characteristics, and so on in different countries, the results of the case study cannot be easily extrapolated to a world-wide scale. As a rough estimate, however, the net saving from system optimization, discussed earlier, may be used. This is about 5 percent of the estimated total distribution system investment costs, or approximately 0.05 percent of the total value added in the Cascavel urban area during the study period. If even half these percentage values were taken on a conservative basis, the net potential savings on total electric power sector investments in the capital-scarce developing countries alone would amount to about (constant 1977) US$400 to 500 million a year, during the next decade.

Additional work must be done in refining the conceptual framework for measuring outage costs and improving the methods of estimation. In particular, the relation between outage expectation and adaptation of consumer behavior must be investigated in the context of indirect versus direct outage costs and long- versus short-run effects. The effect of various pricing policies on optimum reliability levels, through the demand forecast, should also be examined. To test and strengthen the new methodology further, more case studies are required that would cover various aspects of system planning. For example, generation and transmission could be studied in several countries where a different mix of consumers, as well as varied socioeconomic and geographical conditions would be considered. In this context two specific practical difficulties are likely to arise. First, on the supply side, appropriate generation and transmission system reliability indexes, which are meaningful at the consumer level, would have to be computed. (See chapter 2, Introduction to Reliability.) Second, on the demand side, shortcut methods would have to be used to estimate outage costs for the large geographic areas affected by changes in reliability at the generation and transmission level. (See chapter 4, Estimation of Outage Costs.) This would reduce the data-gathering problem to manageable proportions.

Appendixes

Appendix A

~~~~~~

Basic Mathematical Concepts for Reliability Modeling

The ideas developed in this appendix are intended as an aid to understanding the basic mathematical concepts involved in reliability modeling. Therefore, fairly simple cases are considered here in a conceptual way. More detailed treatment of these topics can be found in the references cited below and in chapter 2.

Laws of Probability[1]

The fundamental laws of probability used in reliability modeling may be illustrated by analyzing the two-event case. Let $P(A)$ and $P(B)$ denote the probabilities (each lying between zero and unity) of the occurrence of events A and B, respectively. Furthermore, let $P(A + B)$ represent the probability of either A or B or both taking place: that is, the union of A and B. Also, let the probability of the occurrence of A and B

$$P(A + B) = P(A) + P(B) - P(A \times B).$$

1. For details, see: Athanasios Papoulis, *Probability, Random Variables, and Stochastic Processes* (New York: McGraw-Hill, 1965), chap. 2; or Vijay K. Rohatgi, *An Introduction to Probability Theory and Mathematical Statistics* (New York: John Wiley, 1976), chap. 2.

simultaneously be given by $P(A \times B)$: that is, the intersection of A and B. Then, the following relation holds true:

$$P(A + B) = P(A) + P(B) - P(A \times B).$$

If the events A and B are mutually exclusive, $P(A \times B) = 0$, and therefore the simple additive law of probability is obtained as:

(A.1) $$P(A + B) = P(A) + P(B).$$

Next, let $P(A/B)$ denote the probability of event A taking place, given the fact that B has already occurred. Then the following expression may be written:

$$P(A/B) = P(A \times B)/P(B).$$

If the events A and B are mutually independent:

$$P(A/B) = P(A),$$

and therefore, the simple multiplicative law of probability is derived as:

(A.2) $$P(A \times B) = P(A) \cdot P(B).$$

The probability of the event A not taking place is given by the complementarity rule:

(A.3) $$P(\bar{A}) = 1 - P(A).$$

The above laws may be generalized to obtain the corresponding results for the N event case. Thus, for a set of N mutually exclusive events, equation (A.1) gives rise to:

$$P(A + B + \cdots + N) = P(A) + P(B) + \cdots + P(N).$$

Similarly, if the events are mutually independent, equation (A.2) can be rewritten:

$$P(A \times B \times \cdots \times N) = P(A) \cdot P(B) \cdot \cdots \cdot P(N)$$

Finally, in the long-run context, the expected value of a random variable A_i, which can take on different values for $i = 1, \cdots n$, with corresponding probabilities $P(A_i)$, is given by:

$$E(A_i) = \sum_{i=1}^{n} A_i \cdot P(A_i).$$

Discrete State Continuous Transition Markov Process

Modern reliability studies attempt to represent random equipment failures or outages by means of stochastic models. Therefore the class of discrete state, continuous transition Markov processes is often used for this purpose.[2] A simple generation capacity model is treated below to illustrate the use of this approach.

Consider a single generating unit that at any given moment must be in one of two possible discrete states, depicted in figure A.1: (a) the U or up state, in which the unit is ready and available for use; and (b) the D or down state, in which the unit is off-line and unavailable for use.

The rules governing transitions between the states may be deduced from the following important properties of these states:

(a) The states are mutually exclusive and collectively exhaustive;

(b) The probability of a given transition between states occurring during any small instant of time, Δt, is proportional to Δt, but is independent of the elapsed time, t (this implies that the transition time may be represented by exponential probability density functions of time); and

(c) The probability of transition from a given state depends only on the current state and is independent of the past history of the machine.

At any given time, t, suppose the probability of finding the generator in state, i, is given by $P_i(t)$. From property (a), it follows that:

(A.4) $$P_U(t) + P_D(t) = 1.$$

Let the rate of departure or transition rate out of state i be denoted by λ_i. From property (b), the probability of transferring from state i to the other state during any small duration of time Δt is given by:

$$[\lambda_i \cdot P_i(t) \cdot \Delta t].$$

2. See for example: Chanan Singh and Roy Billinton, "Frequency and Duration Concepts in System Reliability Evaluation," *IEEE Transactions on Reliability*, vol. R-24 (April 1975), pp. 31–36.

Figure A.1. *Basic Markov State-Space Representation of a Single Generator*

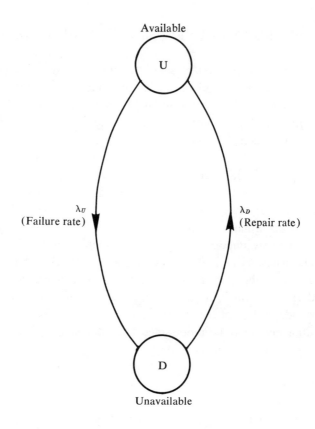

Available

U

λ_U
(Failure rate)

λ_D
(Repair rate)

D

Unavailable

Note: U = upstate; D = down state; and λ_i = transition rate out of state i.

If transitions into and out of state U are considered, it follows that:

$$P_U(t + \Delta t) = P_U(t) - \lambda_U \cdot P_U(t) \cdot \Delta t + \lambda_D \cdot P_D(t) \cdot \Delta t.$$

Rearranging terms, yields:

$$\lambda_D \cdot P_D(t) - \lambda_U \cdot P_U(t) = [P_U(t + \Delta t) - P_U(t)]/\Delta t = \Delta P_U(t)/\Delta t.$$

Assuming steady-state conditions, in the long-run, $\Delta P_U(t) = 0$; and therefore:

(A.5) $\lambda_D \cdot P_D - \lambda_U \cdot P_U = 0$

where P_i is the steady state value of $P_i(t)$.

Equation (A.5) summarizes the fact that for such a Markov process with no trap states, the sum of the rates of transition into a given state, weighted by the availabilities of the originating states, must be equal to the sum of the corresponding weighted rates of departure from that state. This general result also holds true for more than two connected states, and may be represented in the simplified Chapman-Kolmogoroff form:

$$\sum_{All\ j \neq i} \lambda_{j\ to\ i} \cdot P_j = P_i \cdot \sum_{All\ k \neq i} \lambda_{i\ to\ k} \text{ for any given state } i.$$

The steady-state form of equation (A.4) may be written:

(A.6) $P_U + P_D = 1.$

Solving equations (A.5) and (A.6) yields:

$$P_D = \lambda_U / (\lambda_U + \lambda_D)$$

and

$$P_U = \lambda_D / (\lambda_U + \lambda_D).$$

Now this rather abstract mathematical model may be interpreted in terms of quantities commonly encountered in power engineering practice.

Suppose that over a long observation period, data have been gathered on (a) the average time it takes a generator to fail—the time spent in the up state (T_U); and (b) the average time required for repairs following such a failure—time spent in the down state (T_D). Then it follows that:

(A.7)   Availability of the machine $= P_U = T_U / (T_U + T_D)$,

(A.8)   Forced outage rate $= P_D = T_D / (T_U + T_D) = 1 -$ availability,

(A.9)   Failure rate $= \lambda_U = 1/T_U$, and

(A.10)   Repair rate $= \lambda_D = 1/T_D$.

Table A.1. *Characteristics of Two Generators in Parallel*

Capac-ity, C (mega-watts)	Aver-age time to fail-ure, T_U (days)	Aver-age time to repair, T_D (days)	Fail-ure rate, λ_U (per day)	Repair rate, λ_D (per day)	Avail-ability, P_U	Forced outage rate, P_D
40	100	2	0.01	0.5	0.9804	0.0196
60	100	2	0.01	0.5	0.9804	0.0196

Next consider the the operation of two generators in parallel. In this example, to clarify the presentation, numbers are assigned to the two generators as given in the first three columns of table A.1. The state-space diagram for the system consisting of four states is shown in figure A.2. The diagram indicates a limitation of the model. During any small interval of time Δt, only one unit is allowed to change state. For example, when one unit fails or is repaired, the other unit cannot simultaneously fail or be repaired, thus forbidding direct transitions between the 0- and 100-megawatt states, as well as between the 40- and 60-megawatt states.

On the basis of equations (A.7) to (A.10), the numbers in columns 4 to 7 of table A.1 may be computed. Next it is possible to deduce the characteristics of the four system states. For example, the availability or probability of the 0-megawatt state is equal to the probability of both generators being unavailable. Assuming the independence of the failure of the two units and using equation (A.2) yields the availability of the zero capacity state:[3]

$$P_0 = P(40 \text{ megawatt down}) \times P(60 \text{ megawatt down})$$

$$= 0.0196 \times 0.0196$$

$$= 0.00038.$$

3. If the failure of one generation affects the other, then the analysis becomes more complicated, typically involving conditional probabilities. A further complication can arise if common mode failures occur, that is, the simultaneous failure of two or more components which are not consequences of one another, but

Figure A.2. *State-Space Diagram of Two Generators in Parallel*

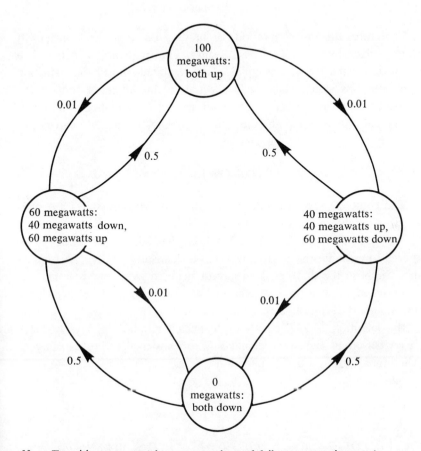

Note: Transition rates are shown as numbers of failures or repairs per day.

As depicted in figure A.2, the total departure rate out of the zero capacity state is equal to the rate of departure to the 40-megawatt state plus the rate of departure to the 60-megawatt state, where equation (A.1) has been used, since these two transitions are mutually exclusive. This result may be written:

which result from a common cause. See, for example, R. N. Allan, E. N. Dialynas, and I. R. Homer, "Modelling Common Mode Failures in the Reliability Evaluation of Power System Networks," *Proceedings of the IEEE Power Engineering Society Winter Meeting, New York, 1979,* paper no. A79040-7.

$$\lambda_0 = 0.5 + 0.5$$

$$= 1.0 \text{ per day.}$$

Therefore, the mean duration, or holding time, in the 0 megawatt state is given by $T_0 = 1/\lambda_0 = 1.0$ days. The frequency of occurrence of the zero capacity state is equal to the weighted sum of the transition rates into this state, which is also equal to the weighted sum of the transition rates out of the 0 megawatt state. (See equation (A.5) and subsequent discussion.) Therefore, the frequency of the zero capacity is given by:

$$F_0 = P_0 \cdot \lambda_0 = 0.00038 \times 1.0 = 0.00038 \text{ per day.}$$

The complete sets of results for all the four Markov states are summarized in table A.2.

Now that the capacity model has been defined, a load model is required to estimate the well-known loss-of-load-probability (LOLP) index. Suppose the daily peak megawatt demand over one year may be represented by a normal distribution with a mean, $\mu = 6$ megawatts, and standard deviation, $\sigma = 10$ megawatts.

By definition, LOLP equals the expected number of days within a given period of time that demand D exceeds availability capacity C. Therefore, during a one-year period:

$$LOLP = 365 \times P(D > C)$$

that is,

$$(A.11) \quad LOLP = 365 \times [P(D > 0) \cdot P_0 + P(D > 40 \text{ MW}) \cdot P_{40}$$

$$+ P(D > 60 \text{ MW}) \cdot P_{60} + P(D > 100 \text{ MW}) \cdot P_{100}] \, .$$

Table A.2. *Characteristics of the Capacity States*

Capacity state, C_i (megawatt)	Avail- ability, P_i	Duration, T_i (days)	Frequency, F_i (per day)
0	0.0004	1.0	0.0004
40	0.0192	1.96	0.0098
60	0.0192	1.96	0.0098
100	0.9612	50.0	0.0192

For a normal distribution:

$$P(D > L) = 1 - (1/\sqrt{2\pi}) \cdot \int_{-\infty}^{(L-\mu)/\sigma} [\exp (-l^2/2)] \cdot dl .$$

These values may be read off a standard statistical table.[4] The four critical values of $(L - \mu)/\sigma$, occurring at $L = 0, 40, 60$, and 100, are: $-6, -2, 0$, and 4.

Evaluation of equation (A.11) yields:

$$LOLP = 365 \times [(1.0 \times 0.0004) + (0.9772 \times 0.0192)$$
$$+ (0.5 \times 0.0192) + (0 \times 0.9612)]$$
$$= 365 \times 0.0288 = 10.5 \text{ days per year.}$$

Therefore, the LOLP is equivalent to 10.5 days per year, which may be interpreted to mean that over a long period, the load is likely to exceed available capacity 10.5 days per year, on the average.

This section concludes with a brief summary of the generalized case. If there are n generators, then there will be a total of 2^n possible combined Markov states. At a more sophisticated level, it is possible to consider multilevel deratings of generators as well, instead of only the simplified up and down states. At any given moment, it is important to know which of the 2^n states have sufficient capacity to meet a given stochastic load, and which do not. The frequency of encountering a capacity deficit state, the duration of such a state, and the magnitude of the deficit are also quantities to be estimated.[5]

The complete Markov process can be described in terms of the fol-

4. Richard S. Burington, *Handbook of Mathematical Tables and Formulas*, fifth edition (New York: McGraw-Hill, 1973), chapter 22 and table 18.

5. Because of the complexity of the calculation, certain simplifying assumptions are usually made. See for example, J. D. Hall, R. J. Ringlee, and A. J. Wood, "Frequency and Duration Methods for Power System Reliability Calculations: Part I—Generation System Model," *IEEE Transactions on Power Apparatus and Systems*, vol. PAS-87 (Sept. 1968), pp. 1787–96; and R. J. Ringlee and A. J. Wood, "Frequency and Duration Methods for Power System Reliability Calculations: Part II—Demand Model and Capacity Reserve Model," *IEEE Transactions on Power Apparatus and Systems*, vol. PAS-88 (April 1969), pp. 375–88. A recent and more rapid Fourier method for calculating the probability density function of capacity shortages, which leads to the estimation of LOLP, is presented in N. S. Rau and Karl F. Schenk, "Application of Fourier Methods for the Evaluation of Capacity Outage Probabilities," *Proceedings of the IEEE Power Engineering Society Winter Meeting, New York, 1979*, paper no. A79103-3.

lowing set of first-order linear differential equations,[6] which are analogous to the one from which equation (A.5) was derived:

$$dP(t)/dt = \underset{\sim}{M} \cdot P(t)$$

where $P(t)$ is a vector of the instantaneous state probabilities, and $\underset{\sim}{M}$ is the state transition matrix, which gives the transition rates between all possible pairs of states.

Monte Carlo Simulation

In the Monte Carlo method, a gaming model of the power system is set up and simulated to determine system performance.[7] The range of application of these models has been discussed in chapter 2, Introduction to Reliability. A simplified version of one type of Monte Carlo simulation of a model of a generation system is described below, to illustrate the use of the Monte Carlo technique in long-run reliability evaluation.

A capacity model may be basically set up along the lines of the sequential simulation approach, with the up and down states of individual represented by randomly drawn numbers, for example, using a random number generating computer subroutine. As an example, consider the 40-megawatt generator described in the previous section on Markov processes, which has average times to failure and repair of 100 and 2 days, respectively.

Given that the machine is up, or available on a particular day, its subsequent state is determined by selecting a random number from the discrete set of integers:

$$U = \{1, 2, - - - - - - -, 99, 100\}.$$

The incidence of failure is associated with one of these integers, say 50. Therefore, if the number 50 is drawn, the generator is deemed to be down on the following day. If any other integer is selected, the machine would be still available.

---

6. See Harvey M. Wagner, *Principles of Operations Research*, second edition (Englewood Cliffs, New Jersey: Prentice-Hall, 1975), chap. 18.

7. See P. L. Noferi, L. Paris, and L. Salvaderi, "Monte Carlo Methods for Power System Reliability Evaluation in Transmission and Generation Planning," *Proceedings of the Annual Reliability and Maintainability Symposiums, Washington, D.C., January 1975*, pp. 460–69.

Similarly, given that the generating unit has failed and is already in the down condition, its state on the next day is determined by the integer set:

$$D = \{1, 2\}.$$

If a random selection from the set D yields the number 1, repairs are assumed to be complete, and the machine would be up; if the integer 2 is selected, the generator would continue in the down state for another day.

It is intuitively clear in the above model that if the machine is available on a given day, the probability of its failing on the next day is 0.01. If the unit is already down, however, the probability of its being up on the following day is 0.5. It can be shown rigorously that this process of random number selection will converge in the long run to yield the desired average times to failure and repair: that is, 100 and 2 days, respectively. The larger the number of such simulations, the more accurately the model represents the state of the machine.

The state of the complete system may be built up by simulating the condition of many interconnected components, including generators, transmission lines, and so on. This procedure gives rise to many possible system states, however, each of which requires several simulations for greater accuracy of the long-run results. Therefore the Monte Carlo approach tends to be relatively time consuming. The random number representation of component behavior could be modified to include the effects of the state of one component on the condition of another distinct but related item of equipment: that is, the states of different components do not necessarily have to be mutually independent.

A typical load may be represented during a given period by a simple probabilistic model of the type also described in the previous section; peak megawatt demand on a particular day of the year might be specified by a normal distribution having a given mean and standard deviation.

The relevant properties of the various capacity states, such as the availability, frequency, and duration (described in the previous section on Markov processes), may be determined through simulation. Reliability indexes can be estimated by comparing these characteristics with the results obtained from the load model. Thus, for example, the *LOLP* of the system may be calculated on the basis of the number of days in which the available supply, as determined by the random model of capacity, is insufficient to meet the demand, which is established by randomly drawing a value from the normally distributed load.

Appendix B

~~~~~~

Shadow Pricing Concepts

Conversion Factors

The conversion factor for a given commodity is the ratio of its border price, in units of the chosen foreign exchange numeraire, to its domestic price. The general case of an electric power sector input is considered below. The input from this sector is also consumed by nonpower sector users and supplied through imports as well as through domestic production.

In figure B.1, WS and DS are the world and domestic supply curves, while $TS = WS + DS$ constitutes the total supply curve. DD is the domestic demand curve of nonpower sector users, and TD is the total domestic demand when the requirements of the power sector PD are included. The effect of the increased demand PD is to drive up the domestic market price of the input from P to $P + \Delta P$; the corresponding world market c.i.f. (import) prices are smaller by a factor $1/(1 + t_m)$, where t_m is the rate of import duty on the input. Without the power sector demand, the level of consumption (from nonpower sector users only) would be $Q = D$, of which M would be supplied through imports and

Note: The framework presented in Lyn Squire and Herman G. van der Tak, is used. (For citation, see footnote 2, this appendix.)

Figure B.1. *Conversion Factor for an Importable Commodity*

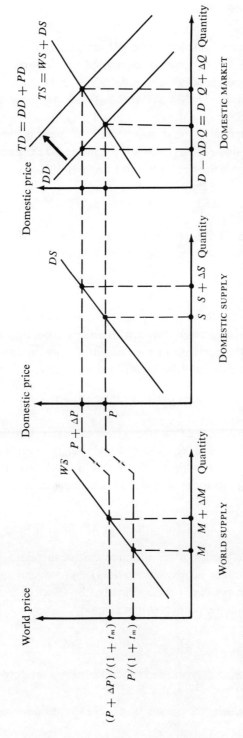

Note: WS = world supply; DS = domestic supply; TS = total supply; DD = domestic demand of nonpower sector users; TD = total domestic demand when the requirements of the power sector PD are included; and t_m = rate of import duty on input.

211

S from domestic production. With PD included, the total domestic consumption is $Q + \Delta Q$, which is composed of nonpower sector demand $D - \Delta D$ and power sector demand $(\Delta Q + \Delta D)$. In this situation, the respective quantities $M + \Delta M$ and $S + \Delta S$ are imported and domestically supplied.[1]

Next, the marginal social cost (MSC) of meeting the power sector demand is considered. First, there is the increased expenditure of foreign exchange, in border prices, for extra imports:

$$\Delta FX = M \cdot \Delta P \cdot (1 + e_w)/(1 + t_m)$$

where $e_w = P\Delta \cdot M/M \cdot \Delta P$ is the price elasticity of world supply. Second, consider the increased resource cost of additional domestic supply:

$$\Delta RC = f \cdot (S \cdot \Delta P \cdot e_d)$$

where $e_d = P \cdot \Delta S/S \cdot \Delta P$ is the price elasticity of domestic supply, and f is the factor that converts the cost of supply from domestic to border price. Third, the decrease in the benefit of consumption of nonpower sector consumers should be considered as a cost:

$$\Delta BD = w_c \cdot (D \cdot \Delta P \cdot n_d)$$

where $n_d = P \cdot \Delta D/D \cdot \Delta P$ is the relevant price elasticity of demand (absolute value), and w_c is the social weight attached to domestic consumption at the relevant consumption level. Fourth, there is the effect resulting from the increase in the income of nonpower sector consumers:

$$\Delta I_c = (b_c - w_c) \cdot [D \cdot \Delta P \cdot (n_d - 1)]$$

where b_c is the border priced resource cost of increasing domestic consumption (of other goods and services) by one unit, and once again w_c is the corresponding benefit. Finally, the effect of increased income accruing to domestic producers is evaluated:

$$\Delta I_p = (b_p - w_p) \cdot (S \cdot \Delta P)$$

where b_p and w_p represent the border-priced resource cost and marginal

---

1. For convenience, the formula is developed in the increments ΔP, ΔQ, and so on.

social benefit (MSB), respectively, of a one-unit increase in the income of the producers.

The total cost of the input to the power sector, in border prices is:

$$\Delta BP = \Delta FX + \Delta RC + \Delta BD + \Delta I_c + \Delta I_p.$$

The corresponding cost of the input in domestic prices is:

$$\Delta DP = P \cdot (\Delta D + \Delta Q) = \Delta P \cdot (D \cdot n_d + S \cdot e_d + M \cdot e_w).$$

Therefore, the expression for the conversion factor may be written:

$$CF_M = \frac{\Delta BP}{\Delta DP}$$

$$= \frac{M[(1 + e_w)/(1 + t_m)] + S(f \cdot e_d + b_p - w_p) + D(b_c \cdot n_d + w_c - b_c)}{M \cdot e_w + S \cdot e_d + D \cdot n_d}.$$

Often, this expression may be considerably simplified for specific situations.

Tradable
Case I. Small country assumption: that is, $e_w \rightarrow \infty$. Therefore:

$$CF_M = \frac{1}{1 + t_m}.$$

Nontradable
Case IIa. No imports and perfectly elastic supply: that is, $M = 0$ (thus $S = D$) and $e_d \rightarrow \infty$,   or

Case IIb. No imports, perfectly inelastic demand, and no income effects: that is $M = 0$, $n_d = 0$, $w_p = b_p$, and $w_c = b_c$. Therefore:

$$CF_2 = f.$$

Case IIIa. No imports and perfectly elastic demand: that is, $M = 0$, $n_d \rightarrow \infty$, or

Case IIIb. No imports, perfectly inelastic supply, and no income effects: that is, $M = 0$, $e_d = 0$, $w_p = b_p$, and $w_c = b_c$. Therefore,

$$CF_3 = b_c.$$

The conversion factor for an electric power sector input that is domestically produced for export as well as for nonpower sector domestic consumption may be derived analogously:

$$CF_x = \frac{X[(n_w - 1)/(1 - t_x)] + S(f \cdot e_d + b_p - w_p) + D(b_c \cdot n_d + w_c - b_c)}{X \cdot n_w + S \cdot e_d + D \cdot n_d}$$

where X represents exports, t_x is the tax rate on exports, n_x is the price elasticity of world demand, and the other symbols are as defined earlier.

Income Effects

If the income of a particular group of consumers is increased by one unit (in domestic prices), the social value of this change in units of the numeraire is $(w - b)$. The interpretation of b and w is discussed below.

The MSC to the economy is represented by b, resulting from the use of the increased income. For example, if all the new income is consumed, then b is the revelant consumption conversion factor or resource cost (in units of the numeraire) of making available to consumers one unit worth (in domestic prices) of the marginal basket of goods they would purchase. In this case, $b = \sum_i g_i \cdot CF_i$, where g_i is the proportion of the ith good in the marginal basket, and CF_i is the appropriate conversion factor.

The corresponding MSB of increased consumption may be broken down further: $w = d/v$; where $1/v$ is the value (in units of the numeraire) of a one-unit increase in domestic-priced consumption accruing to someone at the average level of consumption c. Therefore, v may be roughly thought of as the premium attached to public savings, compared with "average" private consumption. Under certain simplifying assumptions, $b = 1/v$.[2] If $MU(c)$ denotes the marginal utility of consumption at some level c, then $d = MU(c)/MU(c)$. Assuming that the marginal

---

2. If the marginal product of capital equals the consumption rate of interest (See Lyn Squire and Herman van der Tak, *Economic Analysis of Projects* [Baltimore: Johns Hopkins University Press for the World Bank, 1975], p. 68.)

utility of consumption is diminishing, d would be greater than unity for "poor" consumers with $c < \bar{c}$, and would be less than unity for "rich" consumers with $c > \bar{c}$. Two specific values of w are particularly important. First, the level of consumption for which $w = 1$ is called the critical consumption level (CCL). At the CCL the marginal value of domestic priced private consumption is equal to the value of the numeraire. Second, when $w = b$, the income effects cancel out, and social prices become equal to efficiency prices.

As an example, consider the case of the outage costs of residential consumers in the Cascavel case study, which could be treated like foregone income-consumption. In the shadow-pricing analysis conducted in chapter 14, the numeraire was chosen for convenience to be the domestic priced cruzeiro (Cr$). Therefore, it was possible to make the simplifying assumptions that $b = 1$ and $1/v = 1$.

Suppose that OC was the outage cost (in domestic prices) incurred by a household at the consumption level c, which resulted in an equivalent loss of welfare in units of the domestic-priced numeraire. The effect of the income distributional considerations was to introduce an additional correcting factor $OC \cdot (w - b)$, so that the outage cost or negative benefit, measured in social prices, may be written:

$$OC_s = OC \cdot b + OC(w - b) = OC \cdot d.$$

The simplest form of marginal utility function that could be assumed was: $MU(c) = c^{-n}$. Therefore:

$$d = MU(c)/MU(\bar{c}) = (\bar{c}/c)^n.$$

The additional assumption that the distribution parameter $n = 1$ gave:

$$d = \bar{c}/c = \bar{i}/i$$

where $\bar{i}/i$ is the ratio of net incomes that was used as a proxy for the consumption ratio. The appropriate weights were obtained by substituting for $\bar{i}$, the average net income of all households in Cascavel (Cr\$67.7

Income group	Lower	Lower-middle	Upper-middle	Upper
d	3.679	1.419	0.694	0.296

$\times$ 10^3 per year, in 1976), and the corresponding values of i for the various income groups from table 11.1 of chapter 11.

Because all incomes were assumed to increase uniformly at 4 percent every year, while the income structure of the population remained the same, the social weights d were constant over time. Therefore, in the social pricing exercise, all domestically priced outage costs were weighted by the factors d, relevant to the income groups under consideration.

Appendix C

Load Forecasting and Distribution Primary Models

Land Use and Distribution of Population

The load forecast modeling process began by examining maps showing future land use plans and detailed zoning regulations for Cascavel, Brazil. (See figures 10.1 and 10.2 in chapter 10.)

The first part of the Cascavel zoning regulations set out the permitted uses of land for each zoning classification. For example, the ZR1 zone is predominately residential but may also be used for clinics, restaurants, schools, and so on. The second segment of the zoning regulations defines the ratios of buildings to land, the ratios of floor area to land area, and the minimum lot sizes.

The next stage in the development of the model was the division of the area into 0.25-square-kilometer geographic cells as illustrated in figure 10.2 of chapter 10. The fractional area of each cell allocated to the various types of zones was measured and entered into a first-stage data base. Then it was necessary to determine the allocation of consumers, saturation factors, energy usage, load factors, and the time when currently unoccupied outer geographic cells would come into service, as described below.

Allocation of Residential Consumers

For each of the study years, the previously estimated population by income class (see chapter 10, Demand Forecast) was allocated among the various residential areas in the following manner.

First, each class of land was divided into a reasonable mixture of single family, multiple family, commercial, and industrial areas within the restrictions of the zoning regulations, as summarized in table C.1.

Second, the available land for residential use in the above table was then divided among the income levels as shown in table C.2.

Third, reasonable ratios of floor area to land area were determined for multiple family dwellings. These ratios reflected the amount of land occupied by the building and the height of the building or number of floors. For example, the ZR2 zoning regulations permitted two-thirds of the land to be occupied, and the maximum ratio of floor area to land area was 2. By 1996 it was estimated that two-thirds of ZR2 land would be occupied by single-story buildings and one-third by two-story buildings. Therefore the overall ratio of floor to land area would be:

$$\text{Ratio} = (2/3 \times 2/3) + (1/3 \times 4/3) = 0.9.$$

Table C.1. *Land Use, by Zone*

| Type of zone | Percentage of available land allocated to | | | | | | |
| | Residential use | | Commercial use | | | Industrial use | |
	Single family	Multiple family	Light	Medium	Heavy	Service	Main
ZR1	65	20	15	—	—	—	—
ZR2	70	15	15	—	—	—	—
ZR3	90	—	10	—	—	—	—
ZCR	—	80	—	—	20	—	—
SCR	—	80	—	20	—	—	—
ZC	—	—	—	—	100	—	—
SC	—	40	—	60	—	—	—
SL	—	40	—	60	—	—	—
ZI	—	—	—	—	—	—	100
SI	30	—	—	—	—	70	—

The ratios for other zones were determined in a similar manner, as shown in table C.3.

Fourth, the city was divided into the three saturation regions shown in figure 10.2 of chapter 10. For each region, a saturation factor, defined as the ratio of actual to the maximum population allowed by the zoning regulations was determined (see table C.4) to account for the total forecast population, by income class and in any given year (see table 10.1 of chapter 10).

Fifth, data were obtained from COPEL regarding recent trends in lot sizes and apartment floor areas, as summarized in table C.5.

Finally, the number of dwelling units (DU) per cell was determined by income class on the basis of the following expression.

$$DU = (LA \times FAL \times FIC \times LM \times SF)/DA$$

Table C.2. *Allocation of Residential Land, by Income Class*

| Dwelling type | Zone | Income class (percentage) | | | |
		Lower	Lower-middle	Upper-middle	Upper
Single family	ZR1	—	20	50	30
	ZR2	10	50	35	5
	ZR3	70	20	10	—
	SI	70	20	10	—
Multiple family	ZR1	—	20	50	30
	ZR2	10	50	35	5
	SCR	—	60	30	10
	SC	10	40	40	10
	SL	10	40	40	10
	ZCR	—	35	40	25

Table C.3. *Ratio of Floor Area to Land Area*

Zone	Ratio	Zone	Ratio
ZR2	0.9	SC	2.0
ZR1	1.0	SL	2.0
SCR	2.0	ZRC	3.0

Table C.4. *1996 Saturation Factors, by Saturation Region*
(percentage)

| | Saturation factor | | |
Consumer category	Region 1	Region 2	Region 3
Residential			
Lower	73.6	67.2	50.4
Lower-middle	86.1	77.7	58.3
Upper-middle	90.7	82.8	62.1
Upper	92.0	84.0	63.0
Commercial and public illumination	85.6	77.9	58.5

Table C.5. *Average Residential Lot Size and Apartment Floor Area,*
by Income Class

| | Average area (square meters) | |
Income class	Single family lot	Apartment[a]
Lower	400	100
Lower-middle	500	150
Upper-middle	750	225
Upper	1,000	300

a. Includes allowances for common entry ways, stairs, elevators, and halls.

where: LA = residential land area; FAL = fraction of land allocated to single or multiple families (see table C.1); FIC = fraction of land allocated to a given income class (see table B.2); LM = ratio of floor area to land area (see table C.3); SF = saturation factor by region and income class (see table C.4); and DA = average area of dwelling unit by income class (see table C.5).

For example, the number of apartments for upper middle-income families in a given cell in the first saturation region, which contained 100,000 square meters of ZCR land, would be determined as follows:

$$LA = 85 \text{ percent of } 100,000 = 85,000 \text{ square meters}$$

where 15 percent of land has been set aside for streets, sidewalks, and so on; FAL = 80 percent; FIC = 40 percent; LM = 3.0; SF = 90.7 percent; DA = 225 square meters; therefore:

$$DU = (85000 \times 0.8 \times 0.4 \times 3.0 \times 0.907)/225$$

$$= 74011/225$$

$$= 329 \text{ apartments}$$

The total energy and power requirements by income class, by cell, and by year were calculated as the product of the numbers of households by income class, by cell, and by year as determined above, and the corresponding energy and power consumption for each household. (See chapter 10, Demand Forecast.)

The commercial and street lighting load forecasts are described in detail in the following sections, because they were linked closely to the pattern of land use. The other categories of consumption have already been dealt with at length in chapter 10, Demand Forecast.

Commercial Requirements

The commercial sector was divided into three basic types. Light commercial (LC) was confined to residential areas and consisted of such enterprises as shops and professional offices. Medium commercial (SC and SL zones), also referred to as strip commercial, was found along the main streets. Typical strip businesses included supermarkets, motels, restaurants, clinics, offices, and hardware-dry goods stores. Heavy commercial (ZC zone) was concentrated in the center of the city and consisted of high-rise offices, department stores, hotels, and government offices.

The electrical requirements for the three commercial zones were based on the following factors.

(a) The zoned land was divided to reflect multiple usage, as table C.1 indicates.

(b) Saturation factors were determined as the average of the four residential saturation factors in each region (see table C.4), based on the premise that the volume of commercial activity would be directly proportional to population levels.

(c) A reasonable ratio was determined between building area and land area for each type of zone, based on zoning regulations, availability of land, current building trends, and the relation between population and commercial requirements; the selected values are shown in table C.6.

(d) A survey, made to determine the relation between building areas and energy requirements, indicated that large businesses used about 45 kilowatt-hours/square meter/year, small businesses used about 15 kilowatt-hours/square meter/year, and the average was 38.6 kilowatt-hours/square meter/year (table C.7). These figures were used to develop energy requirements for different types of business users, as shown in table C.6.

(e) Load factors for various types of businesses obtained from COPEL billing data. These factors varied from 25 percent for small businesses to 35 percent for large ones, as shown in table C.6.

Street Lighting Requirements

Street lighting electrical requirements were based on the types of streets in Cascavel, COPEL's street lighting standards, and the mixture of streets used in the various zones.

The five types of streets in Cascavel were the following:

(a) Express: for heavy commercial areas
(b) Important: arteries for multifamily residential, medium-commercial, and industrial areas
(c) Main: connector streets for residential, medium-commercial, and industrial areas
(d) Normal: for urban residential areas
(e) Secondary: for fringe urban residential areas

Table C.6. *Commercial Load Forecast Parameters*

Commercial class	Ratio of building to land	Energy consumption density (kilowatt-hours/ year/ square meter)	Annual load factor (percentage)
LC	0.60	15.0	25.0
SL	2.00	15.0	30.0
SC	1.00	35.0	32.5
ZC	2.00	35.0	35.0

For each type of street, COPEL supplies a standard grouping of sodium or mercury vapor lamps as shown in table C.8.

The mixture of streets required to serve the transport needs of the occupants of each zone and the resultant electrical requirements, in kilowatt-hours/square meter/year, are shown in table C.9.

The total street lighting energy requirements for a particular type of land use was computed from the following equation:

$$\text{Energy (kilowatt-hours/year)} = (0.15\, LND) \times SAT \times EN$$

where LND = land area in square meters devoted to the given type of land use, of which 15 percent is assumed to be allocated to streets; SAT = saturation factor same as for commercial load (see table C.8);

Table C.7. *Summary of the Survey of Commercial Consumers*

Type of business	Floor area (square meters)	Annual energy consumption (kilowatt-hours)	Energy consumption density (kilowatt-hours/year/ square meter)
Large			
Appliances and furniture 1	1,870	83,116	44.1
Appliances and furniture 2	600	24,623	41.0
Appliances and furniture 3	1,885	79,630	42.2
Variety and dry goods	850	42,330	49.8
Supermarket	1,560	141,880	90.9
Dry goods and fabrics	1,200	27,860	23.2
Medium and small			
Furniture	600	10,075	16.8
Shoe store	200	5,035	25.2
Dry goods	350	5,360	15.3
Hardware	500	6,660	13.3
Small appliances	115	2,690	23.4
Groceries	500	26,910	53.8
Other			
Bank	1,800	16,930	9.4
Hotel	1,000	28,715	28.7
Newspaper	700	29,125	41.6
Total	13,720	529,938	38.6

Table C.8. *Standard Street Types and Lighting Characteristics*

Type of street	Street width (meters)	Lighting standards[a]	Lamps/ kilo- meter[b]	Kilo- watts/ kilo- meter[c]	Kilo- watts/ square meter[d]	Kilo- watt- hours/ square meter/ year[e]
Express	30	Two 400 watt sv/15m	133	53.2	0.00177	6.46
Impor- tant	25	One 700 watt mv/20m	50	35.0	0.00145	5.29
Main	20	One 400 watt mv/25m	40	16.0	0.00080	2.92
Normal	17.5	One 250 watt mv/25m	40	10.0	0.00057	2.08
Second- ary	15	One 125 watt mv/25m	40	5.0	0.00033	1.22

a. Two 400 watt sv/15 m = two 400-watt sodium vapor lamps every 15 meters; mv = mercury vapor lamps, and so on.

b. Lamps/kilometer = (number of lamps/n meters) $\times$ (1,000/n).

c. Kilowatts/kilometer = (lamps/kilometer) $\times$ (kilowatts/lamp).

d. Kilowatts/square meter = (kilowatts/kilometer) $\times$ (street width in kilometers).

e. Kilowatt-hours/year/square meter = (kilowatts/square meter) $\times$ (3,650 hours), assuming that the lamp will be switched on ten hours a night.

and EN = street lighting energy requirements in kilowatt-hours/square meter/year, for the given type of land use (see table C.9).

Street lighting power demands are derived from the equation:

Demand (kilowatts) = Energy (kilowatt-hours/year)/3,650 (hours of use a year)

For example, street lighting requirements for 100,000 square meters of ZCR in saturation region 1 would be given by:

$$\text{Energy} = (.15 \times 100,000) \times .856 \times 3.62$$
$$= 46480 \text{ kilowatt-hours/year}$$
$$\text{Demand} = 46480/3650 = 12.7 \text{ kilowatts}$$

Land Use and Load Forecast

By 1996, Cascavel will encompass many geographic cells which presently consist of vacant land. The time schedule shown in figure C.1 was

Table C.9. *Allocation of Streets
and Street Lighting Energy Requirements*

Type of land use	Zone	Ex-press	Impor-tant	Main	Nor-mal	Sec-ondary	Kilo-watt-hours/year/square meter
			Allocation (percentage)				
Single	ZR1	—	—	—	100	—	2.08
Family	ZR2	—	—	—	100	—	2.08
Residen-							
tial	ZR3	—	—	—	—	100	1.22
	SI	—	100	—	—	—	5.29
Multiple	ZR2	—	—	—	100	—	2.08
Family	ZR1	—	—	—	100	—	2.08
Residen-							
tial	SCR	—	30	40	30	—	3.38
	SC	—	30	40	30	—	3.38
	SL	—	40	60	—	—	3.87
	ZCR	—	40	30	30	—	3.62
Commer-							
cial	LC	—	—	—	100	—	2.08
	SC	—	30	40	30	—	3.38
	SL	—	40	60	—	—	3.87
	ZC	60	20	20	—	—	5.52
Industrial	SI	—	100	—	—	—	5.29
	ZI	—	40	30	30	—	3.62

developed for serving the cells currently without power, based on discussions with the city authorities and COPEL regarding the expansion of municipal services (roads, water, sewerage, and so on) and the availability of power supply. Currently served geographic cells are shown with a 1976 date, whereas the dates that electricity services will begin are indicated for the other cells.

Finally, land use and electrical loads were forecast, by consumer category and by cell, for the years 1980, 1984, 1988, 1992, and 1996, using a computerized model that implemented the methodology described above.

The residential forecast is summarized in table C.10, and the commercial industrial, public lighting, and special institutions forecasts are summarized in table C.11.

Figure C.1. *Cell Initializing Schedule for Load Forecast, by Cell*

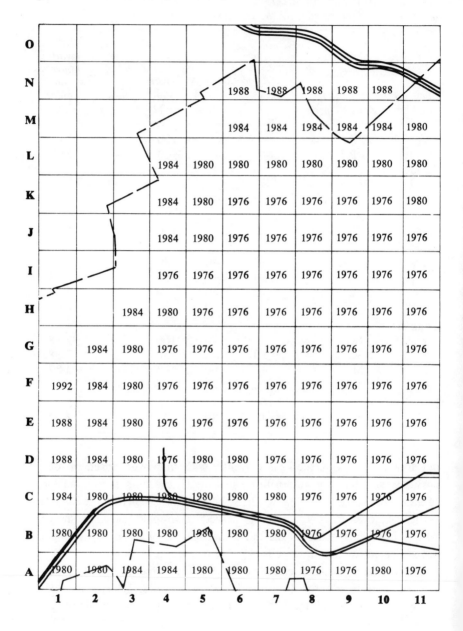

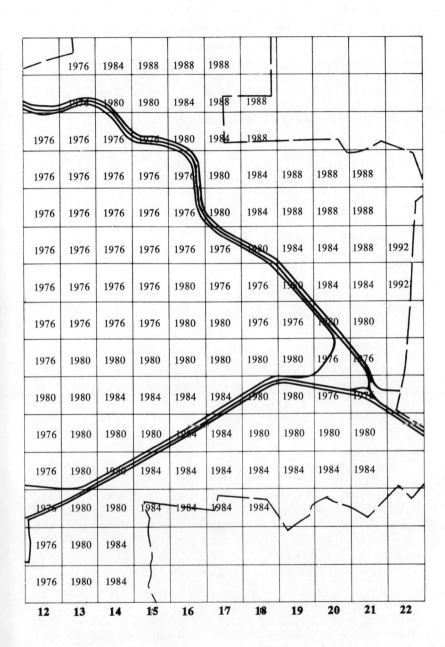

The 1976 Cascavel service area, the 1976 kilowatt demand by cell, and the 1976 load densities are shown in figures C.2, C.3, and C.4, respectively. For comparison, the corresponding set of diagrams for 1996 are shown in figures C.5, C.6, and C.7.

Table C.10. *Summary of the Residential Forecast*

| | | | Income class | | |
Items	Total	Upper	Upper-middle	Lower-middle	Lower
Land use					
(× 10³					
square meters)					
1976	14,840				
1980	23,134				
1984	27,471				
1988	29,321				
1992	29,330				
1996	29,336				
Dwelling units					
1976	10,236	1,333	3,591	4,478	834
1980	19,989	2,267	6,516	8,936	2,270
1984	32,597	3,327	10,108	14,994	4,168
1988	45,888	4,465	14,290	21,319	5,813
1992	61,426	5,492	18,524	27,804	9,605
1996	72,944	6,371	21,561	32,316	12,697
Energy requirements (megawatt-hours)					
1976	14,045	4,377	5,858	3,556	256
1980	28,917	7,978	11,990	8,132	817
1984	51,018	12,508	20,824	15,893	1,792
1988	79,752	18,040	33,010	25,796	2,907
1992	115,897	24,167	47,792	38,370	5,571
1996	152,052	30,732	61,837	50,801	8,685
Demand (kilowatts)					
1976	4,281	1,249	1,783	1,160	90
1980	8,866	2,277	3,650	2,652	287
1984	15,722	3,570	6,339	5,184	629
1988	24,632	5,148	10,049	8,413	1,021
1992	35,917	6,897	14,548	12,515	1,957
1996	47,214	8,771	18,824	16,569	3,051

Distribution Primary Model

The distribution primary model (DPM) that was used in the planning, design, and operation of the Cascavel distribution system consisted of a data base and a group of modular programs for data entry, data editing, and system analysis (see figure C.8).

The modeling process began with the division of the primary feeders (or circuits) into nodes and sections. Nodes are points on a circuit such as branches, changes in conductor size or number of phases, location of major loads, and so on. Sections are the lines between the nodes. Numbers were then assigned to the nodes and sections. Figure C.9

Table C.11. *Summary of the Forecast: Commercial, Industrial, Public Lighting, Special Institutions, and No Load Forecast*

Items	Com-mer-cial	Indus-trial	Public light-ing	Special institu-tion	No load
Land use					
(× 10³					
square meters)					
1976	5,282	1,404	3,799	84	3,092
1980	6,669	5,325	6,199	138	6,533
1984	7,312	5,596	7,126	213	10,031
1988	7,561	5,625	7,501	288	12,202
1992	7,565	5,622	7,512	363	12,807
1996	7,557	5,621	7,502	438	12,795
Energy require-ments (mega-watt-hours)					
1976	13,500	22,428	3,001	588	0
1980	28,300	34,946	4,897	976	0
1984	51,399	53,901	7,197	1,446	0
1988	82,799	85,001	9,399	1,918	0
1992	122,500	135,098	11,500	2,361	0
1996	164,472	216,962	13,534	2,750	0
Demand (kilowatts)					
1976	4,855	9,715	820	139	0
1980	10,176	15,675	1,339	233	0
1984	18,481	24,320	1,973	348	0
1988	29,773	38,353	4,241	710	0
1992	44,050	60,958	5,189	871	0
1996	59,149	97,895	3,708	676	0

Figure C.2. *Service Area in 1976*

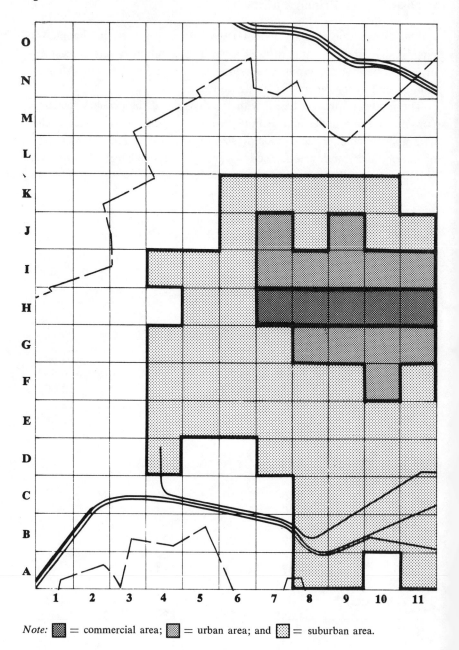

Note: ■ = commercial area; ▨ = urban area; and ▫ = suburban area.

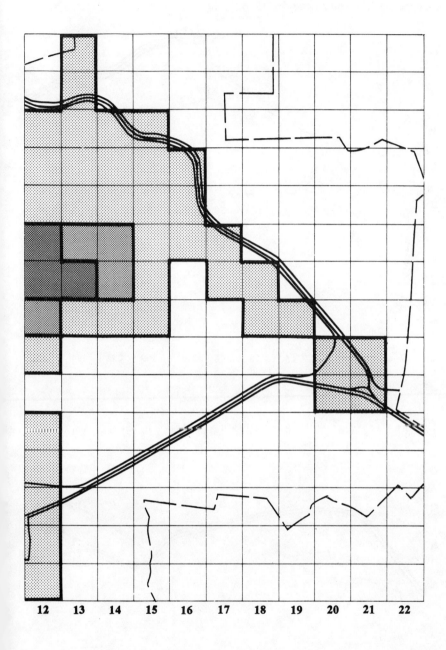

12   13   14   15   16   17   18   19   20   21   22

Figure C.3. *Kilowatt Demand in 1976, by Cell*

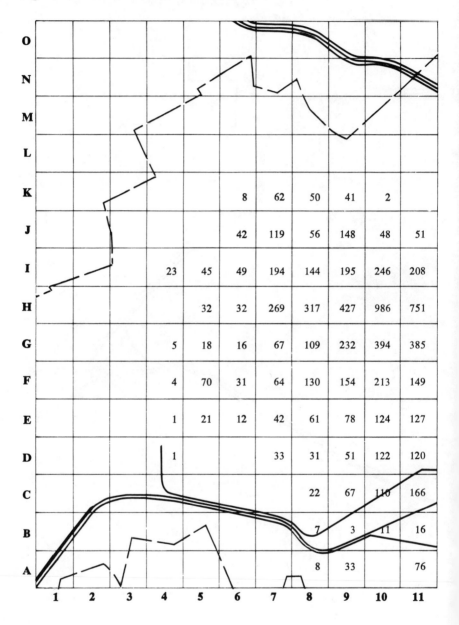

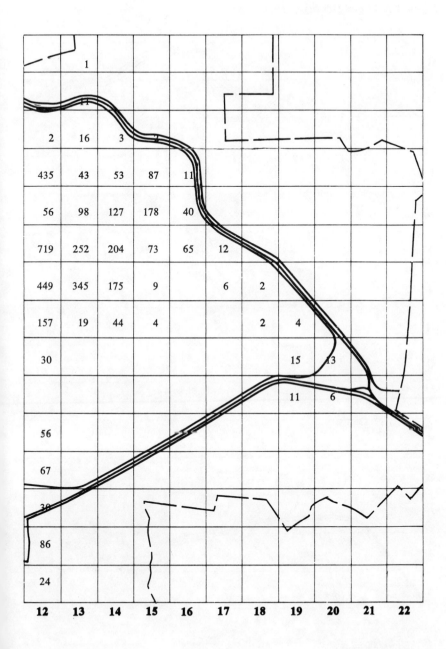

Figure C.4. *Load Density in 1976*

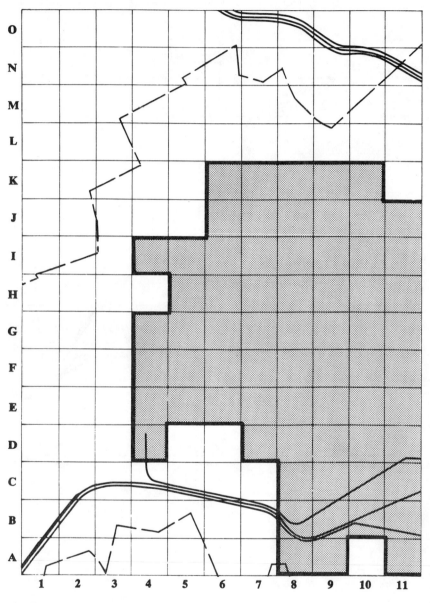

(0 to 1,000 kilowatts)

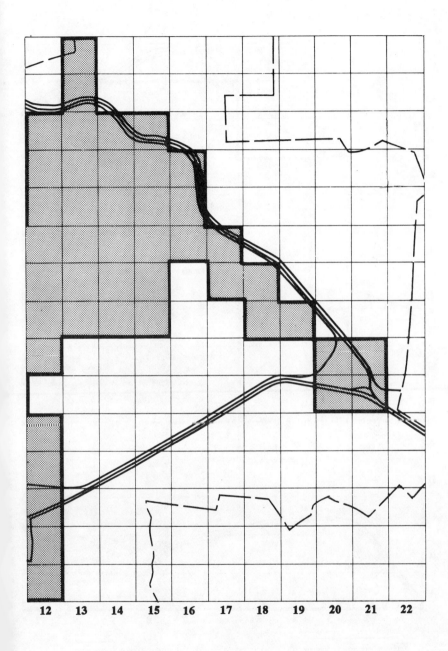

Figure C.5. *Service Area in 1996*

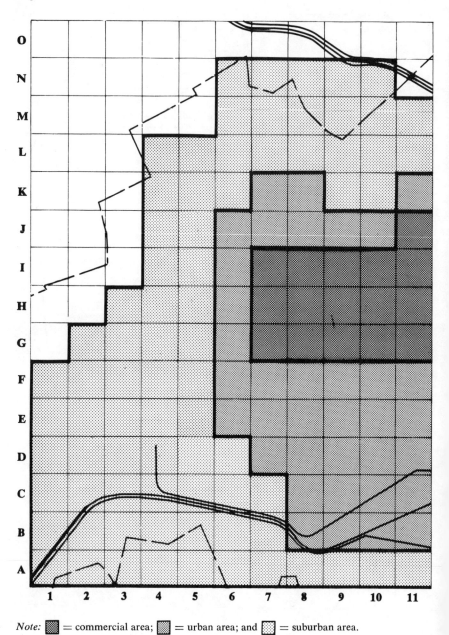

Note: ▓ = commercial area; ▒ = urban area; and ░ = suburban area.

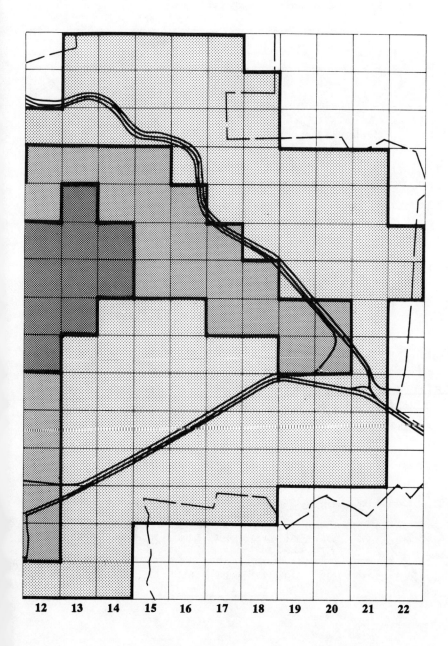

| 12 | 13 | 14 | 15 | 16 | 17 | 18 | 19 | 20 | 21 | 22 |

Figure C.6. *Kilowatt Demand in 1996, by Cell*

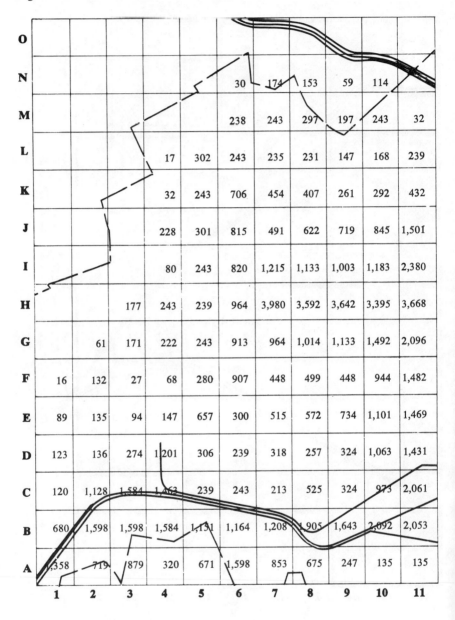

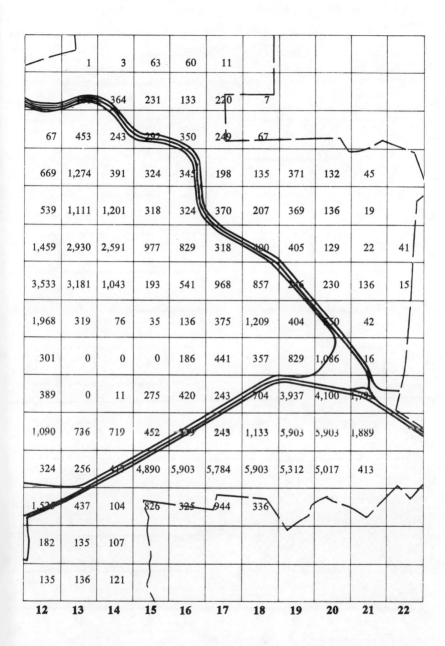

	1	3	63	60	11					
		364	231	133	220	7				
67	453	243		350	249	67				
669	1,274	391	324	345	198	135	371	132	45	
539	1,111	1,201	318	324	370	207	369	136	19	
1,459	2,930	2,591	977	829	318	400	405	129	22	41
3,533	3,181	1,043	193	541	968	857		230	136	15
1,968	319	76	35	136	375	1,209	404	50	42	
301	0	0	0	186	441	357	829	1,086	16	
389	0	11	275	420	243	704	3,937	4,100	1,792	
1,090	736	719	452		243	1,133	5,903	5,903	1,889	
324	256		4,890	5,903	5,784	5,903	5,312	5,017	413	
1,520	437	104	826	325	944	336				
182	135	107								
135	136	121								
12	13	14	15	16	17	18	19	20	21	22

Figure C.7. *Load Densities in 1996*
(kilowatts)

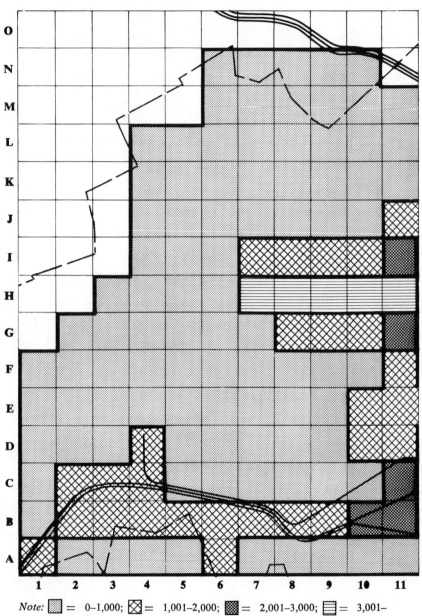

Note: ▨ = 0–1,000; ▧ = 1,001–2,000; ▦ = 2,001–3,000; ▤ = 3,001–
4,000; ▧ = 4,001–5,000; and ▨ = over 5,000 kilowatts.

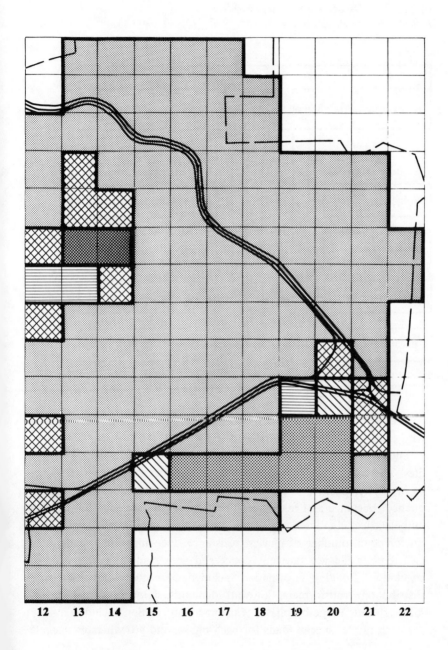

Figure C.8. *Distribution System Model:*
Data Bank and Program Modules

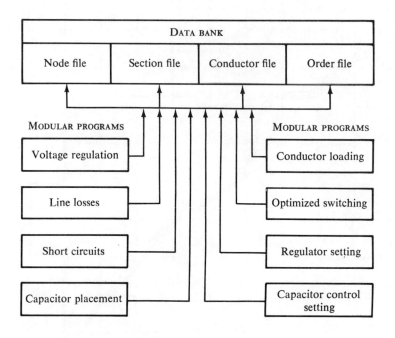

depicts a typical circuit that has been divided into nodes and sections with appropriate numbers assigned.

The data base consisted of conductor, section, node, and order set files. The conductor file contained major conductor characteristics such as ampacity, positive sequence resistance and reactance, and zero sequence resistance and reactance. The section file contained the physical and electrical characteristics of the line sections such as the length, conductor code, number of phases, resistance, reactance, and spacing.

The node file was basically concerned with loading, customers, and regulation. Loading information included connected kilovolt-amps of distribution transformers, kilowatt demands, kilovar[1] demands, and kilowatt-hour usage by phases. Customer information included number for each phase, special loads for each phase, and growth rates. Regula-

---

1. Kilovar = reactive kilovolt-ampere.

Figure C.9. *Cascavel Distribution System:*
Circuit Number 4

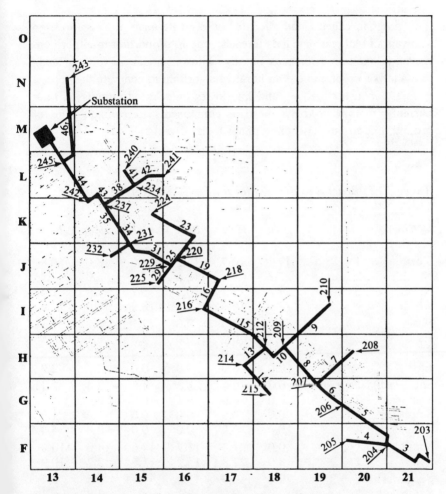

Note: Node numbers are indicated by an arrow; other numbers
identify the sections.

tion involved the use of line regulators or boosters to provide voltage control on the system. The order set file contained digital maps of each circuit.

A program called "load allocate" used an iterative process to assign kilowatt and kilovar demands to each node in proportion to either connected kilovolt-amps or peak monthly kilowatt-hours. A voltage/load/loss analysis program used an iterative algorithm to compute the voltage profile, conductor loading, and line losses on selected circuits. A fault current program used symmetrical components to compute line-to-ground, line-to-line, and three-phase fault currents.

Table C.12. *Lengths of Feeders for the Low-Reliability System* (kilometers)

Circuits		1976	1980	1984	1988	1992	1996
North	1	17.1	10.7	13.7	11.0	13.0	10.8
North	2	22.2	9.8	12.0	7.9	5.0	7.3
North	3	21.4	13.7	10.6	6.7	4.0	2.4
North	4	12.9	16.0	9.2	10.9	11.0	11.4
East	1	0.0	0.0	0.0	12.1	8.1	8.1
East	2	0.0	0.0	0.0	4.0	6.1	10.5
East	3	0.0	0.0	0.0	0.0	2.9	2.9
East	4	0.0	0.0	0.0	0.0	2.9	2.9
Southeast	1	0.0	0.0	8.3	2.8	2.8	2.3
Southeast	2	0.0	0.0	6.1	6.6	0.6	1.2
Southeast	3	0.0	0.0	0.0	0.0	6.2	1.6
Southeast	4	0.0	0.0	0.0	0.0	0.0	4.4
South	1	0.0	21.7	11.7	14.6	14.9	10.2
South	2	0.0	22.8	15.2	11.6	12.2	10.9
Southwest	1	0.0	0.0	11.4	8.9	6.5	8.7
Southwest	2	0.0	0.0	9.1	8.7	3.8	5.3
Southwest	3	0.0	0.0	0.0	0.0	13.4	7.6
Southwest	4	0.0	0.0	0.0	0.0	0.0	10.2
Northwest	1	0.0	0.0	0.0	10.2	7.0	2.3
Northwest	2	0.0	0.0	0.0	10.7	12.7	15.3
Central	1	0.0	0.0	0.0	0.0	5.3	3.1
Central	2	0.0	0.0	0.0	0.0	5.8	6.1
Central	3	0.0	0.0	0.0	0.0	0.0	5.6
Central	4	0.0	0.0	0.0	0.0	0.0	7.3
Averages		18.4	15.8	10.7	9.1	7.2	6.6

Table C.13. *Lengths of Feeders for the High-Reliability System* (kilometers)

Circuits		1976	1980	1984	1988	1992	1996
North	1	17.1	10.9	16.8	11.2	12.0	8.9
North	2	22.2	6.2	6.2	4.6	5.0	3.9
North	3	21.4	5.1	5.1	5.1	4.0	3.1
North	4	12.9	10.4	10.4	8.1	8.0	8.0
North	5	0.0	0.0	0.0	0.0	0.0	5.9
East	1	0.0	0.0	0.0	12.4	8.2	8.2
East	2	0.0	0.0	0.0	2.6	7.2	1.7
East	3	0.0	0.0	0.0	2.4	1.6	10.9
East	4	0.0	0.0	0.0	0.0	1.4	1.2
East	5	0.0	0.0	0.0	0.0	0.0	.9
East	6	0.0	0.0	0.0	0.0	0.0	.9
Southeast	1	0.0	0.0	5.9	2.8	2.8	1.1
Southeast	2	0.0	0.0	2.6	1.1	1.1	1.3
Southeast	3	0.0	0.0	0.0	6.3	6.9	2.8
Southeast	4	0.0	0.0	0.0	0.0	4.6	2.1
Southeast	5	0.0	0.0	0.0	0.0	0.0	7.7
Southeast	6	0.0	0.0	0.0	0.0	0.0	.6
Southeast	7	0.0	0.0	0.0	0.0	0.0	2.3
South	1	0.0	8.8	8.8	11.6	9.8	8.2
South	2	0.0	11.6	11.6	7.4	8.6	6.1
South	3	0.0	8.0	8.3	8.3	6.8	5.3
South	4	0.0	15.1	13.2	7.0	8.8	4.7
South	5	0.0	0.0	0.0	0.0	0.0	7.4
Southwest	1	0.0	13.3	10.1	10.6	13.6	8.8
Southwest	2	0.0	7.8	6.5	4.7	4.7	3.8
Southwest	3	0.0	0.0	8.8	3.6	7.3	3.8
Southwest	4	0.0	0.0	0.0	5.4	5.9	5.9
Southwest	5	0.0	0.0	0.0	0.0	0.0	5.9
Southwest	6	0.0	0.0	0.0	0.0	0.0	3.4
Northwest	1	0.0	0.0	0.0	5.4	4.8	3.9
Northwest	2	0.0	0.0	0.0	9.1	7.4	4.7
Northwest	3	0.0	0.0	0.0	7.3	5.5	4.4
Northwest	4	0.0	0.0	0.0	0.0	0.0	3.0
Central	1	0.0	0.0	0.0	0.0	3.2	4.7
Central	2	0.0	0.0	0.0	0.0	5.5	3.3
Central	3	0.0	0.0	0.0	0.0	0.0	5.5
Central	4	0.0	0.0	0.0	0.0	0.0	3.3
Averages		18.4	9.7	8.8	6.5	6.2	4.8

Alternative System Configurations

The data bases of the load forecast and primary system models were correlated through a group of interface programs. As described in chapter 11, Long-Range Distribution System Planning, the 1996 loads were imposed on the existing distribution system, and an analysis was made to pinpoint voltage, loading, and loss problems. The primary network was then expanded by adding substations and feeders until the analysis indicated that reliability and voltage criteria had been met. This process is repeated for the low-, medium-, and high-reliability systems during each of the study years.

Tables C.12 and C.13 show the length of feeder for the low- and high-reliability systems. In both cases the average length of the feeders decreased over time, which was caused by an ever-increasing load density. The decreasing exposure reduced outages and thus increased the average level of future reliability for both plans.

Figure C.10 shows the areas served by the four 1976 circuits. Figures C.11 and C.12 depict the cells served by the circuits of the low-reliability system for 1988 and 1996, and figures C.13 and C.14 show the areas served by the circuits of the high-reliability system for the same two years.

Comparison of figures C.11 with C.13, and C.12 with C.14, shows that, on the average, the high-reliability system serves smaller areas for each circuit, and therefore it has less exposure per feeder and less outages per consumer.

Details of the method of calculating outages for the different systems were given in chapter 11. These outage results are summarized in tables C.14 and C.15.

Figure C.10. *Areas Served by Four Existing Circuits in 1976*

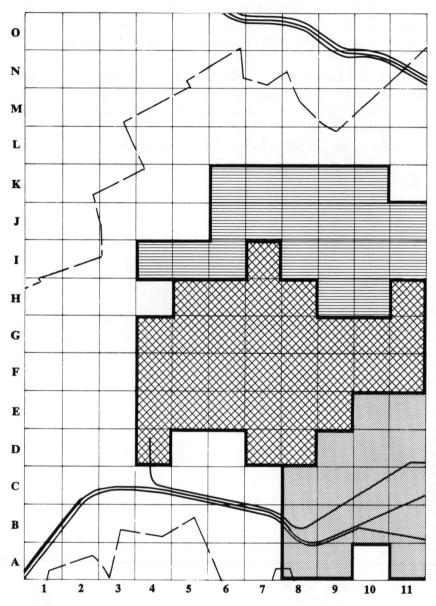

Note: The substation is indicated by the solid black square. Each pattern identifies a separate circuit.

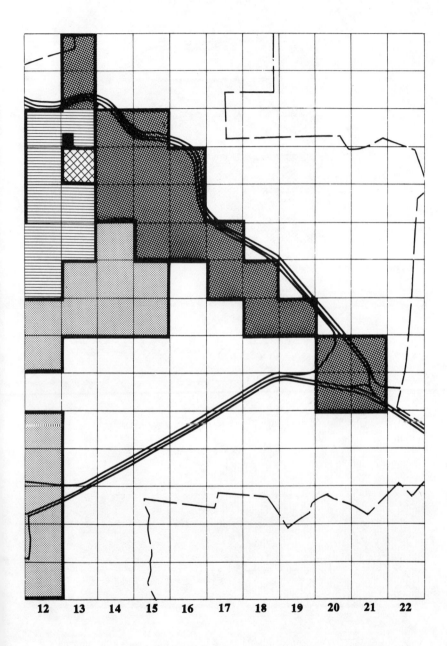

Figure C.11. *Areas Served by Low- and Medium-Reliability Circuits in 1988*

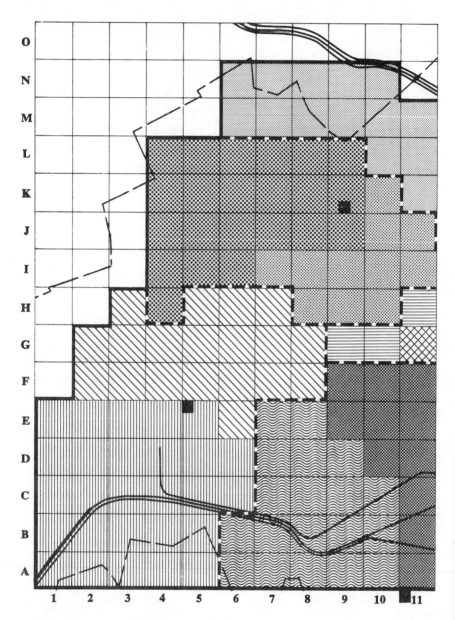

Note: Substations are indicated by solid black squares. Each pattern identifies a separate circuit.

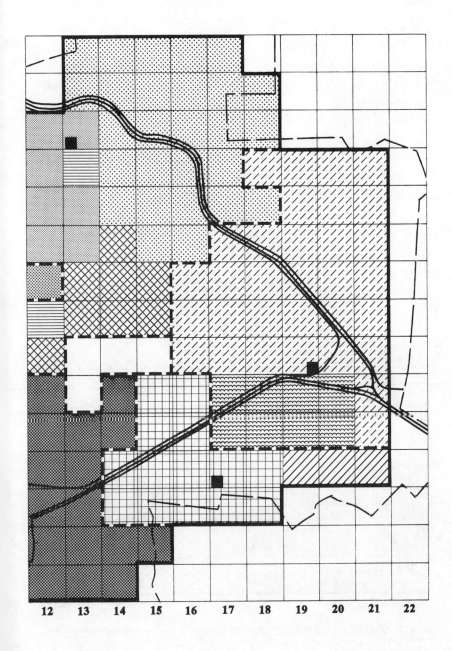

12   13   14   15   16   17   18   19   20   21   22

Figure C.12. *Areas Served by Low- and Medium-Reliability Circuits in 1996*

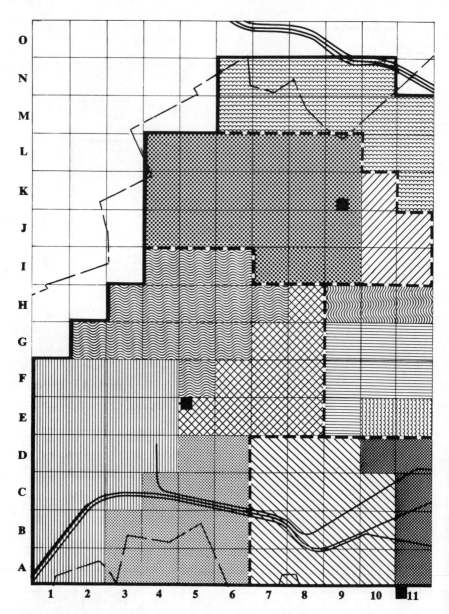

Note: Substations are indicated by solid black squares. Each pattern identifies a separate circuit.

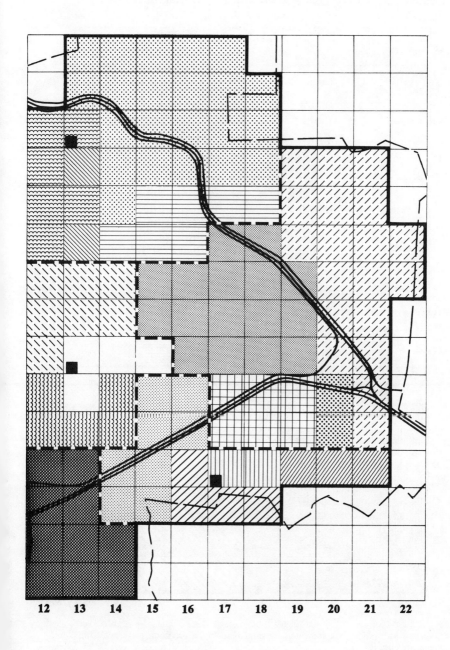

12   13   14   15   16   17   18   19   20   21   22

Figure C.13. *Areas Served by High-Reliability Circuits in 1988*

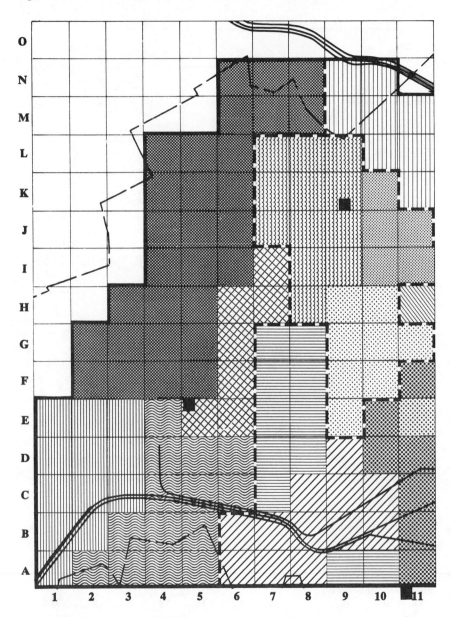

Note: Substations are indicated by solid black squares. Each pattern identifies a separate circuit.

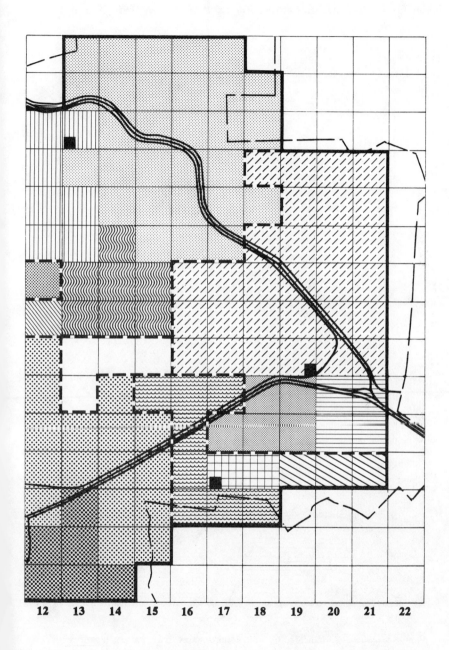

12   13   14   15   16   17   18   19   20   21   22

Figure C.14. *Areas Served by High-Reliability Circuits in 1996*

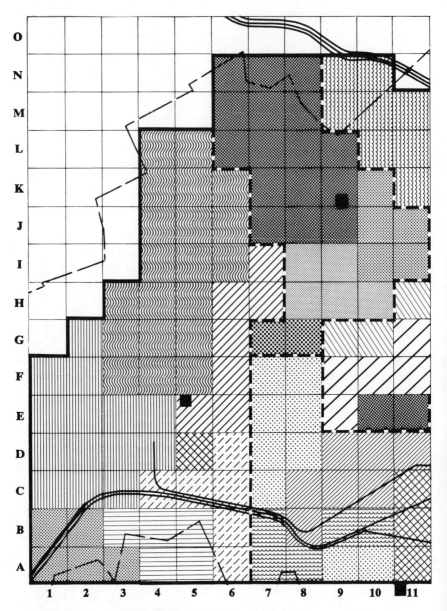

Note: Substations are indicated by solid black squares. Each pattern identifies a separate circuit.

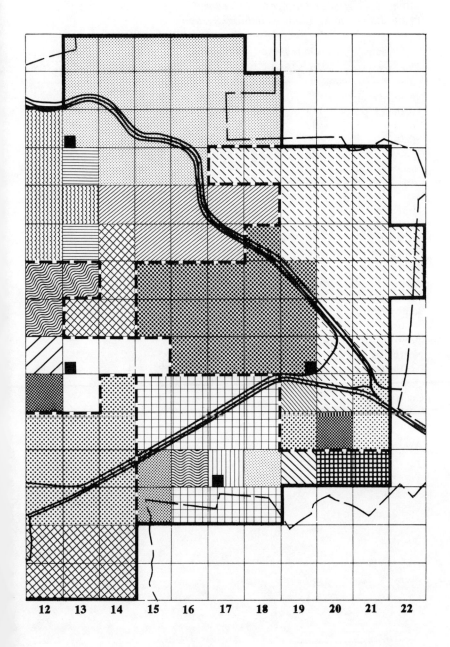

Table C.14. *Annual Outages, by Feeder,*
for the Low- and Medium-Reliability Systems

Feeders		Daily Period, 0001–0800						Daily period,	
		1976	1980	1984	1988	1992	1996	1976	1980
North	1	12	8	10	8	9	8	31	20
North	2	16	7	9	6	4	5	41	18
North	3	9	11	8	5	3	2	39	25
North	4	—	—	7	8	8	8	24	29
East	1	—	—	—	9	6	6	—	—
East	2	—	—	—	3	4	8	—	—
East	3	—	—	—	—	2	2	—	—
East	4	—	—	—	—	2	2	—	—
Southeast	1	—	—	6	2	2	2	—	—
Southeast	2	—	—	4	5	1	1	—	—
Southeast	3	—	—	—	—	4	1	—	—
Southeast	4	—	—	—	—	0	3	—	—
South	1	—	16	8	10	11	7	—	40
South	2	—	16	11	8	9	8	—	42
Southwest	1	—	—	7	6	5	6	—	—
Southwest	2	—	—	—	6	3	4	—	—
Southwest	3	—	—	—	—	10	5	—	—
Southwest	4	—	—	—	—	—	7	—	—
Northwest	1	—	—	—	7	5	2	—	—
Northwest	2	—	—	—	8	9	11	—	—
Central	1	—	—	—	—	4	2	—	—
Central	2	—	—	—	—	4	4	—	—
Central	3	—	—	—	—	—	4	—	—
Central	4	—	—	—	—	—	5	—	—
Averages		13	11	8	7	5	5	34	29

0801–1800				Daily period, 1801–2400					
1984	1988	1992	1996	1976	1980	1984	1988	1992	1996
25	20	24	20	17	11	13	11	13	11
22	15	9	13	22	10	12	8	5	7
20	12	7	4	21	13	10	7	4	2
17	20	20	21	13	16	9	11	11	11
—	22	15	15	—	—	—	12	8	8
—	7	11	19	—	—	—	4	6	10
—	—	5	5	—	—	—	—	3	3
—	—	5	5	—	—	—	—	3	3
15	5	5	4	—	—	8	3	3	2
11	12	1	2	—	—	6	6	1	1
—	—	11	3	—	—	—	—	6	2
—	—	—	8	—	—	—	—	—	4
22	27	27	19	—	21	12	14	15	10
28	21	22	20	—	22	15	11	12	11
21	16	12	16	—	—	11	9	6	9
17	16	7	10	—	—	9	9	4	5
—	—	25	14	—	—	—	—	13	7
—	—	—	19	—	—	—	—	—	10
—	19	13	4	—	—	—	10	7	2
—	20	23	28	—	—	—	11	12	15
—	—	10	6	—	—	—	—	5	3
—	—	11	11	—	—	—	—	6	6
—	—	—	10	—	—	—	—	—	6
—	—	—	13	—	—	—	—	—	7
20	17	13	12	18	16	11	9	7	6

Table C.15. *Annual Outages, by Feeder, for the High-Reliability System*

Feeders		Daily period, 0001–0800						Daily period,	
		1976	1980	1984	1988	1992	1996	1976	1980
North	1	12	8	12	8	9	6	31	20
North	2	16	4	4	3	4	3	41	11
North	3	15	4	4	4	3	2	29	9
North	4	9	7	7	6	6	6	24	19
North	5	—	—	—	—	—	4	—	—
East	1	—	—	—	9	6	6	—	—
East	2	—	—	—	2	5	1	—	—
East	3	—	—	—	2	1	8	—	—
East	4	—	—	—	—	1	1	—	—
East	5	—	—	—	—	—	1	—	—
East	6	—	—	4	—	—	1	—	—
Southeast	1	—	—	2	2	2	1	—	—
Southeast	2	—	—	—	1	1	1	—	—
Southeast	3	—	—	—	5	5	2	—	—
Southeast	4	—	—	—	—	3	2	—	—
Southeast	5	—	—	—	—	—	6	—	—
Southeast	6	—	—	—	—	—	0	—	—
Southeast	7	—	—	—	—	—	2	—	—
South	1	—	6	6	8	7	6	—	16
South	2	—	8	8	5	6	4	—	21
South	3	—	6	6	6	5	4	—	—
South	4	—	11	9	5	6	3	—	28
South	5	—	—	—	—	—	5	—	—
Southwest	1	—	10	7	8	10	6	—	24
Southwest	2	—	6	5	3	3	3	—	14
Southwest	3	—	—	6	3	5	3	—	—
Southwest	4	—	—	—	4	4	4	—	—
Southwest	5	—	—	—	—	—	4	—	—
Southwest	6	—	—	—	—	—	2	—	—
Northwest	1	—	—	—	4	3	3	—	—
Northwest	2	—	—	—	7	5	3	—	—
Northwest	3	—	—	—	5	4	3	—	—
Northwest	4	—	—	—	—	—	2	—	—
Central	1	—	—	—	—	2	3	—	15
Central	2	—	—	—	—	4	2	—	—
Central	3	—	—	—	—	—	4	—	—
Central	4	—	—	—	—	—	2	—	—
Averages		13	7	6	5	4	3	34	18

LOAD FORECASTING AND DISTRIBUTION PRIMARY MODELS 261

0801–1800				Daily period, 1801–2400					
1984	1988	1992	1996	1976	1980	1984	1988	1992	1996
31	21	22	26	17	11	17	11	12	9
11	8	9	7	22	6	6	5	5	4
9	9	7	6	21	5	5	5	4	3
19	15	15	15	13	10	10	8	8	8
—	—	—	11	—	—	—	—	—	6
—	23	15	15	—	—	—	12	8	8
—	5	13	3	—	—	—	3	7	2
—	4	3	20	—	—	—	2	2	11
—	—	3	2	—	—	—	—	1	1
—	—	—	2	—	—	—	—	—	1
—	—	—	2	—	—	—	—	—	1
11	5	5	2	—	—	6	3	3	1
5	2	2	2	—	—	3	1	1	1
—	12	13	5	—	—	—	6	7	3
—	—	8	4	—	—	—	—	5	2
—	—	—	14	—	—	—	—	—	8
—	—	—	1	—	—	—	—	—	1
—	—	—	4	—	—	—	—	—	2
16	21	18	15	—	9	9	11	10	8
21	14	16	11	—	11	11	7	8	6
15	15	13	10	—	8	8	8	7	5
24	13	16	9	—	15	13	7	9	5
—	—	—	14	—	—	0	0	—	7
19	20	25	16	—	13	10	10	13	9
12	9	9	7	—	8	6	5	5	4
16	7	13	7	—	—	9	4	7	4
—	10	11	11	—	—	—	5	6	6
—	—	—	11	—	—	—	—	—	6
—	—	—	6	—	—	—	—	—	3
—	10	9	7	—	—	—	5	5	4
—	17	14	9	—	—	—	9	7	5
—	13	10	8	—	—	—	7	5	4
—	—	—	6	—	—	—	—	—	3
—	—	6	9	—	—	—	—	3	5
—	—	10	6	—	—	—	—	5	3
—	—	—	10	—	—	—	—	—	5
—	—	—	6	—	—	—	—	—	3
16	12	11	9	18	10	9	6	6	5

Appendix D

▄▄

Outage and Supply Cost Computations

Outage Costs and Energy

The expected annual frequency and duration[1] of outages corresponding to each system plan were available for the three daily periods—0001 to 0800, 0801 to 1800, and 1801 to 2400 hours—by geographic cell over the twenty-year period, 1976 to 1996. These values were used to estimate disaggregate outage costs and outage energy for the nineteen types of consumers in each of the 247 geographic cells at the four-year intervals: 1976, 1980, 1984, 1988, 1992, and 1996. Corresponding results for intermediate years were determined by linear interpolation.[2] The detailed outage costs could then be aggregated in various ways for further analysis.

The following formulas were used in the computerized model that generated outage costs and energy loss caused by outages.

---

1. A more refined analysis would use a spread of values for outage duration based on some probability density function. In this study, however, the mean outage duration is used, because the quality of available data does not warrant a more sophisticated measure of outage duration.

2. This procedure involves negligible error, because of the smooth evolution over time of the system planning process and the simulations carried out.

$$OC_{1,i,t}^{R} = n_{1,i,t} * y_{l,t} * (s^{R} * f_{3,i,t} * d_{3,i,t})$$

$$OC_{j,i,t}^{I} = q_{j,i,t} * \sum_{m=1}^{3} [S_{m}^{I} * f_{m,i,t} * \mathrm{OCF}_{j,m}(d_{m,i,t})]$$

$$OC_{i,t}^{P} = g * k_{i,t} * \sum_{m \neq 2} (S_{m}^{P} * f_{m,i,t} * d_{m,i,t})$$

$$OC_{i,t}^{H} = v * B_{i,t} * \sum_{m \neq 2} (S_{m}^{H} * f_{m,i,t} * d_{m,i,t})$$

$$OE_{1,i,t}^{R} = n_{l,i,t} * \sum_{m=1}^{3} (e_{l,m,t}^{R} * f_{m,i,t} * d_{m,i,t})$$

$$OE_{j,i,t}^{I} = q_{j,i,t} * \sum_{m=1}^{3} [e_{j,m}^{I} * S_{m}^{I} * f_{m,i,t} * \{d_{m,i,t} + \gamma_{j}(d_{m,i,t})\}]$$

$$OE_{k,i,t}^{C} = E_{k,i,t}^{C} * \sum_{m=2}^{3} (S_{m}^{C} * f_{m,i,t} * d_{m,i,t})$$

$$OE_{i,t}^{P} = E_{i,t}^{P} * \sum_{m \neq 2} (S_{m}^{P} * f_{m,i,t} * d_{m,i,t})$$

$$OE_{i,t}^{H} = B_{i,t} * \sum_{m \neq 2} (e_{m}^{H} * S_{m}^{H} * f_{m,i,t} * d_{m,i,t})$$

$$OE_{i,t}^{S} = E_{i,t}^{S} * (S^{S} * f_{2,i,t} * d_{2,i,t})$$

where superscripts R = residential; I = industrial; C = commercial; P = public illumination; H = hospitals; S = schools; and where subscripts $i = 1, \ldots, 247$ (city geographic cell index); $j = 1, \ldots, 10$ (industrial sector index); $k = 1, \ldots, 3$ (commercial class index); $l = 1, \ldots, 4$ (residential income class index); $m = 1$ (0001 to 0800 hours), 2 (0801 to 1800 hours), 3 (1801 to 2400 hours) − (daily period index); and $t = 1, \ldots, 21$ (year index).

Variables and coefficients which depend on the above indexes are:

$OC_{i,t}^{a}$ and $OC_{b,i,t}^{a}$ = annual outage costs for consumer category a, subcategory b (Cr$);

$OE_{i,t}^{a}$ and $OE_{b,i,t}^{a}$ = annual outage energy for consumer category a, subcategory b (kilowatt-hours);

$f_{m,i,t}$ = annual frequency of outages;
$d_{m,i,t}$ = mean duration of outages (hours);
$n_{l,i,t}$ = number of households;
$y_{l,t}$ = mean income earning rate (Cr\$ per hour);
$q_{j,i,t}$ = annual value added (Cr\$ a year);
OCF_j = industrial outage cost function (see table 12.3);
$K_{i,t}$ = value of capital stock used for public illumination (Cr\$);
$B_{i,t}$ = number of hospital beds;
$E^R_{l,m,t}$ = mean kilowatt-hour consumption per hour for each household;
$E^I_{j,m}$ = mean kilowatt-hour consumption per hour of operation for every unit value added;
j = restart time function;

$E^C_{k,i,t}$, $E^P_{i,t}$ and $E^S_{i,t}$ = total kilowatt-hour consumption for each hour;
e^H_m = mean kilowatt-hour consumption per hour per hospital bed;
s^a or s^a_m = scale factor, if normal hours of activity by customer category a does not correspond to hours falling within time period m;
g = annuitizing factor for public illumination (Cr\$ per hour of usage per Cr\$ of capital stock);
v = outage cost per hour for each hospital bed (Cr\$ per hour per bed).

Typical computer printouts of disaggregate results are presented in table D.1. Tables D.2 to D.10 and figures D.1 to D.3 show these results aggregated in different ways (for example, by cell, by consumer type, discounted over time, and so on).

Supply Costs and Sensitivity Testing

The stream of distribution system costs corresponding to the four basic plans are shown in tables D.11 to D.14, which include the effects of shadow wage rates, applied to the labor component of costs as described in chapter 14. Some sensitivity testing was also carried out. The parameter that had the greatest effect on the computations was the discount rate. Figure D.4 summarizes the effect of using three different discount rates—8, 10, and 12 percent—to represent the opportunity cost of capital. Although the actual present discounted values changed, the major results and conclusions regarding the optimum range of reliability levels were basically unaltered. Using a shadow wage rate of 0.8 times the market wage rate for the unskilled component of labor in the evaluation of supply costs also had negligible effect on the results. Finally, a variation of the shadow exchange rate in the range 1.0 to 1.25 times the official exchange rate did not affect the results, because there were hardly any imported items.

Table D.1. *Medium-Reliability Plan B: Disaggregate Data*

	Residental, by income				Special instiutions	
	Lower	Lower-middle	Upper-middle	Upper	Hospitals	School
Plan 2, year 1, cell 96, square 454, feeder 0.						
Outage cost	274.36	417.88	1,308.64	1,022.87	0.00	0.00
Outage energy	8.37	13.00	40.07	26.89	0.00	0.00
Total energy	3,067.75	4,762.46	14,681.58	9,850.01	0.00	0.00
Outage rate	0.2730	0.2730	0.2730	0.2730	—	—
Plan 2, year 1, cell 97, square 455, feeder 0.						
Outage cost	0.00	0.00	0.00	0.00	0.00	0.00
Outage energy	0.00	0.00	0.00	0.00	0.00	0.00
Total energy	0.00	0.00	0.00	0.00	0.00	0.00
Outage rate	—	—	—	—	—	—
Plan 2, year 1, cell 98, square 456, feeder 0.						
Outage cost	254.77	948.52	1,530.20	633.20	0.00	0.00
Outage energy	7.77	29.43	46.82	16.63	0.00	0.00
Total energy	4,601.63	17,462.36	27,731.88	9,850.01	0.00	0.00
Outage rate	0.1688	0.1688	0.1688	0.1688	—	—
Plan 2, year 1, cell 99, square 457, feeder 0.						
Outage cost	101.91	948.52	1,440.19	422.14	0.00	0.00
Outage energy	3.11	29.48	44.06	11.09	0.00	0.00
Total energy	1,840.65	17,462.36	26,100.60	6,566.67	0.00	0.00
Outage rate	0.1688	0.1688	0.1688	0.1688	—	—
Plan 2, year 1, cell 88, square 446, feeder 0.						
Outage cost	22.21	4,679.58	9,769.76	11,316.49	0.00	0.00
Outage energy	0.68	145.16	298.33	296.62	0.00	0.00
Total energy	306.78	65,880.72	135,396.84	134,616.76	0.00	0.00
Outage rate	0.2203	0.2203	0.2203	0.2203	—	—
Plan 2, year 1, cell 89, square 447, feeder 0.						
Outage cost	0.00	4,566.82	9,769.76	11,316.49	0.00	0.00
Outage energy	0.00	141.66	298.33	296.62	0.00	0.00
Total energy	0.00	64,293.23	135,396.84	134,616.76	0.00	0.00
Outage rate	—	0.2203	0.2203	0.2203	—	—
Plan 2, year 1, cell 90, square 448, feeder 0.						
Outage cost	0.00	3,946.63	8,828.10	10,212.44	0.00	0.0
Outage energy	0.00	122.43	269.58	267.68	0.00	0.0
Total energy	613.55	61,118.26	127,240.40	121,483.42	92,667.00	0.0
Outage rate	—	0.2203	0.2203	0.2203	—	—
Plan 2, year 1, cell 91, square 449, feeder 0.						
Outage cost	44.42	4,341.30	9,181.22	10,212.44	785.55	0.0
Outage energy	1.35	134.67	280.36	267.68	133.64	0.0
Total energy	613.55	61,118.26	127,240.40	121,483.42	92,667.00	0.0
Outage rate	0.2203	0.2203	0.2203	0.2203	0.1442	—

		Main industry, by kind				
Metallurgy and mechanical	Non-metallic minerals	Wood	Vegetable oils	Food and beverage	Other	Public illumina-tion
0.94	1.88	48.63	98.34	51.61	18.25	29.68
0.04	0.16	0.64	4.00	2.31	0.80	68.30
21.68	68.55	369.67	461.86	278.40	105.64	19,552.00
0.1742	0.2326	0.1742	0.8658	0.8288	0.7580	0.3493
0.00	0.00	0.00	0.00	0.00	0.00	0 .00
0.00	0.00	0.00	0.00	0.00	0.00	0 .00
0.00	0.00	0.00	0.00	0.00	0.00	0 .00
—	—	—	—	—	—	—
0.62	1.24	32.15	63.91	33.99	12.06	22.96
0.02	0.11	0.43	2.62	1.52	0.53	52.84
23.29	73.65	397.15	496.19	299.09	113.49	24,885.00
0.1072	0.1431	0.1072	0.5287	0.5071	0.4664	0.2123
0.00	0.00	0.00	0.00	0.00	0.00	24.60
0.00	0.00	0.00	0.00	0.00	0.00	56.61
0.00	0.00	0.00	0.00	0.00	0.00	26,662.00
—	—	—	—	—	—	0.2123
37.73	75.24	1,946.94	3,964.12	2,076.44	730.45	36.15
1.51	6.38	25.79	161.21	93.00	32.06	83.19
1,091.73	3,452.75	18,618.54	23,261.66	14,021.45	5,320.52	29,625.00
0.1385	0.1849	0.1385	0.6930	0.6632	0.6024	0.2808
81.20	161.92	4,190.02	8,531.20	4,468.73	1,572.01	36.15
3.25	3.75	55.50	346.94	200.14	68.99	83.19
2,349.51	7,430.68	40,069.07	50,061.57	30,175.65	11,450.33	29,625.00
0.1385	0.1849	0.1385	0.6930	0.6632	0.6025	0.2808
9.91	19.75	511.16	1,040.75	545.16	191.77	36.15
0.40	1.68	6.77	42.33	24.42	8.42	83.19
286.63	906.50	4,888.18	6,107.20	3,681.24	1,396.87	29,625.00
0.1385	0.1849	0.1385	0.6930	0.6632	0.6025	0.2808
7.68	15.33	396.75	807.82	423.14	148.85	35.71
0.31	1.30	5.25	32.85	18.95	6.53	82.19
222.48	703.61	3,794.14	4,740.34	2,857.34	1,084.23	29,269.00
0.1385	0.1849	0.1385	0.6930	0.6632	0.6025	0.2808

Table D.1 (continued)

		Service industry, by kind			Commercial, by kir	
	Tele-phone	Water and sewer-age	Metallurgy and mechanical	Other	Light	Medium

Plan 2, year 1, cell 96, square 454, feeder 0.
Outage cost	0.00	0.00	0.00	0.00	0.00	0.00
Outage energy	0.00	0.00	0.00	0.00	38.25	0.00
Total energy	0.00	0.00	0.00	0.00	17,990.00	0.00
Outage rate	—	—	—	—	0.2126	—

Plan 2, year 1, cell 97, square 455, feeder 0.
Outage cost	0.00	0.00	0.00	0.00	0.00	0.00
Outage energy	0.00	0.00	0.00	0.00	0.00	0.00
Total energy	0.00	0.00	0.00	0.00	0.00	0.00
Outage rate	—	—	—	—	—	—

Plan 2, year 1, cell 98, square 456, feeder 0.
Outage cost	0.00	0.00	0.00	0.00	0.00	0.00
Outage energy	0.00	0.00	0.00	0.00	8.25	185.63
Total energy	0.00	0.00	0.00	0.00	6,286.00	141,512.00
Outage rate	—	—	—	—	0.1312	0.1312

Plan 2, year 1, cell 99, square 457, feeder 0.
Outage cost	303.73	0.00	0.00	98.35	0.00	0.00
Outage energy	12.30	43.28	54.10	3.94	22.18	87.75
Total enregy	6,774.50	40,363.49	50,449.30	3,675.85	16,906.00	66,897.00
Outage rate	0.1815	0.1072	0.1072	0.1072	0.1312	0.1312

Plan 2, year 1, cell 88, square 446, feeder 0.
Outage cost	0.00	0.00	0.00	0.00	0.00	0.00
Outage energy	0.00	0.00	0.00	0.00	36.55	17.53
Totalenergy	0.00	0.00	0.00	0.00	21,458.00	10,292.00
Outage rate	—	—	—	—	0.1703	0.1703

Plan 2, year 1, cell 89, square 447, feeder 0.
Outage cost	0.00	0.00	0.00	0.00	0.00	0.00
Outage energy	0.00	0.00	0.00	0.00	38.76	0.00
Total energy	0.00	0.00	0.00	0.00	22,759.00	0.00
Outage rate	—	—	—	—	0.1703	—

Plan 2, year 1, cell 90, square 448, feeder 0.
Outage cost	0.00	0.00	0.00	0.00	0.00	0.00
Outage energy	0.00	0.00	0.00	0.00	41.81	0.00
Total energy	0.00	0.00	0.00	0.00	24,547.00	0.00
Outage rate	—	—	—	—	0.1703	—

Plan 2, year 1, cell 91, square 449, feeder 0.
Outage cost	0.00	0.00	0.00	0.00	0.00	0.00
Outage energy	0.00	0.00	0.00	0.00	36.11	49.11
Total energy	0.00	0.00	0.00	0.00	21,201.00	28,832.00
Outage rate	—	—	—	—	0.1703	0.1703

Table D.2. *Medium-Reliability Plan B:*
Residential, Public Illumination, and Hospital Outage Costs, by Year
(thousands of Cr$)

| Year | Residential, by income group | | | | | Public illumi-nation | Hospi-tals |
	Lower	Lower-middle	Upper-middle	Upper	Total		
1976	10.78	144.58	241.38	212.13	608.87	4.13	5.72
1977	21.75	230.63	362.47	296.23	911.09	5.13	6.11
1978	32.73	316.69	483.57	380.32	1,213.31	6.12	6.50
1979	43.71	402.74	604.66	464.42	1,515.52	7.12	6.88
1980	54.68	488.80	725.75	548.51	1,817.74	8.11	7.27
1981	59.06	534.64	778.92	575.72	1,948.33	7.98	8.59
1982	63.44	580.48	832.08	602.92	2,078.92	7.86	9.90
1983	67.82	626.32	885.25	630.12	2,209.51	7.73	11.21
1984	72.20	672.16	938.41	657.32	2,340.10	7.61	12.53
1985	85.06	762.93	1,049.02	706.91	2,603.92	8.02	12.10
1986	97.91	853.70	1,159.64	756.51	2,867.74	8.44	11.67
1987	110.76	944.46	1,270.25	806.09	3,131.56	8.85	11.24
1988	123.61	1,035.23	1,380.86	855.68	3,395.38	9.27	10.82
1989	147.16	1,079.75	1,418.40	851.10	3,496.41	9.51	11.27
1990	170.71	1,124.27	1,455.95	846.51	3,597.44	9.76	11.73
1991	194.27	1,168.79	1,493.49	841.93	3,698.47	10.00	12.19
1992	217.82	1,213.31	1,531.04	837.35	3,799.50	10.24	12.65
1993	241.88	1,310.96	1,677.96	923.69	4,154.48	10.22	13.46
1994	265.94	1,408.61	1,824.88	1,010.04	4,509.46	10.20	14.27
1995	290.00	1,506.26	1,971.80	1,096.38	4,864.44	10.18	15.08
1996	314.07	1,603.91	2,118.72	1,182.73	5,219.42	10.16	15.89

Table D.3. *Medium-Reliability Plan B:*
Industrial Outage Costs, by Year and Kind of Industry
(thousands of Cr$)

	Main industry, by kind						
Year	Metal-lurgy and me-chani-cal	Nonme-tallic min-erals	Wood	Vege-table oils	Food and bev-erages	Other	Total
1976	9.02	17.98	465.37	938.12	493.66	174.60	2,098.75
1977	11.38	22.62	513.67	1,265.19	589.58	206.45	2,608.90
1978	13.75	27.26	561.98	1,592.27	685.50	238.30	3,119.05
1979	16.11	31.90	610.28	1,919.34	781.42	270.15	3,629.21
1980	18.48	36.54	658.59	2,246.41	877.34	302.01	4,139.36
1981	17.00	33.58	574.42	2,052.71	790.94	272.52	3,741.17
1982	15.52	30.63	490.25	1,859.01	704.55	243.03	3,342.98
1983	14.04	27.68	406.07	1,665.30	618.15	213.55	2,944.79
1984	12.56	24.73	321.90	1,471.60	531.75	184.06	2,546.60
1985	13.35	26.31	314.40	1,605.41	555.41	190.03	2,704.92
1986	14.15	27.91	306.89	1,739.22	579.07	196.00	2,863.24
1987	14.95	29.50	299.39	1,873.03	602.72	201.97	3,021.56
1988	15.74	31.09	291.88	2,006.84	626.38	207.95	3,179.88
1989	15.78	31.14	272.00	1,874.30	609.05	203.08	3,005.36
1990	15.81	31.20	252.13	1,741.76	591.73	198.22	2,830.84
1991	15.85	31.25	232.25	1,609.22	574.40	193.36	2,656.32
1992	15.88	31.31	212.37	1,476.67	557.08	188.49	2,481.81
1993	17.71	34.91	215.20	1,717.66	602.95	203.33	2,791.76
1994	19.54	38.51	218.03	1,958.64	648.83	218.16	3,101.71
1995	21.37	42.11	220.85	2,199.62	694.70	233.00	3,411.65
1996	23.20	45.72	223.68	2,440.60	740.58	247.83	3,721.60

	Service industry, by kind				
Tele-phone	Water and sewerage treatment	Metallurgy and mechanical	Other	Total	Industry total
32.57	0.00	0.00	10.45	43.02	2,141.77
41.92	0.00	0.00	13.27	55.19	2,664.10
51.28	0.00	0.00	16.09	67.37	3,186.42
60.63	0.00	0.00	18.92	79.54	3,700.75
69.98	0.00	0.00	21.74	91.72	4,231.08
67.46	0.00	0.00	21.24	88.70	3,829.87
64.94	0.00	0.00	20.73	85.67	3,428.65
62.42	0.00	0.00	20.23	82.65	3,027.44
59.90	0.00	0.00	19.73	79.63	2,626.23
67.56	0.00	0.00	22.82	90.38	2,795.30
75.22	0.00	0.00	25.90	101.12	2,964.36
82.89	0.00	0.00	28.99	111.87	3,133.43
90.55	0.00	0.00	32.08	122.62	3,302.50
111.83	0.00	0.00	40.22	152.05	3,157.41
133.11	0.00	0.00	48.37	181.49	3,012.33
154.40	0.00	0.00	56.52	210.92	2,887.24
175.68	0.00	0.00	64.67	240.35	2,722.16
182.92	0.00	0.00	69.40	252.32	3,044.07
190.15	0.00	0.00	74.14	264.29	3,365.99
197.38	0.00	0.00	78.88	276.26	3,687.91
204.61	0.00	0.00	83.61	288.23	4,009.83

Table D.4. *Medium-Reliability Plan B:*
Present Discounted Values of Outage Costs
(thousands of Cr$)

Dis-count rate	Residential, by income group					Public illumi-nation
	Lower	Lower-middle	Upper-middle	Upper	Total	
0.08	1,432.82	9,571.52	13,044.84	8,292.33	32,341.51	97.58
0.10	1,078.92	7,475.60	10,260.74	6,646.71	25,461.98	80.62
0.12	833.10	5,983.41	8,273.23	5,458.70	20,548.45	68.10
0.14	658.72	4,897.01	6,821.65	4,580.56	16,957.93	58.65

Dis-count rate	Special institutions		Commercial, by kind			
	Hospi-tals	Schools	Light	Medium	Heavy	Total
0.08	126.39	—	—	—	—	—
0.10	102.91	—	—	—	—	—
0.12	85.82	—	—	—	—	—
0.14	73.07	—	—	—	—	—

—, Negligible.

			Main industry, by kind			
Metallurgy and mechanical	Nonmetallic minerals	Wood	Vegetable oils	Food and beverages	Other	Total
193.76	382.75	4,900.78	21,915.50	8,056.47	2,755.84	38,205.11
160.34	316.85	4,349.12	18,244.75	6,833.28	2,342.61	32,246.95
135.93	268.69	3,916.67	15,541.24	5,921.10	2,033.95	27,817.59
117.63	232.60	3,569.67	13,498.74	5,223.30	1,797.45	24,439.40

		Service industry, by kind			
Telephone	Water and sewerage treatment	Metallurgy and mechanical	Other	Total	Industry total
1,178.30	0.00	0.00	427.94	1,606.24	39,811.35
923.09	0.00	0.00	330.14	1,253.23	33,500.17
742.85	0.00	0.00	261.75	1,004.60	28,822.18
612.65	0.00	0.00	212.87	825.53	25,264.92

Table D.5. *Medium-Reliability Plan B:*
Present Discounted Values of Outage Energy
(megawatt-hours)

Dis-count rate	Residential, by income group					Public illumi-nation
	Lower	Lower-middle	Upper-middle	Upper	Total	
0.08	83.08	552.97	703.70	382.09	1,721.83	224.59
0.10	62.60	432.61	556.84	308.69	1,360.74	185.54
0.12	48.37	346.82	451.59	255.38	1,102.16	156.73
0.14	38.28	284.28	374.40	215.75	912.70	134.97

Dis-count rate	Special institutions		Commercial, by kind			
	Hospi-tals	Schools	Light	Medium	Heavy	Total
0.08	21.50	2.02	178.04	378.17	504.32	1,060.53
0.10	17.51	1.53	139.04	298.61	403.80	841.44
0.12	14.60	1.18	111.39	241.64	331.32	684.35
0.14	12.43	0.93	91.34	199.93	277.80	569.08

Main industry, by kind						
Metallurgy and mechanical	Nonmetallic minerals	Wood	Vegetable oils	Food and beverages	Other	Total
7.77	32.13	67.17	667.62	367.99	120.91	1,263.59
6.43	26.60	59.55	564.60	311.74	102.78	1,071.70
5.45	22.57	53.58	487.92	269.83	89.24	928.58
4.71	19.54	48.79	429.37	237.80	78.86	819.07

Service industry, by kind					
Telephone	Water and sewerage treatment	Metallurgy and mechanical	Other	Total	Industry total
47.75	119.93	235.60	17.15	420.43	1,684.02
37.40	95.92	181.74	13.23	328.30	1,400.00
30.10	78.77	144.09	10.49	263.45	1,192.03
24.82	66.24	117.17	8.53	216.77	1,035.84

Table D.6. *Medium-Reliability Plan B:*
Present Discounted Values of Total Energy
(megawatt-hours)

Dis-count rate	Residential, by income group					Public illumi-nation
	Lower	Lower-middle	Upper-middle	Upper	Total	
0.08	35,476.61	256,069.68	328,299.09	180,792.91	800,638.29	92,818.21
0.10	26,233.53	195,030.37	252,343.16	141,217.87	614,824.93	73,938.12
0.12	19,871.61	152,232.23	198,966.69	113,124.86	484,095.38	60,367.79
0.14	15,404.13	121,582.40	160,397.85	92,734.31	390,118.68	50,389.69

Dis-count rate	Special institutions		Commercial, by kind			
	Hospi-tals	Schools	Light	Medium	Heavy	Total
0.08	17,865.94	1,739.19	117,423.62	276,962.35	441,747.71	836,133.67
0.10	14,305.84	1,346.20	89,646.58	211,507.06	337,393.01	638,546.65
0.12	11,729.74	1,068.15	70,176.01	165,606.47	264,205.49	499,987.98
0.14	9,822.65	867.08	56,234.03	132,725.64	211,771.25	400,730.91

Main industry, by kind

Metal-lurgy and mechani-cal	Nonme-tallic minerals	Wood	Vege-table oils	Food and beverages	Other	Total
17,042.28	53,703.16	96,375.59	245,557.35	148,025.01	56,112.28	616,815.66
12,676.73	39,951.67	77,452.55	186,949.03	112,693.67	42,719.25	472,442.90
9,677.42	30,503.30	63,863.91	146,184.74	88,119.57	33,404.10	371,753.04
7,574.30	23,877.71	53,875.12	117,216.16	70,656.47	26,784.56	299,984.32

Service industry, by kind

Tele-phone	Water and sewerage treatment	Metal-lurgy and mechani-cal	Other	Total	Industry total
24,267.45	112,075.27	234,380.65	17,061.92	387,785.28	1,004,600.94
18,319.33	86,006.77	174,286.81	12,688.07	291,300.97	763,743.87
14,201.62	67,799.96	133,013.15	9,683.92	224,698.64	596,451.68
11,290.24	54,803.20	104,081.58	7,578.02	177,753.04	477,737.36

Table D.7. *Medium-Reliability Plan B:
Present Discounted Values of Outage Rates*
[(outage energy/total energy) × 100]

| Dis-count rate | Residential, by income group | | | | | Public illumi-nation |
	Lower	Lower-middle	Upper-middle	Upper	Total	
0.10	0.2342	0.2159	0.2143	0.2113	0.2151	0.2420
0.10	0.2386	0.2218	0.2207	0.2186	0.2213	0.2509
0.12	0.2434	0.2278	0.2271	0.2258	0.2277	0.2596
0.14	0.2485	0.2338	0.2334	0.2327	0.2340	0.2679

| Dis-count rate | Special institutions | | Commercial, by kind | | | |
	Hospi-tals	Schools	Light	Medium	Heavy	Total
0.08	0.1203	0.1160	0.1516	0.1078	0.0750	0.1268
0.10	0.1224	0.1134	0.1986	0.1412	0.0982	0.1318
0.12	0.1245	0.1106	0.2537	0.1803	0.1254	0.1369
0.14	0.1266	0.1076	0.3166	0.2250	0.1564	0.1420

		Main industry, by kind				
Metallurgy and mechanical	Nonmetallic minerals	Wood	Vegetable oils	Food and beverages	Other	Total
0.0456	0.0598	0.0697	0.2719	0.2486	0.2155	0.2049
0.0507	0.0666	0.0769	0.3020	0.2766	0.2406	0.2268
0.0563	0.0740	0.0839	0.3338	0.3062	0.2671	0.2498
0.0622	0.0818	0.0906	0.3663	0.3366	0.2944	0.2730

		Service industry, by kind			
Telephone	Water and sewerage treatment	Metallurgy and mechanical	Other	Total	Industry total
0.1967	0.1070	0.1005	0.1005	0.1084	0.1676
0.2042	0.1115	0.1043	0.1043	0.1127	0.1833
0.2119	0.1162	0.1083	0.1083	0.1172	0.1999
0.2199	0.1209	0.1126	0.1126	0.1220	0.2168

Table D.8. *Medium-Reliability Plan B:*
Present Discounted Values of Outage Costs
(Cr$/kilowatt-hours lost)

Dis-count rate	Residential, by income group					Public illumi-nation
	Lower	Lower-middle	Upper-middle	Upper	Total	
0.08	17.25	17.30	18.54	21.70	18.78	0.43
0.10	17.23	17.28	18.43	21.53	18.71	0.43
0.12	17.22	17.25	18.32	21.37	18.64	0.43
0.14	17.21	17.23	18.22	21.23	18.58	0.43

Dis-count rate	Special institutions		Commercial, by kind			
	Hospi-tals	Schools	Light	Medium	Heavy	Total
0.08	5.88	—	—	—	—	—
0.10	5.88	—	—	—	—	—
0.12	5.88	—	—	—	—	—
0.14	5.88	—	—	—	—	—

—, Negligible.

		Main industry, by kind				
Metallurgy and mechanical	Nonmetallic minerals	Wood	Vegetable oils	Food and beverages	Other	Total
24.95	11.91	72.96	32.83	21.89	22.79	30.24
24.95	11.91	73.03	32.31	21.92	22.79	30.09
24.95	11.91	73.10	31.85	21.94	22.79	29.96
24.95	11.90	73.17	31.44	21.97	22.79	29.84

Service industry, by kind

Telephone	Water and sewerage treatment	Metallurgy and mechanical	Other	Total	Industry total
24.68	0.00	0.00	24.95	3.82	23.64
24.68	0.00	0.00	24.95	3.82	23.93
24.68	0.00	0.00	24.95	3.81	24.18
24.68	0.00	0.00	24.95	3.81	24.39

Table D.9. *Medium-Reliability Plan B: Grand Total, by Year*

Year	Outage costs (thousands of Cr$)	Outage energy (mega-watt-hours)	Total energy (mega-watt-hours)	Outage rate $\left(\dfrac{outage\ energy}{total\ energy} \times 100 \right)$	Outage cost (Cr$/ kilowatt-hours lost)
1976	2,760.49	161.19	53,490.19	0.3013	17.13
1977	3,586.42	206.28	64,532.89	0.3197	17.39
1978	4,412.35	251.37	75,575.59	0.3326	17.55
1979	5,238.27	296.47	86,618.29	0.3423	17.67
1980	6,064.20	341.56	97,660.99	0.3497	17.75
1981	5,794.77	338.73	114,869.91	0.2949	17.11
1982	5,525.34	335.89	132,078.82	0.2543	16.45
1983	5,255.90	333.06	149,287.74	0.2231	15.78
1984	4,986.47	330.23	166,496.65	0.1983	15.10
1985	5,419.34	359.63	189,420.69	0.1899	15.07
1986	5,852.22	389.03	212,344.73	0.1832	15.04
1987	6,285.09	418.43	235,268.78	0.1779	15.02
1988	6,717.97	447.83	258,192.82	0.1734	15.00
1989	6,674.61	459.10	290,316.28	0.1581	14.54
1990	6,631.26	470.36	322,439.74	0.1459	14.00
1991	6,587.91	481.63	354,563.20	0.1358	13.68
1992	6,544.55	492.89	386,686.66	0.1275	13.28
1993	7,222.24	532.15	427,328.90	0.1245	13.57
1994	7,899.93	571.40	467,971.14	0.1221	13.83
1995	8,577.61	610.66	508,613.38	0.1201	14.05
1996	9,255.30	649.91	549,255.61	0.1183	14.24

Table D.10. *Medium-Reliability Plan B:*
Present Discounted Values of the Grand Totals

Discount rate	Outage costs (thousands of Cr$)	Outage energy (megawatt-hours)	Total energy (megawatt-hours)	Outage rate $\left(\dfrac{outage\ energy}{total\ energy} \times 100\right)$	Outage cost (Cr$/kilowatt-hours lost)
0.08	72,376.82	4,714.49	2,753,796.25	0.1712	15.35
0.10	59,145.68	3,806.76	2,106,705.61	0.1807	15.54
0.12	49,524.55	3,151.05	1,653,700.71	0.1905	15.72
0.14	42,354.57	2,665.96	1,329,666.36	0.2005	15.89

Figure D.1. *Medium-Reliability Plan B:*
Present Discounted Value of Outage Energy, by Cell
(megawatt-hours)

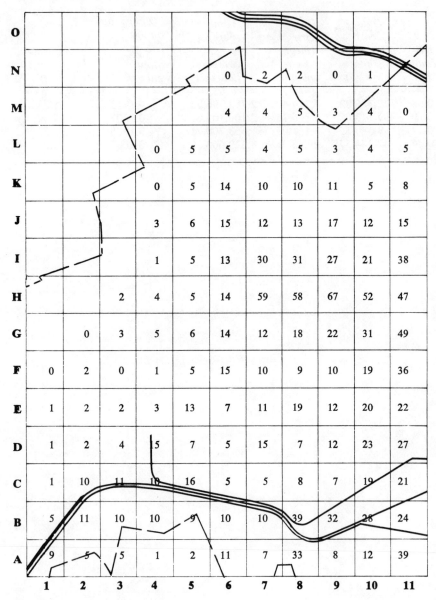

Note: Discount rate = 12 percent.

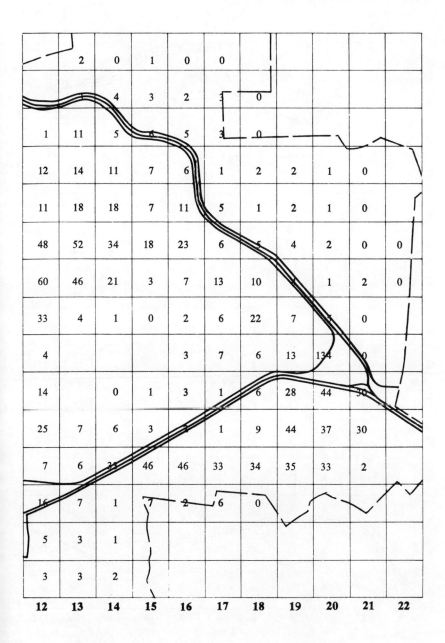

Figure D.2. *Medium-Reliability Plan B:*
Present Discounted Value of Total Energy, by Cell
(gigawatt-hours)

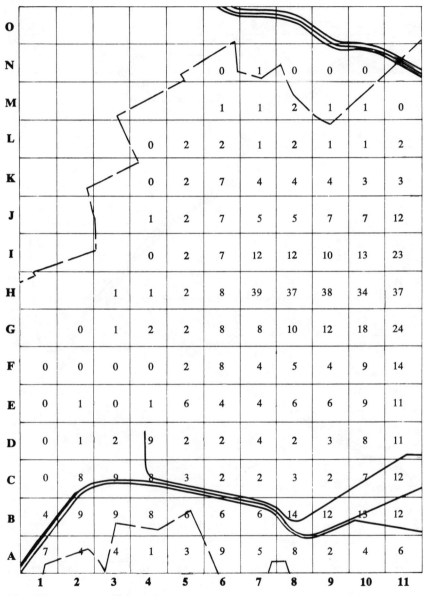

	1	2	3	4	5	6	7	8	9	10	11
O											
N						0	1	0	0	0	
M						1	1	2	1	1	0
L					0	2	2	1	2	1	1	2
K					0	2	7	4	4	4	3	3
J					1	2	7	5	5	7	7	12
I					0	2	7	12	12	10	13	23
H			1	1	2	8	39	37	38	34	37
G		0	1	2	2	8	8	10	12	18	24
F	0	0	0	0	2	8	4	5	4	9	14
E	0	1	0	1	6	4	4	6	6	9	11
D	0	1	2	9	2	2	4	2	3	8	11
C	0	8	9	8	3	2	2	3	2	7	12
B	4	9	9	8	6	6	6	14	12	13	12
A	7	4	4	1	3	9	5	8	2	4	6

Note: Discount rate = 12 percent.

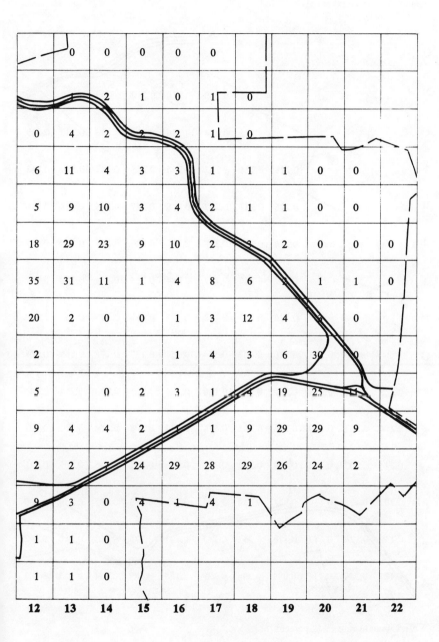

Figure D.3. *Medium-Reliability Plan B:*
Outage Rate, by Cell
[(outage energy/total energy) × 100]

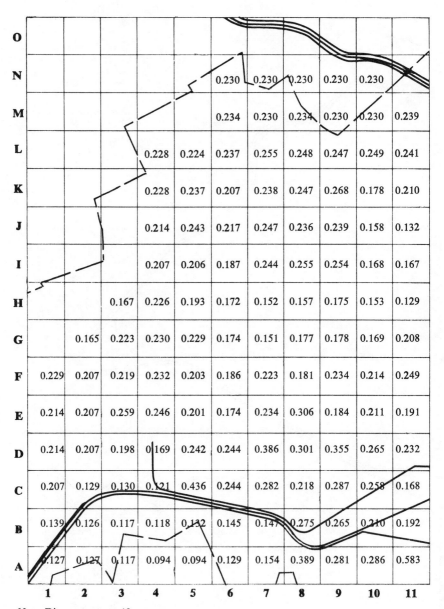

	1	2	3	4	5	6	7	8	9	10	11
O											
N						0.230	0.230	0.230	0.230	0.230	
M						0.234	0.230	0.234	0.230	0.230	0.239
L				0.228	0.224	0.237	0.255	0.248	0.247	0.249	0.241
K				0.228	0.237	0.207	0.238	0.247	0.268	0.178	0.210
J				0.214	0.243	0.217	0.247	0.236	0.239	0.158	0.132
I				0.207	0.206	0.187	0.244	0.255	0.254	0.168	0.167
H			0.167	0.226	0.193	0.172	0.152	0.157	0.175	0.153	0.129
G		0.165	0.223	0.230	0.229	0.174	0.151	0.177	0.178	0.169	0.208
F	0.229	0.207	0.219	0.232	0.203	0.186	0.223	0.181	0.234	0.214	0.249
E	0.214	0.207	0.259	0.246	0.201	0.174	0.234	0.306	0.184	0.211	0.191
D	0.214	0.207	0.198	0.169	0.242	0.244	0.386	0.301	0.355	0.265	0.232
C	0.207	0.129	0.130	0.121	0.436	0.244	0.282	0.218	0.287	0.258	0.168
B	0.139	0.126	0.117	0.118	0.132	0.145	0.147	0.275	0.265	0.210	0.192
A	0.127	0.127	0.117	0.094	0.094	0.129	0.154	0.389	0.281	0.286	0.583

Note: Discount rate = 12 percent.

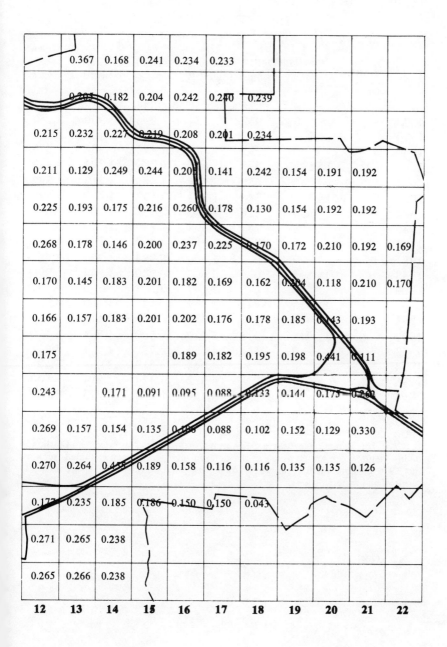

Table D.11. *Low-Reliability Distribution System Costs*
(1976 Cr$ · 10³) and Losses

	Investment costs		Recur-rent costs	Total costs	Losses Kilo-watts	Losses Mega-watt-hours
Year	Stations	Lines				
1977	0	828	16	844	719	1,851
1978	0	962	34	996	906	2,287
1979	0	1,118	55	1,173	1,124	2,793
1980	0	1,295	79	1,375	1,376	3,379
1981	15,515	576	695	16,787	1,394	3,479
1982	0	655	709	1,365	1,413	3,593
1983	15,515	743	1,333	17,592	1,436	3,723
1984	0	828	1,370	2,198	1,462	3,870
1985	0	781	1,364	2,145	1,416	3,750
1986	15,515	870	1,986	18,372	1,365	3,615
1987	0	977	2,006	2,984	1,308	3,464
1988	15,515	1,089	2,635	19,240	1,244	3,295
1989	0	679	2,647	3,327	1,356	3,591
1990	15,515	743	3,267	19,526	1,480	3,924
1991	5,973	832	3,531	10,336	1,615	4,281
1992	11,946	915	4,039	16,900	1,764	4,680
1993	0	686	4,053	4,739	1,901	5,041
1994	0	750	4,068	4,819	2,051	5,435
1995	5,973	818	4,332	11,124	2,214	5,866
1996	0	894	4,350	5,244	2,393	6,336
1997–2006	0	0	4,350	4,350	2,393	6,336

Note: The annual expenses are associated with new substations and primary mains. Items which are common to the different plans have been excluded, such as the 1976 existing plant, primary laterals, distribution transformers, secondaries, services, and meters.

Table D.12. *Medium-Reliability A Distribution System Costs* (1976 Cr\$ · 10³) *and Losses*

Year	Investment costs Stations	Investment costs Lines	Recurrent costs	Total costs	Losses Kilowatts	Losses Megawatthours
1977	0	876	16	892		
1978	0	1,018	34	1,052		
1979	0	1,183	57	1,240	Same losses as	
1980	0	1,368	84	1,452	for low-	
1981	15,515	662	703	16,880	reliability	
1982	0	753	716	1,469	distribution	
1983	15,515	854	1,341	17,710	system	
1984	0	977	1,360	2,337		
1985	0	1,038	1,380	2,418		
1986	15,515	1,157	2,009	18,681		
1987	0	1,300	2,033	3,333		
1988	15,515	1,449	2,668	19,632		
1989	0	875	2,685	3,560		
1990	15,515	957	3,309	19,781		
1991	5,973	1,071	3,576	10,620		
1992	11,946	1,177	4,092	17,215		
1993	0	930	4,109	5,039		
1994	0	1,013	4,130	5,143		
1995	5,973	1,108	4,307	11,478		
1996	0	1,210	4,422	5,632		
1997–2006	0	0	4,422	4,422		

Note: See note to table D.1.

Table D.13.　*Medium-Reliability B Distribution System Costs*
(1976 Cr$ · 10³) and Losses

	Investment costs		Recur-rent costs	Total costs	Losses	
					Kilo-watts	Mega-watt-hours
Year	Stations	Lines				
1977	0	877	16	893	582	1,499
1978	0	1,019	34	1,053	734	1,852
1979	0	1,185	58	1,243	910	2,262
1980	0	1,370	84	1,454	1,115	2,737
1981	15,515	809	708	17,032	1,129	2,818
1982	0	916	726	1,642	1,145	2,910
1983	15,515	1,033	1,358	17,906	1,163	3,016
1984	0	1,156	1,383	2,539	1,184	3,135
1985	0	1,045	1,403	2,448	1,147	3,038
1986	15,515	1,165	2,034	18,714	1,106	2,928
1987	0	1,312	2,058	3,370	1,059	2,806
1988	15,515	1,464	2,695	19,674	1,008	2,669
1989	0	932	2,713	3,645	1,098	2,909
1990	15,515	1,019	3,340	19,874	1,199	3,178
1991	5,973	1,142	3,610	10,725	1,308	3,468
1992	11,946	1,253	4,130	17,329	1,429	3,791
1993	0	932	4,147	5,079	1,540	4,083
1994	0	1,020	4,168	5,188	1,661	4,402
1995	5,973	1,117	4,436	11,526	1,793	4,751
1996	0	1,224	4,461	5,685	1,938	5,132
1997–2006	0	0	4,461	4,461	1,938	5,132

Note: See note to table D.1.

Table D.14. *High-Reliability Distribution System Costs* (1976 Cr$ · 10³) *and Losses*

	Investment costs		Recur- rent costs	Total costs	Losses	
	Stations	Lines			Kilo- watts	Mega- watt- hours
1977	0	1,613	28	1,642	531	1,405
1978	0	1,875	61	1,937	500	1,323
1979	18,887	2,179	727	21,793	464	1,227
1980	0	2,522	774	3,296	422	1,117
1981	0	631	784	1,415	486	1,286
1982	18,887	718	1,426	21,032	559	1,480
1983	0	814	1,441	2,255	642	1,698
1984	0	931	1,457	2,389	736	1,949
1985	18,887	1,204	2,105	22,196	736	1,948
1986	0	1,343	2,127	3,470	735	1,946
1987	18,887	1,509	2,780	23,177	735	1,944
1988	0	1,680	2,810	4,491	733	1,942
1989	18,887	817	3,450	23,155	856	2,267
1990	0	893	3,467	4,360	994	2,632
1991	14,025	999	4,037	19,061	1,142	3,024
1992	9,350	1,100	4,323	14,773	1,307	3,462
1993	14,025	1,223	4,895	20,143	1,393	3,690
1994	4,675	1,335	4,973	10,983	1,488	3,939
1995	4,675	1,458	5,055	11,189	1,590	4,211
1996	0	1,592	5,082	6,674	1,702	4,508
1997–2006	0	0	5,082	5,082	1,702	4,508

Note: See note to table D.1.

Figure D.4.   *Relation between Costs and Outage Rate*

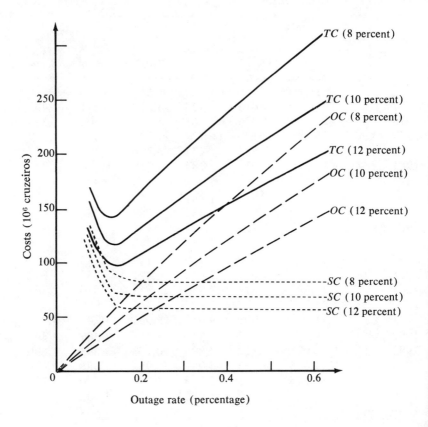

Note: Discount rate given in parentheses. *TC* = total cost, *OC* = outage cost, and *SC* = supply cost.

Appendix E

~~~~~~

Comparison with Previous Studies

Comparing the results of this study with previous studies is difficult because, in the latter, outage costs have been calculated on the basis of many different units: that is, dollars for each kilowatt lost, dollars per kilowatt-hour lost, dollars an hour, total dollar value, and so on. Therefore, wherever possible, all the results have been reduced to outage cost for each kilowatt-hour lost, for standardized outage durations of 0.33 hours (20 minutes) and 1.5 hours, respectively, corresponding to representative values of duration for the high- and low-reliability systems described in the case study. This information is presented in tables E.1 and E.2. All money values have been converted to US$ on the basis of official exchange rates prevailing when the studies were undertaken, and the U.S. deflator of GDP has been used to adjust for the effects of inflation up to 1977.[1]

Given the lack of uniformity in the methodologies adopted, as well as the differences among the countries and in the timing of the previous studies, the range of outage costs per kilowatt-hour lost (that is, US$0 to 7 for each kilowatt-hour) for the various types of industries examined

---

1. More refined inflation adjustments, including the use of the actual rates of inflation by industrial sector in the different countries, followed by conversion to US$ at the 1977 exchange rates, would not be worthwhile, given the inaccuracies inherent in the original outage cost estimates.

Table E.1. *Industrial Outage Costs*

Study	Industry type	Costs in US$ for each kilowatt-hour lost for an outage of duration		Comments
		0.333 hours	1.5 hours	
Sweden[a] (1948)	All	1.97	0.96	Very aggregate level
Sweden[b] (1969)	Mines	0.81	0.54	Based on the results
	Smelting	0.05	0.10	of a survey of sev-
	Iron and steel	0.34	0.41	enty firms repre-
	Workshop	2.26	3.03	senting 28 percent
	Quarrying	0.17	1.31	of total industrial
	Timber	0.38	0.45	consumption.
	Pulp and paper	0.41	0.22	
	Graphic	1.96	6.03	
	Food	0.63	0.63	
	Textiles	3.49	1.98	
	Rubber	2.96	1.00	
	Chemical	0.53	0.29	
	All	0.75	0.74	
Chile[c] (1973)	Paper	0.20	0.17	Based on an input-
	Basic metal	0.42	0.35	output approach,
	Nonmetallic minerals	0.52	0.43	using direct plus indirect average
	Printing	0.86	0.71	kilowatt-hour
	Metal products	1.11	0.91	requirements to
	Textiles	1.17	0.96	produce unit
	Nonelectrical machinery	1.33	1.33	value of output; therefore outage
	Chemicals	1.83	1.83	costs are average
	Lumber	1.86	1.86	rather than mar-
	Rubber	2.01	2.01	ginal.
	Leather	2.26	2.26	
	Miscellaneous	2.28	2.28	
	Furniture	2.28	2.28	
	Transport	2.56	2.56	
	Electrical machinery	2.57	2.57	
	Foodstuffs	2.84	2.84	
	Petroleum and coal	3.01	3.01	
	Shoes and clothing	3.20	3.20	

Table E.1 (continued)

Study	Industry type	Costs in US$ for each kilowatt-hour lost for an outage of duration		Comments
		0.333 hours	1.5 hours	
	Beverages	3.90	3.90	
	Tobacco	8.11	8.11	
IEEE,	Large plant	4.99	2.43	
North	Small plant	26.69	15.49	
America[d]				
(1973)				
Taiwan[e]	Aluminum	0.03	0.03	Based on direct
(1975)	Fertilizer	0.05	0.05	average kilowatt-
	Alkali and acid	0.05	0.05	hour requirements
	Steel	0.06	0.06	to produce unit
	Paper	0.16	0.16	value of output;
	Chemical	0.42	0.42	therefore outage
	Cement	1.22	1.22	costs are average rather than marginal.
Ontario-	Large user	5.37	2.67	
Hydro,	Small manufacturer	8.71	4.55	
Canada[f]	Commercial user	0.99	1.03	
(1976)				
Cascavel,	Telephone	1.98	1.97	Based on a detailed
Brazil	Nonmetallic			theory and survey
(1977)	minerals	1.00	1.10	of twenty firms.
	Mechanical and			
	metallurgy	2.00	2.00	
	Vegetable oils	1.02	2.77	
	Food and	2.10	3.89	
	beverages			
	Wood	4.74	2.76	
	Other	1.78	1.29	

a. Dahlin Lolander, "Memorandum Concerning Estimation of the Costs of the National Economy in the Event of a Loss of Supply" (Vattenfall, 1948).

b. Swedish Joint Committee for the Electricity Council, "Cost of Interruptions in Electricity Supply" (Stockholm: September 1969).

c. Pablo Jaramillo and Esteban Skoknic, "Costo Social de Las Restricciones Energía Eléctrica," Oficina de Planificación (Chile: August 1973).

d. IEEE, Reliability Subcommittee at Industrial and Commercial Power System Committee, "Report on Reliability Survey of Industrial Plants. Part 2—Cost of

(Footnotes continue on the following page)

298   APPENDIXES

Power Outages, Plant Restart Time, Critical Service Loss Duration Time, and Type of Load Loss vs. Time of Power Outages," May 1973.
   e. Taiwan Power Company, "Evaluation of Generating Capacity Reserve for Taiwan Power Company."
   f. Ontario-Hydro, "Survey on Power System Reliability: Viewpoint of Large Users," report no. PMA 76-5, Ontario, Canada, 1976; processed.

Table E.2. *Residential Outage Costs*

Study	Outage costs (US$ per kilowatt-hour lost)	Comment
Sweden[a] (1948)	0.38 to 0.64	Estimated approximately as a percentage of industrial outage costs.
Sweden[b] (1969)	0.74 to 1.48	Based on estimated costs of interrupted household activities; not verified empirically.
Chile[c] (1973)	0.30	Based on annuitized value of household appliances made idle.
California, U.S.[d] (1977)	0.1	Based on household appliances made idle
England[d] (1977)	0.5 to 1.5	Related to earning rate
Jamaica[e] (1976)	0.06	Based on annuitized value of household appliances made idle.
Cascavel, Brazil (1977)	1.3 to 2.0	Based on an explicit household utility maximizing model and verified empirically by the willingness-to-pay of consumers.

   a. Same as *a*, table E.1.
   b. Same as *b*, table E.1.
   c. Same as *c*, table E.1.
   d. Systems Control Inc., "Analysis of Electric Power System Reliability" (prepared for the California Energy Resources Conservation and Development Commission, Palo Alto, Calif., 1978; processed).
   e. De Anne S. Julius, "The Economic Cost of Power Outages: Methodology and Application to Jamaica," report no. RES7, The World Bank, Energy, Water and Telecommunications Department (a restricted-circulation document) (Washington, D.C., August 1976).

is quite comparable with the results of the Cascavel study. The residential outage costs are considerably higher than the corresponding results for the previous studies, however, because they ignored the value of foregone leisure. The 1969 Swedish study that also considered lost leisure explicitly is the only exception.

Appendix F

~~~~~~

Survey Questionnaires

Residential Consumers

The information from this survey will be used by COPEL[1] to analyze and improve the quality of electricity services to customers. All responses will be treated as strictly confidential.

1. What was your average monthly electricity consumption during the last three months:

    .... kilowatt-hours per month .... Cr$ per month

2. Do you feel that:

    (a) Your electricity supply is good   Yes   No

    (b) There are many electricity power outages   Yes   No

3. (a) On the average, how many minutes of unexpected outages per month have you experienced during the last three months:

    .... minutes per month

    (b) During what hours is electricity essential for the enjoyment of your leisure: ....

    (c) Approximately what fraction of outages occurred during these critical hours:

    .... percent

4. If an unexpected outage occurred during these critical hours while you were enjoying your leisure (for example, watching television,

---

1. The electric power company, Compania Paranaense de Energía Eléctrica.

listening to the radio, reading, having dinner, and so forth), how much extra would you be willing to pay to avoid:

(a) A one-minute interruption . . . . Cr$
(b) A five-minute interruption . . . . Cr$
(c) A thirty-minute interruption . . . . Cr$
(d) A sixty-minute interruption . . . . Cr$
(e) A ninety-minute interruption . . . . Cr$
(f) A two-hour interruption . . . . Cr$

5. If an unexpected outage occurred at any other time (for example, while housekeeping) how much extra would you be willing to pay to avoid:

(a) A one-minute interruption . . . . Cr$
(b) A five-minute interruption . . . . Cr$
(c) A thirty-minute interruption . . . . Cr$
(d) A sixty-minute interruption . . . . Cr$
(e) A ninety-minute interruption . . . . Cr$
(f) A two-hour interruption . . . . Cr$

6. Do you feel that:

(a) Electricity is an important service   Yes   No
(b) The service is too expensive   Yes   No

7. On average, how do you spend your evening/night-time leisure hours:

(a) Watching television   . . . . hours
(b) Listening to the radio   . . . . hours
(c) Reading   . . . . hours
(d) Having dinner   . . . . hours
(e) In conversation   . . . . hours
(f) Going out   . . . . hours
(g) Other   . . . . hours

8. When do you normally go to sleep: . . . . P.M./A.M.

9. If we were to reduce the incidence of unexpected outages to half its present level, how much extra would you be willing to pay on your monthly electricity bill:

. . . . Cr$ per month

10. How many persons live in this household:

. . . . persons

11. (a) What are your principal sources of income:

(b) What was the average monthly income (gross of taxes) of your household during the last three months:

. . . . Cr$ per month

12. If the level of unexpected outages were to double, what reduction in your monthly electricity bill would you consider to be fair:
.... Cr$ per month

Industrial Consumers

1. Name of firm and principal outputs produced.
2. Name(s) and title(s) of official(s) interviewed.
3. (a) If there is an unexpected interruption in the supply of electricity, what is the value of materials and products that are spoiled?
   (b) Does this value vary with the duration of the outage?
4. (a) While the power is out, what percentage of normal output is not produced?
   (b) Does this vary with the duration of the outage?
5. (a) After the power is restored, how long is it before production can begin again?
   (b) Does this restart time vary with the duration of the outage?
   (c) What percentage of normal output is not produced during this restart period?
   (d) Does this percentage vary with the duration of the outage?
6. Is there any slack productive capacity, and if so, how much more could be produced per hour of work following the outage than is normally produced?
7. (a) What is this firm's yearly value added?
   (b) What are your normal working hours?
   (c) What is your overtime pay rate?
   (d) Do you own alternative energy sources, and, if so, how much did they cost, and how often have they been used?
   (e) Have you altered your production techniques to reduce outage costs?
8. If your output is reduced because of an outage, will you make it up by working overtime?
9. What are this firm's expansion plans for the next twenty years, and how rapidly will its output increase during this period?

Glossary

~~~~~~

Aggregation: Adding together or combining, for example, the electrical loads of different consumers.

Auto-consumption: The consumption, within a household, of self-produced goods and services that do not enter the market.

Busbar: A conductor or group of conductors that serves as a common connecting point for two or more electrical circuits, for example, in a substation.

Captive generation: The generation of electricity by private individuals using their own plant, instead of drawing power from the main electricity grid (also called auto-generation).

Cold reserve: Reserve generating capacity available for service, only after a specified time has elapsed, because the generators are not maintained at operating conditions (see also **Hot reserve**).

Cross section data: Data relating to several different objects at a given point in time (see also **Time series data**).

Demand side: Considerations relating to the demand for electricity.

Direct outage costs: Economic costs incurred during outages (see also **Outage costs**).

Disaggregation: Breaking up into smaller components, for example, a load forecast.

Elasticity of demand with respect to price (or income): The percentage change in demand divided by the percentage change in price (or income).

Fault: The malfunction of an electrical circuit in a power system, for example, the short-circuiting of a line.

Forced outage: The unexpected failure of a component in a power system, for example, a generator (see also **Planned outage**).

303

Growth pole: A geographic center for economic growth and development.

Hot reserve: Reserve thermal generating capacity available for service promptly, because the generators are maintained at operating conditions (see also **Cold reserve**).

Indirect outage costs: Economic costs incurred as a result of actions designed to avoid the effects of anticipated outages (see also **Outage costs**).

Iterate: To run through a modeling procedure repeatedly.

Load shedding: Deliberate removal of specific loads from the system to avoid system failure during a power supply shortage.

Matrix model (for load forecasting): A mathematical model involving representation and manipulation of probabilistic data in matrix format.

Nonspinning reserve: Reserve generating capacity not connected to the busbars, but able to carry the load only after a specified time has elapsed.

Numeraire: A common unit of account or yardstick for measuring the economic value of goods and services.

Objective function: A mathematical expression used in an analytical model, the value of which is usually maximized or minimized.

Operating reserve: Reserve generating capacity, normally consisting of both the spinning and nonspinning reserves.

Outage (of a component): The condition of a power system component when it cannot perform its function satisfactorily because of an event associated directly with the component.

Outage (at the point of use): Unavailability of electric power to the consumer.

Outage costs: The economic costs resulting from a shortage of electricity supply, including frequency and voltage fluctuations, as well as interruptions of supply. These costs consist of both direct and indirect outage costs.

Parametrize: To define a curve or mathematical function in terms of one or more parameters.

Pareto optimal: An economic condition that occurs when no one can be made better off without making someone else worse off.

Peak suppression: The suppression of peaks in the electricity demand curve, for example, by shedding load.

Piecewise linear: The property of a graph or mathematical function indicating that it is composed of several linear segments.

Planned outage: The preplanned unavailability of a component in a power system, usually for preventive maintenance or construction (also called scheduled outage).

Rating period: Time interval during the day or season of the year, within which a specific price (or rate) is charged for electricity consumption.

Ring main busbar: A busbar designed in the form of a loop to provide redundancy.

Spinning reserve: Reserve generating capacity connected to the busbars and ready to meet the load immediately.

Stochastic process: A process that is random in time.

Supply side: Considerations relating to the supply of electricity.

Time horizon: A future period for which forecasts or plans are made.

Time series data: Data relating to a given object, during several successive time periods (see also **Cross section data**).

References

The word *processed* indicates works that are reproduced by mimeograph, Xerox, or any other manner other than conventional typesetting and printing.

Allan, R. N., E. N. Dialynas, and I. R. Homer. "Modelling Common Mode Failures in the Reliability Evaluation of Power System Networks." *Proceedings of the IEEE Power Engineering Society Winter Meeting, New York, 1979.* Paper no. A79040-7.

Allan, R. N., E. N. Dialynas, and I. R. Homer. "Modelling and Evaluating the Reliability of Distribution Systems." *IEEE Transactions on Power Apparatus and Systems,* vol. PAS-98 (May–June 1979).

Allan, R. N., and F. N. Takieddine. "Generation Modelling in Power System Reliability Evaluation." *Reliability of Power Supply Systems.* IEE Conference Publication no. 148. London: Institute of Electrical Engineers, February 1977.

Allan, R. N., and F. N. Takieddine. "Network Limitations on Generating Systems Reliability Evaluation Techniques." *Proceedings of the IEE Power Engineering Society Winter Meeting, New York, January–February 1978.* Paper no. A78070-5.

Anderson, Dennis. "Models for Determining Least Cost Investments in Electricity Supply." *The Bell Journal of Economics and Management Science,* vol. 3 (Spring 1972), pp. 267–301.

ANSI Publication no. C84.1, 1970.

Aoki, H. "New Method of Long Range or Very Long Range Demand Forecast of Energy, Including Electricity, Viewed from a Worldwide Standpoint." Electric Power Development Company, Ltd., Tokyo, Japan, 1974.

Backlund, Yngve, and Janis A. Bubenko. "Computer-Aided Distribution System Planning." *Electrical Power and Energy Systems,* vol. 1 (April 1979), pp. 35–45.

Balasko, Yves. "On Designing Public Utility Tariffs with Applications to Electricity." *Electricité de France Report,* Paris (1974).

Balassa, Bela. "Estimating the Shadow Price of Foreign Exchange in Project Appraisal." *Oxford Economic Papers*, vol. 26 (July 1974), pp. 147–68.

Bator, Francis J. "General Equilibrium, Welfare, and Allocation." *American Economic Review* (March 1957), pp. 22–59.

Bazovsky, Igor. *Reliability Engineering and Practice*. Prentice-Hall Space Technology Series. Englewood Cliffs, N.J.: Prentice-Hall, 1961.

Becker, Gary. "A Theory of the Allocation of Time." *Economic Journal*, vol. 75 (September 1965), pp. 493–517.

Berntsen, Tor-odd, and Arne T. Holen. "Security Control in Network System Operation." *Reliability of Power Supply Systems*. IEE Conference Publication no. 148. London: Institute of Electrical Engineers, February 1977.

Billinton, Roy. "Bibliography on the Application of Probability Methods in Power System Reliability Evaluation." *IEEE Transactions on Power Apparatus and Systems*, vol. PAS-91 (March–April 1972), pp. 649–60.

Billinton, Roy. "Composite System Reliability Evaluation." *IEEE Transactions on Power Apparatus and Systems* (April 1969), pp. 276–80.

Billinton, Roy. *Power System Reliability Evaluation*. New York: Gordon and Breach, 1970.

Billinton, Roy, and G. Hamond. "Considerations in Including Uncertainty in LOLE Calculations for Practical Systems." *Proceedings of the IEEE Power Engineering Society Winter Meeting, New York, 1979*. Paper no. A79075-3.

Billinton, Roy, and P. G. Harrington." Reliability Evaluation in Energy Limited Generating Capacity Studies." *Proceedings of the IEEE Power Engineering Society Winter Meeting, New York, January–February 1978*. Paper no. F78004-4.

Billinton, Roy, T. K. P. Medicherla, and M. S. Sachdev. "Adequacy Indexes for Composite Generation and Transmission System Reliability Evaluation." *Proceedings of the IEEE Power Engineering Society Winter Meeting, New York, 1979*. Paper no. A79024-1.

Billinton, Roy, Robert J. Ringlee, and Allen J. Wood. *Power System Reliability Calculations*. Cambridge, Mass.: MIT Press, 1973.

"Blackout '77: Once More with Looting." *Time*, vol. 110 (July 25, 1977), pp. 12–26.

Brown, Gardner, Jr., and M. Bruce Johnson. "Public Utility Pricing and Output Under Risk." *American Economic Review* (March 1969), pp. 119–28.

Bruce, Colin. "Social Cost-Benefit Analysis: A Guide for Country and Project Economists to the Derivation and Application of Economic and Social Accounting Prices." World Bank Staff Working Papers, no. 239. Washington, D.C.: World Bank, August 1976.

Burington, Richard S. *Handbook of Mathematical Tables and Formulas*, fifth edition. New York: McGraw-Hill, 1973.

Calabrese, G. "Generating Reserve Capacity Determined by the Probability Method." *AIEE Transactions*, vol. 66 (1947), pp. 1439–50.

Canadian International Development Agency. *Regional Power Systems Engineering Seminar, Kathmand, Nepal, February–March 1977*

Chow, Gregory C. "Tests of Equality Between Subsets of Coefficients in Two Linear Regressions." *Econometrica*, vol. 28 (July 1960), pp. 591–605.

Christensen, Laurits. "The Production Function Method II." *Marginal Costing and Pricing of Electric Energy, Proceedings of the State-of-the-Art International Conference, Montreal, May 1978*, pp. 107–13.

Crew, Michael A., and Paul R. Kleindorfer. "Peak Load Pricing with Diverse Technology." *The Bell Journal of Economics* (Spring 1976), pp. 207–31.

Crew, Michael A., and Paul R. Kleindorfer. "Reliability and Public Utility Pricing." *American Economic Review* (March 1978), pp. 31–40.

CURA. "Pesquisa Fisico-Socio-Economica." Prepared for the Cascavel City Government, 1975–76.

Dasgupta, Partha, Amartya Sen, and Stephen Marglin. *Guidelines for Project Evaluation* (UNIDO). New York: United Nations, 1972.

Dasgupta, Partha, and Joseph Stiglitz. "Benefit Cost Analysis and Trade Policies." *Journal of Political Economy*, vol. 82 (January–February 1974), pp. 1–33.

Debs, A. R., and A. S. Benson. "Security Assessment of Power Systems." *Systems Engineering for Power: Status and Prospects, USERDA Conference, Henniker, New Hampshire, August 1975*. NTIS no. CONF-750867, pp. 144–76.

Dhar, S. B. "Power System Long-Range Decision Analysis Under Fuzzy Environment." *IEEE Transactions on Power Apparatus and Systems*, vol. PAS-98 (March/April 1979), pp. 588–96.

Dhrymes, Phoebus J., and Mordecai Kurtz. "Technology and Scale in Electricity Generation." *Econometrica*, vol. 32 (July 1965), pp. 287–315.

Di Capro, U., and R. Marconato. "Automatic Load Shedding in Multiarea Elastic Power Systems." *Electric Power and Energy Systems*, vol. 1 (April 1979), pp. 21–29.

Dixon, G. F. L. "British and French Views on Security of Supply." *Electrical Review* (November 1971), pp. 735–37.

DyLiacco, Thomas E. "The Emerging Concept of Security Control." *Proceedings of the 1970 Symposium on Power Systems*. Lafayette, Ind.: Purdue University, May 1970.

Fabres, J., and A. Bonnardot. "The Cost of Energy Not Applied in Electrical Networks." *Electrical Review* (November 1971), pp. 737–39.

Federal Power Commission. *The Methodology of Load Forecasting*. 1970 National Power Survey. Washington, D.C., 1970.

Fischl, Robert. "Optimal System Expansion Planning: A Critical Review." *Systems Engineering for Power: Status and Prospects, USERDA Conference, Henniker, New Hampshire, August 1975*. NTIS no. CONF-750867, pp. 233–60.

Fisher, Franklin M. "Tests of Equality Between Sets of Coefficients in Two

Linear Regressions: An Exposition Note." *Econometrica*, vol. 38 (March 1970), pp. 361–66.

Ford, Lester R., and Delbert R. Fulkerson. *Flows in Networks*. Princeton: Princeton University Press, 1962.

Galatin, M. *Economies of Scale and Technical Change in Thermal Power Generation*. Amsterdam: North-Holland, 1968.

Galiana, Frank D. "Short Term Load Forecasting." *Systems Engineering for Power: Status and Prospects, USERDA Conference, Henniker, New Hampshire, August 1975*. NTIS no. CONF-750867, pp. 105–14.

Gronau, Reuben. "The Intra-Family Allocation of Time: The Value of the Housewives' Time." *American Economic Review*, vol. 63 (September 1973), pp. 634–51.

Hajdu, L. P., and R. Podmore. "Security Enhancement for Power Systems." *Systems Engineering for Power: Status and Prospects, USERDA Conference, Henniker, New Hampshire, August 1975*. NTIS no. CONF-750867, pp. 177–95.

Hall, J. D., R. J. Ringlee, and A. J. Wood. "Frequency and Duration Methods for Power System Reliability Calculations: Part I—Generation System Model." *IEEE Transactions on Power Apparatus and Systems*, vol. PAS-88 (April 1969).

Harberger, Arnold C. *Project Evaluation*. London: Macmillan and Co., 1972.

Harris, John R., and Michael P. Todaro. "Migration, Unemployment, and Development." *American Economic Review*, vol. 60 (March 1970), pp. 126–42.

Hayes, T. P., R. P. Webb, and J. T. Day. "A Quantitative Method for Transmission System Reliability Calculations." *Proceedings of the IEEE Power Engineering Society Summer Meeting, Los Angeles, July 1978*. Paper no. A78566-2.

Holt, Stewart B., Jr., and Dale M. Crawford. "Distribution Substation Planning Using Optimization Methods." *Application of Optimization Methods in Power System Engineering*. IEEE Tutorial Course Text no. 76CH1107-2-PWR. New York, 1976.

Huck, G. E. "Load Forecast Bibliography—Phase I." *Proceedings of the IEEE Power Engineering Society Summer Meeting, Vancouver, July 1979*. Paper no. F79650-3.

IAEA. *Nuclear Power Planning Study for Indonesia*. Vienna, 1976.

IEEE, Reliability Subcommittee of Industrial and Commercial Power System Committee. "Report on Reliability Survey of Industrial Plants. Part 2—Cost of Power Outages, Plant Restart Time, Critical Service Loss Duration Time, and Type of Load Loss vs. Time of Power Outages." May 1973.

IEEE Standard. No. 346-1973. New York: IEEE, 1973.

IEEE-PES Working Group. "Reliability Indices for Use in Bulk Supply Adequacy Evaluation." *IEEE Transactions on Power Apparatus and Systems*, vol. PAS-97 (July–August 1978), pp. 1097–1103.

Jamaica Public Service Company Planning Department. "Reliability Dollar Value Analysis."

Jamaica Public Service Company Planning Department. "The Selection of a Generation (Static) Reliability Criteria for the Jamaican Public Service Company, Ltd." November 1975.

Janac, Karel. "Control of Large Power Systems Based on Situation Recognition and High Speed Simulation." *IEEE Transactions on Power Apparatus and Systems*, vol. PAS-98 (May/June 1979), pp. 710–15.

Jaromillo, Pablo, and Esteban Skoknic. "Costo Social de Las Restricciones Energía Eléctrica." Oficina de Planificación, Chile. August 1973.

Johnston, J. *Econometric Methods*. New York: McGraw-Hill, 1972.

Julius, DeAnne S. "The Economic Cost of Power Outages: Methodology and Application to Jamaica." Report no. RES7, the World Bank, Energy, Water, and Telecommunications Department. A restricted-circulation document. Washington, D.C., August 1976. Processed.

Kaufman, Alvin. "Reliability Criterion—A Cost-Benefit Analysis." Office of Research, New York State Public Service Commission. August 1975.

Knight, Upton G. *Power System Engineering and Mathematics*. New York: Pergamon Press, 1972.

Kohm, Gregory C. "A Survey of Disruption and Consumer Costs Resulting from a Major Residential Power Outage." Argonne National Laboratory, report no. ANL/EES-TM-29. Argonne, Illinois, June 1978.

Kohm, Gregory C. "Costs of Interruptions of Electrical Service in the Commercial Sector." Argonne National Laboratory, report no. ANL/EES-TM-30. Argonne, Illinois, September 1978.

Lal, Deepak. *Methods of Project Analysis*. World Bank Staff Occasional Papers, no. 16. Baltimore: Johns Hopkins University Press for the World Bank, 1974.

Lalander, Dahlin. "Memorandum Concerning Estimation of the Costs of the National Economy in the Event of a Loss of Supply." Vattenfall, 1948.

Lancaster, Kevin. "A New Approach to Consumer Behavior." *Journal of Political Economy*, vol. 74 (April 1966), pp. 132–57.

Le, Khai D. "Conventional Probability Methods and Monte Carlo Simulation Techniques: A Comparison of Results." *Proceedings of the IEEE Power Engineering Society Winter Meeting, New York, January–February 1978*. Paper no. A78238-8.

Little, Ian M. D., and Jan A. Mirrlees, *Project Appraisal and Planning for Developing Countries*. New York: Basic Books, 1974.

Luenberger, David G. *Introduction to Linear and Non-Linear Programming*. Reading, Mass.: Addison-Wesley, 1973.

Lundberg, L. *Quality of Service from the Consumer's Point of View*. Report of the Group of Experts, no. 60/D1, International Union of Producers and Distributors of Electrical Energy. Paris: UNIPEDE, 1972.

Manichaikul, Y., and F. C. Schweppe. "Physically Based Industrial Load." *IEEE Transactions on Power Apparatus and Systems*, vol. PAS-98 (July/August 1979), pp. 1439–50.

Marglin, Stephen A. *Public Investment Criteria*. London: George, Allen, and Unwin, 1967.

Marglin, Stephen R. "The Social Rate of Discount and the Optimal Rate of Investment." *Quarterly Journal of Economics* (1963).

Marko, G. E. "A Method of Combining High Speed Contingency Load Flow Analysis with Stochastic Probability Methods to Calculate a Quantitative Measure of Overall Power System Reliability." *Proceedings of the IEEE Power Engineering Society Summer Meeting, Los Angeles, July 1978.* Paper no. A78053-1.

McCoy, Fred. "The Production Function Method I." *Marginal Costing and Pricing of Electrical Energy, Proceedings of the State-of-the-Art International Conference, Montreal, May 1978.*

Mishan, Ezra J. *Cost Benefit Analysis.* New York: Praeger, 1976.

Moore, Edwin A. "Electricity Supply Forecast for the Developing Countries." Energy, Water, and Telecommunications Department, the World Bank. A restricted-circulation document. Washington, D.C., December 1978. Processed.

Munasinghe, Mohan. "A New Approach to Power System Planning." *IEEE Transactions on Power Apparatus and Systems,* vol. PAS-99 (January/February 1980).

Munasinghe, Mohan. "Costs Incurred by Residential Electric Consumers Due to Power Failures." *Journal of Consumer Research* (March 1980).

Munasinghe, Mohan. "Electric Power Pricing Policy." *LDC Energy Management Training Seminar, State University of New York–Brookhaven National Laboratory, Stony Brook, New York, November 1978.*

Munasinghe, Mohan. "The Leisure Cost of Electric Power Failures." World Bank Staff Working Paper, no. 285. Washington, D.C.: World Bank, June 1978.

Munasinghe, Mohan, and Mark Gellerson. "Economic Criteria for Optimizing Power System Reliability Levels." *The Bell Journal of Economics* (Spring 1979), pp. 353–65.

Munasinghe, Mohan, and Jeremy J. Warford. "Shadow Pricing and Power Tariff Policy." *Marginal Costing and Pricing of Electrical Energy, Proceedings of the State-of-the-Art International Conference, Montreal, May 1978,* pp. 159–80.

Munasinghe, Mohan, and Colin J. Warren. "Rural Electrification, Energy Economics, and National Policy in Developing Countries." *Proceedings of the IEE International Conference on Future Energy Concepts, London, January–February 1979.* IEE Conference Publication no. 171.

Noferi, P. L., L. Paris, and L. Salvaderi. "Monte Carlo Methods for Power System Reliability Evaluation in Transmission and Generation Planning." *Proceedings of the Annual Reliability and Maintainability Symposium, Washington, D.C., January 1975,* pp. 460–69.

Oi, Walter. "Labor as a Quasi-Fixed Factor." *Journal of Political Economy* (December 1962), pp. 538–55.

Ontario-Hydro. "Survey on Power-System Reliability: Viewpoint of Large Users." Report no. PMA 76-5. Ontario, Canada, 1976. Processed.

Pang, C. K., R. L. Watt, and J. A. Bruggeman. "Multi-Area Generation Reliability Studies." *Proceedings of the IEEE Power Engineering Society Summer Meeting, Los Angeles, July 1978.* Paper no. A78546-4.

Papoulis, Anthanasios. *Probability, Random Variables, and Stochastic Processes.* New York: McGraw-Hill, 1965.

Paris, L., and L. Salvaderi. "Optimization of the Basic Characteristics of Pumped Storage Plants." *Proceedings of the IEEE Power Engineering Society Winter Meeting, New York, January–February 1974.* Paper no. C74158-2.

Patton, A. D., and A. K. Ayoub. "Reliability Evaluation." *Systems Engineering for Power: Status and Prospects, USERDA Conference, Henniker, New Hampshire, August 1975.* NTIS no. CONF-750867, pp. 275–89.

Prasad, N. R., John M. Perkins, and G. Nesgos. "A Markov Process Applied to Forecasting. Part II. The Demand for Electricity." *Proceedings of the Power Engineering Society Summer Meeting, Vancouver, July 1973.*

Prasad, N. R., John M. Perkins, and G. Nesgos. "A Markov Process Applied to Forecasting. Part II. The Demand for Electricity." *Proceedings of the IEEE Power Engineering Society Winter Meeting, New York, January 1974.*

Prefeitura Municipal de Cascavel. *Plano Diretor de Desenvolvimento.* Parana, Brazil, 1975.

Priestman, D. "The Cost of a Long Term Electrical Energy Shortage Due to Under Planning." Paper presented at the Eleventh Annual Pacific Northwest Regional Economic Conference, May 1977, Eugene, Oregon. Processed.

Raiffa, H. *Decision Analysis: Introductory Lectures on Choices Under Uncertainty.* Reading, Mass.: Addison-Wesley, 1970.

Rau, N. S., and Karl F. Schenk. "Application of Fourier Methods for the Evaluation of Capacity Outage Probabilities." *Proceedings of the IEEE Power Engineering Society Winter Meeting, New York, 1979.* Paper no. A79103-3.

Reguly, Z. "Costs Evaluation of Power Supply Reliability." *Reliability of Power Supply Systems.* IEE Conference Publication no. 148. London: Institute of Electrical Engineers, 1977.

Reppen, N. D., R. J. Ringlee, B. F. Wollenberg, A. J. Wood, and K. A. Clements. "Probabilistic Methodologies—A Critical Review." *Systems Engineering for Power: Status and Prospects, USERDA Conference, Henniker, New Hampshire, August 1975.* NTIS no. CONF-750867, pp. 290–310.

Rohatgi, Uijay K. *An Introduction to Probability Theory and Mathematical Statistics.* New York: John Wiley, 1976.

Sassone, Peter G. "Shadow Pricing in CBA Mathematical Programming and Economic Theory." *The Engineering Economist,* vol. 22 (Spring 1977), pp. 219–33.

Schlaifer, R. *Analysis of Decision Under Uncertainty.* New York: McGraw-Hill, 1969.

Schulte, S. "Problems in the Evaluation of Costs Incurred Due to Electricity Supply Failures." *Elektrizitotswirtschaft*, vol. 70, no. 23 (November 1971), pp. 656–61.

Schwartz, Hugh, and Richard Berney (eds.). *Social and Economic Dimensions of Project Evaluation*. Washington, D.C.: Inter-American Development Bank, 1977.

Scott, Walter G. "Computer Model Forecasts Future Loads." *Electrical World* (September 15, 1972), pp. 114–16.

Scott, Walter G. "Rural System Engineering and Computer Models" (no. C76408-OIA). Paper presented at the IEEE National Rural Electric Conference, April 1976, Atlanta, Georgia. Processed.

Sherman, Roger, and Michael Visscher. "Second Best Pricing with Stochastic Demand." *American Economic Review* (March 1978), pp. 41–53.

Shipley, R. Bruce, Alton D. Patton, and John J. Denison. "Power Reliability Cost vs. Worth." *IEEE Transactions on Power Apparatus and Systems*, vol. PAS-91 (September/October 1972), pp. 2204–12.

Singh, Chanan, and Roy Billinton. "Frequency and Duration Concepts in System Reliability Evaluation." *IEEE Transactions on Reliability*, vol. R-24 (April 1975), pp. 31–36.

Squire, Lyn, and Herman G. van der Tak. *Economic Analysis of Projects*. Baltimore: Johns Hopkins University Press for the World Bank, 1975.

Stanton, K. N. "Medium Range, Weekly, and Seasonal Peak Demand Forecasting by Probability Methods." *IEEE Transactions on Power Apparatus and Systems*, vol. PAS-71 (May 1971), pp. 1183–89.

Stott, B. "Review of Load-Flow Calculation Methods." *Proceedings of IEEE*, vol. 62 (July 1974), pp. 916–29.

Sugarman, Robert. "New York City's Blackout: A $350 Million Drain." *IEEE Spectrum* (November 1978), pp. 44–46.

Sullivan, Robert L. *Power System Planning*. New York: McGraw-Hill International, 1977.

Svelflow, James. *Public Utility Accounting: Theory and Applications*. East Lansing: Michigan State University, 1973.

Swedish Joint Committee for the Electricity Council. "Cost of Interruptions in Electricity Supply." Stockholm: September 1969.

Systems Control Inc. "Analysis of Electric Power System Reliability." Prepared for the California Energy Resources Conservation and Development Commission, Palo Alto, California, 1978. Processed.

Systems Control Inc. "Impact Assessment of the 1977 New York City Blackout." U.S. Department of Energy Report, no. HCP/T5103-01. Arlington, Virginia, July 1978. Processed.

Taiwan Power Company. "Evaluation of Generating Capacity Reserve for Taiwan Power Company."

Taylor, Lester. "The Demand for Electricity: A Survey." *The Bell Journal of Economics*, vol. 6 (Spring 1975), pp. 74–110.

Taylor, Lester. "Power System Supply Costs." Chapter 8.

Telson, Michael L. "The Economics of Alternative Levels of Reliability for Electric Power Generation Systems." *The Bell Journal of Economics,* vol. 6 (Fall 1975), pp. 675–94.

Turvey, Ralph, and Dennis Anderson. *Electricity Economics.* Baltimore: Johns Hopkins University Press for the World Bank, 1977.

"Twenty-ninth Annual Electrical Industry Forecast." *Electrical World* (September 15, 1978), pp. 61–76.

Vardi, Joseph, Jacob Zahavi, and Benjamin Avi-Itzhak. "Variable Load Pricing in the Face of Loss of Load Probability." *The Bell Journal of Economics,* vol. 8 (Spring 1977), pp. 270–88.

Vemuri, S. "An Annotated Bibliography of Power System Reliability Literature." *Proceedings of the IEEE Power Engineering Society Summer Meeting, Los Angeles, July 1978.* Paper no. A78548-0.

Wagner, Harvey M. *Principles of Operations Research,* second edition. Englewood Cliffs, New Jersey: Prentice-Hall, 1975.

Wall, D. L., G. L. Thompson, and J. E. D. N. Green. "An Optimization Model for Planning Radial Distribution Networks." *IEEE Transactions on Power Apparatus and Systems,* vol. PAS 98 (May/June 1979), pp. 1061–68.

Warr, Peter. "On the Shadow Pricing of Traded Commodities." *Journal of Political Economy,* vol. 85 (1977), pp. 865–72.

Webb, Michael. "The Determination of Reverse Generating Capacity Criteria in Electricity Supply Systems." *Applied Economics* (March 1977), pp. 19–31.

Weber, H. "Evaluation of the Damage to the Economy Caused by Losses of Electricity Supply." *Energetik,* vol. 2 (1966), pp. 22–26.

Weckstein, Richard S. "Shadow Prices and Project Evaluation in Less-Developed Countries." *Economic Development and Cultural Change* (April 1972), pp. 474–94.

Werts, R. W. "International Criteria and Practices for System Reliability." *Symposium on Reliability Criteria for System Dynamic Performance.* IEEE Publication no. CH1221-1-1PWR. New York, 1977.

Westinghouse Distribution Systems Reference Book. East Pittsburgh: Westinghouse Corporation, 1959.

Willig, Robert D. "Consumers' Surplus Without Apology." *American Economic Review,* vol. 66 (September 1976), pp. 589–97.

Wilson, G. L., and P. Zarakas. "Anatomy of a Power Failure." *IEEE Spectrum* (February 1978), pp. 39–46.

Wismer, David A. *Optimization Methods for Large Scale Systems.* New York: McGraw-Hill, 1971.

World Bank, EMENA Projects Division. "Appraisal of the Istanbul Power Distribution Project, Istanbul Electricity, Tramway, and Tunnel Company (IETT), Turkey." A restricted-circulation document. Washington, D.C., April 1973. Processed.

Index

~~~~~~

315

high, 11
oscillations in, 16
reduction in, 11, 14, 15, 16, 20
standards of, for distribution systems,
  137–39
variation in, 64

Welfare maximizer, 31

Willingness-to-pay, 49, 50, 51, 62, 71,
  82, 83, 164, 168, 169, 194, 301
World Bank, The, xv, 117
Worst case concept, 96
Worst-fault design, 8

XLOL. *See* Expected loss of load